Right vs. Wrong

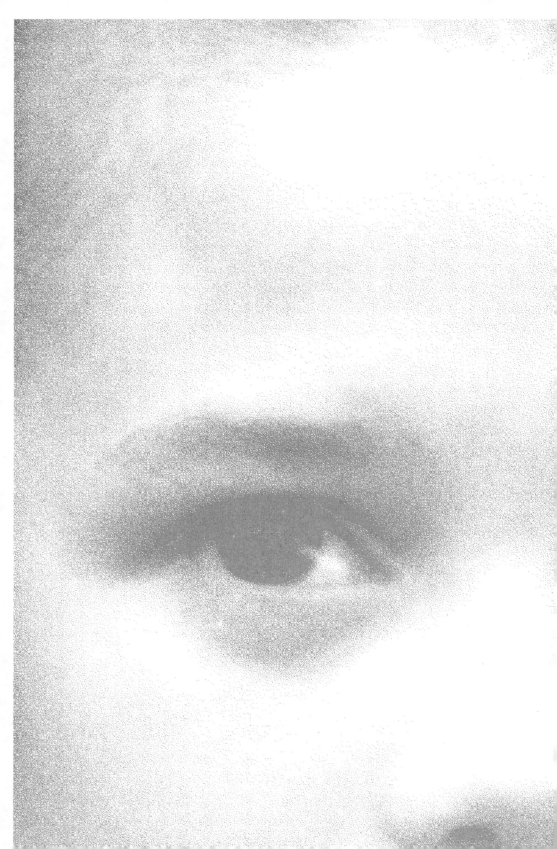

Right vs. Wrong—
Raising a Child with a Conscience

BARBARA M. STILWELL, M.D.
MATTHEW R. GALVIN, M.D.
S. MARK KOPTA, PH.D.

INDIANA UNIVERSITY PRESS
BLOOMINGTON AND INDIANAPOLIS

This book is a publication of

Indiana University Press
601 North Morton Street
Bloomington, IN 47404-3797 USA

http://www.indiana.edu/~iupress

Telephone orders　800-842-6796
Fax orders　812-855-7931
Orders by e-mail　iuporder@indiana.edu

© 2000 by Barbara M. Stilwell, Matthew R. Galvin, and S. Mark Kopta

Manufactured in the United States of America

Library of Congress Cataloging-in-Publication Data

Stilwell, Barbara M.
Right vs. wrong — raising a child with a conscience /
Barbara M. Stilwell, Matthew R. Galvin, S. Mark Kopta.
p.　cm.
Includes bibliographical references and index.
ISBN 0-253-33709-7 (cloth : alk. paper) — ISBN 0-253-21368-1
(paper : alk. paper)
1. Conscience. 2. Moral development. 3. Moral education (Elementary)
4. Moral education (Secondary)　I. Title: Right versus wrong.　II. Galvin,
Matthew.　III. Kopta, S. Mark, date　IV. Title.

BJ1471 .S69 2000
649'.7—dc21　　　　　　　　　　　　　　　　99-054311

1　2　3　4　5　05　04　03　02　01　00

This book is dedicated to all of the children and adolescents who taught us about the development of conscience.

CONTENTS

Foreword:
What to Expect from This Book

WRITTEN FOR WHOM?

This book is written mainly for parents who want their children to grow up recognizing the moral dimensions of their lives—to be fully aware of their consciences. It is also written for any adult who wants to become more conscience-sensitive, but particularly for adults who influence children and adolescents in their everyday work. We include in that group child-care workers, grandparents, teachers, pastoral and psychological counselors, public policy makers, and those who influence our children through media, mall, and entertainment arenas. That includes about all of us.

WRITTEN ABOUT WHAT?

In this book, we define *conscience* as the moral part of our being—the part of us that generates our sense of *oughtness*. We describe how children and adolescents mentally coordinate their memories and ongoing experiences with caretakers and peers, their emotional responsiveness, their value judgments and rule-making logic, and their sense of individual worth and will-power into a highly personal concept of conscience. Conscience is a "working concept" that gets updated in light of new experiences and maturation. We describe how this concept, a product of dynamic, moral meaning-making, changes with development, moving progressively through five stages in childhood and adolescence. Although each individual conscience is as unique as each individual personality, we describe universal developmental features.

This book confines itself to the normal development of conscience. Although we do discuss developmental crises, we do not discuss conscience development in children or adolescents suffering from mental or character disorders. We save that discussion for another book. In this book, we describe how moral development unfolds in ordinary children living in American homes where parents have the energy to nurture their children's sense of good and bad, right and wrong. We offer suggestions to parents for enhancing the process at each of the five stages.

BASED ON WHAT EXPERIENCE?

The ideas in this book are the product of three authors: two child psychiatrists and one clinical psychologist. More precise credentials follow in the section below. We speak from the experience of professional training, clinical experience, research, and teaching, as well as personal child-rearing experiences including parenting, step-parenting, and grandparenting. We speak from a reservoir of fervent interest in child development, psychopathology, and maltreatment; moral philosophy, religion, and ethics; bioevolutionary concepts, neuroscience, and therapeutic interventions. Our collective voice gains confidence from our published empirical studies of children and adolescents with normal and disturbed conscience development, but is humbled by ideas not yet considered, scientific flaws, competing theories, and human fallibility.

WRITTEN BY WHOM?

Each contributor to this book came to address conscience development from a somewhat different background. Dr. Galvin is Clinical Associate Professor of Child and Adolescent Psychiatry at Indiana University School of Medicine. He is a voluntary faculty member in the Section of Child and Adolescent Psychiatry as well as the Indiana University School of Medicine Program in Medical Ethics. Dr. Kopta is Professor of Psychology and Chairman of the Psychology Department at the University of Evansville. Dr. Stilwell is a semi-retired Associate Professor of Child and Adolescent Psychiatry in the Department of Psychiatry at Indiana University School of Medicine.

We would like to introduce ourselves by telling how the process of conscience development came to be important to each of us.

Dr. Galvin:

Before attending medical school I earned an undergraduate degree in philosophy at Indiana University. Much of my study pertained to moral philosophy. It was interrupted by the war in Vietnam, where I served as a medic. Like so many others who emerged from adolescence into young adulthood during that era, I was sensitized to the moral dilemmas posed by the war. In the course of my experience as a medic, I also became aware that prolonged exposure to traumatic stress can change a person. At that time post-traumatic stress disorder was a condition without a name. The condition itself was hardly recognized and poorly understood. Though difficult to describe or place in a conceptual framework, changes were nonetheless there to be observed, I thought, perhaps at a biological as well as a psychological level. This awareness and some associated ideas lasted, with occasional elaboration, through my medical school and general psychiatry training.

As a child psychiatry fellow, with Dr. Stilwell as a research mentor, and later faculty colleague, I joined in the Conscience Study, developing a particular interest in how a child's prolonged exposure to traumatic stress (especially maltreatment) can affect moral development at biological as well as psychological levels. I continue to work with maltreated children according to conscience-sensitive treatment plans. I also find applications of our study to teaching conscience-centered professional ethics to health care professionals.

Dr. Kopta:

My interest in the conscience began before I entered college, when I worked manual-labor jobs and when later I was an acrobat with the circus. I would observe how people behaved in situations that involved making moral decisions (for example, whether or not to tell the truth, steal, or fight) and wondered what thinking processes guided them to take certain actions. In addition, I became curious about how their particular values about "right" and "wrong" had developed over their lifetimes. To be sure, I also applied these questions to myself. While on the faculty at the University of Evansville, Dr. Stilwell and I met at a parents' reception and realized we had a common interest. Despite my being busy with my psychotherapy research as well as administrative and teaching responsibilities, her work was so fascinating that I could not resist getting involved. Since then, we have collaborated on this research, which, in many ways, has become more like a pleasant hobby for me. Our research has also given my students a chance to learn valuable research skills and make intriguing discoveries about their own consciences as well as those of others.

Dr. Stilwell:

Conscience development piqued my curiosity in the late 1970s and early 1980s, while my former husband and I were rearing three children in a home where I also had an office in child and adolescent psychiatry. I became curious about the links between normal and disturbed development as well as the relationship of mental health to character formation. As I moved back and forth between the "office" and the "home" part of the house, I was aware of both subtle transitions and glaring differences. Some problems were no more than developmental crises. Other problems were clearly related to aberrant developmental experiences and brain pathology.

I pondered over the wellness-versus-sickness dichotomy and continuum that defines mental illness. Simultaneously, I pondered over the goodness-seeking/badness-seeking dichotomy and continuum that defines character. I began to design questions for children and adolescents that would cross the boundaries between normal and abnormal development. Suddenly, it dawned on me that every child with whom I talked could readily describe her or his conscience. Although younger ones did not use the term *conscience*, they had definite ideas about right and wrong, good and bad, expressed in words or play, all the way down to two years of age. These observations led to a consuming interest in studying conscience in all of its normal and abnormal trajectories.

WRITTEN IN WHAT STYLE?

This book is written in the voice of "we parents," speaking of "our children." By joining into the voice of parents, we authors fully identify with the frustrations and uncertainties of parenting. We commiserate when things don't go well and grin when they do.

We have chosen an alternating style for dealing with gender, when necessary. Although we believe that gender differences are important in all aspects of development, they are not addressed directly in this book. We are aware of the justice-versus-caring gender differences that were first highlighted by Carol Gilligan. In response, we pay attention to each child's descriptions of these dimensions.

ADVOCATING WHAT?

With regard to parents rearing children under normal circumstances, we believe that, with some consciousness-raising about the conscience, parents will pursue a course that they find right for them and will be pleased with their efforts. We believe that there are multiple right ways to rear children so that they will become persons of conscience.

A special feature of this book is that it is anchored in development. It is an effort to help us adults find the right thing to do at the right time. Hence, the second half of most chapters is entitled, "Developmental Considerations." It is here that we advocate specific considerations for specific stages of development—five in all. The advice we give comes from our professional and personal experiences with children and adolescents at all ages, but especially from those children and adolescents who participated in our research. You will encounter many quotes from these research subjects.

Knowing full well that many children are not being reared under normal circumstances, we are also passionate advocates of the rights and needs of all children and adolescents to receive moral nurturance. You will notice while reading that we periodically are seized by an attack of oughtness. During these attacks, our collective conscience demands that we speak of the rightful needs of all children instead of just "our children." On those occasions, the heading "The Advocate" warns you that a statement of passionate advocacy is forthcoming. Please read every one of them.

WITH GRATITUDE TOWARD WHOM?

We are grateful to all the children, adolescents, and parents in our research study as well as some youngsters in treatment who helped us build the empirical foundation for our "Advice to Parents." We are also grateful to Indiana University Press, especially our sponsoring editor, Bob Sloan, who carefully guided us through the publication process.

Right vs. Wrong

The Moral Theme in Development

Most of our children's developmental experiences contribute to the moral meaning they find in life. If we as parents become more aware of the moral theme in our children's day-to-day experiences, we will probably nurture their search for moral meaning more successfully.

Generally, we want our children to grow up

- physically healthy;
- feeling loved and valued;
- curious about the world;
- enjoying emotional well-being;
- thinking and communicating logically;
- appreciative of heritage;
- capable of having stable human relationships;
- making meaningful commitments to work, love, and play; and
- having the energy to pursue valued commitments.

A moral theme is interwoven into each of these parenting desires. Highlighting the moral theme, we want our children

- to recognize goodness;
- to pursue it in rightful ways; and
- to feel a sense of "oughtness" about the pursuit.

To say it in even fewer words, we want our children to develop a well-functioning conscience.

Chapter by chapter, this book will expand the meaning of conscience. Each chapter will describe a different domain of conscience, based on how children and adolescents have described various aspects of learning about morality to us. As we describe developmental landmarks, we will explore ways that parents can most fully support children's pursuit of moral meaning.

For a starting definition of conscience, let's simply say that it is our awareness of good and bad, right and wrong.

GROWING UP

THE MORAL THEME IN DEVELOPMENT

Imagine that we are attending the high school graduation of our eighteen-year-old son, Dan. During the procession, mental snapshots of Dan's development keep flashing through our minds. In the first one, he is our precious infant suckling at his mother's breast. We remember thinking, "This is perfection, a gift from God; are we worthy of this joy?" Next he is a two-year-old, pounding his head and fists on the floor. We thought, "Will he ever learn to live with his emotions?" When he was a first-grader, he would literally bounce into the house, waving a school paper with a smiling face on it as big as his own. We marveled at how every day he learned something new. We remember how important it was for him to please us. When he was twelve, he spontaneously offered to help an elderly neighbor set out her trash and recycling bins at the curb every week. We delighted in his caring attitude. We seldom saw him when he turned fifteen. When vibrating music came blaring through his closed bedroom door, we thought, "What happened to consideration?" Now, as we watch him marching in the procession, we think, "What a nice young man he has become!" We brace ourselves for his entry into a larger world. We hope we have done a decent job of preparing him for it. We hope we will continue to be a supportive resource in his life.

A moral theme is interwoven into each of Dan's developmental snapshots. His moral fiber grew a little each time he gained more self-control, took pride in learning, responded to other people's needs, developed individuality, and prepared for future responsibility. Every day, whether we consciously thought about it or not, we were nurturing his conscience. On those occasions when Dan's behavior really puzzled us, we became very much aware of our conscience-nurturing responsibilities. At those times, we pondered long and hard about possible mistakes. Whether we found ourselves faulty or not, we worked harder at being good parents. We realized that we and our son had a definite characteristic in common: moral imperfection. Moral imperfection invites forgiveness and self-forgiveness. As parents we need to keep that in mind.

PURSUING GOODNESS

Conscience is more than awareness of good and bad, right and wrong. It motivates us to pursue goodness in rightful ways. Using a child-appealing example (we promise a more refined definition shortly), let's define candy as good, but stealing as a wrong way to pursue it. For the sake of this example, let's pretend that five-year-old Sarah is growing up in a family that values limiting or, better yet, eliminating refined sugar from the diet. What her parents define as "bad for you," Sarah defines as good.

Sarah finds candy irresistibly tasty and in short supply, available only in stores and friends' homes. Is there a rightful way for her to pursue candy? If her parents forbid it, rightful options are nil. If her parents believe in limited access to candy, she may be able to acquire it through earn-a-reward behavior or the delayed-gratification method of waiting for special occasions. Depending on opportunity and her temptation/resistance ratio, she may decide to steal it. She may accidentally run into good fortune: her grandparents may innocently—or not so innocently—bring her sweet treats when they visit.

PURSUING MORAL GOODNESS

We present Sarah's scenario to make the following point: Moral goodness is context-bound; it is defined within the rules of human relationships. Living alone in a magical land where candy can be plucked from trees removes it from the moral arena. Complying with parental rules designed to protect children's health makes candy a listen-to-your-elders moral issue. Sharing short-of-supply candy with other children makes it a fairness-and-caring moral issue. Gaining permission to personally test the value of candy makes it an individual-rights moral issue. (Will it rot my teeth, or make me first hyperactive and then lethargic?) Leaving candy wrappers strewn around on the ground makes it a community moral issue. Therefore, the moral goodness of candy resides not in the candy itself, nor even in the eating of it, but in the relational agreements regarding getting and eating the candy.

DEVELOPING THE MORAL CONNECTION

Let's say that around the age of seven our candy-loving Sarah begins to willingly refuse sweet treats. Her candy refusal begins to occur in the presence of her parents, when they are out of the room, when her grandparents visit, when she is with her friends at school recess, and on overnight stays at her cousins' house, where candy abounds. Why?

Sarah has not been severely punished; she has not been bribed; and she has not had such an adverse experience with candy (for example, pigging out on it till she got sick) that she never wants another piece. Somehow she has accepted her parents' belief that sugar is not good for her. Let's not distract ourselves with whether or not she cheats once in a while. She may. The point is that she has accepted her parents' rule. When her parents are not present, her conscience says, "You ought not eat candy." This rule of oughtness, or in this case, ought-not-ness, has developed through the strength of attachment she feels to her parents. Sarah's strong feeling of connectedness to her parents, sealed by loving care from the moment she was conceived, allows her to internalize their rules as though they are coming from a part of herself, that is, her conscience. She has faith in their knowledge of moral goodness. "Developing the Moral Connection" is the domain of conscience described in Chapter 2.

MORALIZATION OF BEHAVIOR

Throughout this book, we often say that a particular behavior has become *moralized*. We mean that this activity, formerly considered neither good nor bad, is now imbued with oughtness. It's something we are impelled to do if we want to continue feeling like a good person. It is a matter of right and wrong, a matter of conscience. For example, playing with fire is not a moral issue in young children's minds until they learn that it can endanger people's lives and property. They need not experience the harm to believe it. They can trust their parents' knowledge. By either route, making a personal discovery or accepting parent moral wisdom, playing with fire becomes moralized. Candy is a stickier issue to moralize than fire!

GOOD AND BAD FEELINGS

Imagine that our now candy-resistant Sarah begins to feel good about her sugarless state. Reinforced by marveling statements from adult relatives and neighbors, she begins to feel sweet when she resists candy. Sugar-free goodness becomes equated with emotional well-being. She develops an "am good–feel good" inner state of peacefulness and harmony as long as she keeps her hands away from those boxes of sweetened cereal. When her restraining power is high, she feels good. When it is low, she feels bad. Bad feelings equate to being a bad person. Emotions like shame, guilt, anger, and disgust ruin her day. After yielding to temptation, she has to do something to make things right and to make herself feel better. She wants to stay in a state of moral-emotional equilibrium. She wants to feel like a good person.

Sarah's parents may see her sugar-free lapses only in terms of health. They may think she is irritable because she is in a sugar funk. (She may be, but to debate that point would distract us from the moral point.) With an empty box of candy beside her, Sarah judges herself to have done something wrong. Doing bad, feeling bad, and being bad mesh together. She must make amends to get back to her am good–feel good state. "Developing Moral-Emotional Responsiveness" is the domain of conscience described in Chapter 3.

MORAL WEIGHTS

Imagine that candy-resistant Sarah is now eleven years old. She has been invited to spend the summer with relatives in a distant state. She is excited because this family with many cousins lives on a farm. They all ride horses. Her parents ask that she not be treated like a guest. They want her vacation to be a learning experience. They want her to fit into their relatives' family like a true member. She is to respect her aunt and uncle as though they are her parents. She is to carry her weight of chores and responsibilities. She is to participate in whatever the family does for fun and spiritual well-being.

Sarah's parents completely forget that this side of the family all have a rarely satisfied sweet tooth. Hard physical work allows them to eat what they want without worry. Sarah is continuously being offered sweet, gooey pastries and sugared cereals for breakfast. Her relatives aren't tempting her; they simply value sugar differently than her parents do. Sarah finds herself caught in a value clash. How will she handle this moral dilemma?

Sarah may, in her eleven-year-old mind, try to weigh one value against another. Her relatives are good people; they just do things differently. Her parents told her that they wanted her to fit into this family like a member. Her cousins will think she is weird if she doesn't do what they do. It would be impolite to expect different food from what the family eats.

Will Sarah see the sugar issue as an absolute wrong? as situationally de- pendent? as one value in the midst of many more important ones? as a silly value in need of discarding? as an opportunity to test her parents' convictions? In giving moral weight to her various thoughts, she will be affected by the pricking of her conscience as well as by her relationship with new authority figures in her summer life. The beliefs and feelings of her cousins and their friends will be important. Her own sense of choice will be important.

Chapters 4, 5, and 6 each deal with the domain of moral valuation—how we morally weigh different perspectives of any particular situation. Chapter 4, "Developing the Authority of Conscience," describes how we morally weigh issues in terms of lineage, status, traditions, and the wisdom of our elders. Chapter 5, "Developing the Golden Rule of Conscience," deals with how concepts of fairness and caring are interwoven into our conscience. Moral self-worth is dealt with in Chapter 6, "Developing Moral Willpower."

MORAL WILLPOWER

Sarah had a very good summer. After the first week, sugar slipped into the back of her mind. None of the relational aspects of morality that had made candy-avoidance an issue of oughtness at home existed in her summer environment. She didn't have to go to the dentist. No one found her hyperactive or lethargic. Her active lifestyle and metabolism evidently handled any carbohydrate overloads. Out of habit, she avoided stuffing herself with desserts.

Sweetness re-emerged as a sticky issue when she returned home. She found it difficult to turn off her morning urges for pastry and sugared cereal. What had formerly been a matter of automatic compliance now became an issue of debate, decision making, and will. As Sarah entered adolescence, sugar wasn't the only issue of debate, decision making, and will that cropped up. Finding her own moral pathway became very important to her. The way in which free will interweaves with conscience functioning is also described in Chapter 6.

Sugar was chosen as an issue in this vignette because it is debatable, metaphorical, and, we hope, humorous. We all agree that stealing candy is wrong. As parents, we have a less unified opinion about whether children should clean their plates before receiving dessert; to what extent sugar consumption is a health issue; and whether or not the sweets of life should all be earned. We have many decisions to make in guiding our children's conscience development. Some are sweet; some are sour. That's our moral burden.

MORAL MEMORY: CHAINS OF AUTOBIOGRAPHICAL STORIES

Moral development is complex and changing. When the conscience is challenged, many networks of brain functioning turn on. We use attention, emotion, reasoning, judgment, volition, language, and memory, one at a time or together, to differentiate the good from the bad, to figure out the right thing to do, to avoid harmful consequences. Fortunately, many decisions are as automatic as habits. Others require consultation with our encyclopedic conscience. Still others require on-the-spot, pioneer-like discovery. Where is moral knowledge stored? How is it organized? How does it get updated? In other words, just where does the conscience live within us? We believe that the conscience resides within chains and chains of autobiographical stories. We'll explain.

Stories captivate our attention and organize our memories. They are rich in meaning when they contain characters with interesting traits, beliefs, and vulnerabilities; when they present unusual provoking events and action choices; and when they surprise us with unusual complications and outcomes. We are more likely to remember stories in which we can identify with one of the characters, vicariously live through the challenges and rescue efforts, or accept a resolution of fate. Almost every story's resolution contains a moral lesson — hence the moral of the story. Sometimes it affirms a value in which we already believe. At other times it may pique our moral curiosity in new ways, leading us to new considerations.

Autobiographical stories organize moral themes at critical points in our development. As our brain functions mature, characters, provoking events, action choices, consequences, and resolutions take on more complex meaning. When old memories pop up for review, new insights about rightful ways to pursue the good may emerge. As parents, we are always having déjà vu experiences when our children challenge us in ways very similar to the ways in which we challenged our own parents. We may react to the current incident in the same way, convinced of the righteousness of our own rearing. Or we may do things differently. Child rearing is an opportunity to improve on the past. Sometimes we only make new mistakes.

Picture the moral theme of life as a chain of autobiographical stories, the morals of which keep getting reorganized through development. Conscience is a mental storehouse of our latest synthesis of moral meaning. It is a changing, developing formulation. Sometimes conscience may come to life like a real character in our life story. At other times it serves as a reference book. The progress and development of moral meaning-making is presented in summary form in Chapter 7, "Developing the Meaning of Conscience."

Conscience is an important part of our being, but it is not our whole being. Our whole being is better captured by the term "personality." We will describe our understanding of what personality is and how conscience fits into personality.

PERSONALITY: OUR SIGNATURE STATEMENT

Personality is both universal and unique. In the midst of universal features, we each make an individual statement to the world. We express our personality. The desire to get to know other people, to capture the essence of their personalities, is a common human quest. Students in their early teens sometimes exchange spiral-bound notebooks known as "Personality Books" in class.

The purpose of these books is to get to know each other in a fun and safe way. Many of these students may actually have known each other since kindergarten, but childhood getting-to-know-yous are different from emerging adolescent getting-to-know-yous. The latter type of will-you-or-won't-you-tell information is invested in popularity, sexual attraction, physical and social power, and other growing-up mysteries of instinct, body, and relationships.

Each page of the notebook has a question written at the top, with consecutive numbers written down the left-hand side. The numbers code individual respondents, identified on the last page of the book. The queries have to do with various preferences — some humdrum, others full of emotional meaning. "What is your favorite color, food, and music? What do you think about when you're alone? Who do you most want to be with on Friday night at the mall?"

As the book is surreptitiously passed from person to person in the classroom, the recipient chooses a line number and enters all answers to the questions on that particular line on each page. When an "interesting" response is noted on another line, the curious person can peek at the code page to see whose name matches that numbered line.

This rudimentary exercise in personality assessment is always done during school hours, when students are supposed to be focused on photosynthesis or geometry instead of each other's preferences and popularity. Their intense motivation to get to know each other through the safety of spiral-bound notebooks highlights the importance we all place on personality. These emerging teenagers want to know what others think and feel, as well as what others think and feel *about them.* They want to reveal themselves to others, too, but very, very cautiously! What is this thing called personality? Intuitively, they know that it has the power to drive friendship, animosity, gossip, fame, popularity, or ostracism. They want that social power under their command.

Today's behavioral scientists explore personality in terms of traits, types, and disorders. The *Diagnostic and Statistical Manual* of the American Psychiatric Association defines personality as a collection of dependably present traits within an individual, "enduring patterns of perceiving, relating to and thinking about the environment and oneself, . . . exhibited in a wide variety of important social and personal contexts." Individual differences in personality are influenced by the interactions of genetics, experience, and development.

If personality traits were not stable within individuals, we would have a hard time recognizing and figuring out how to relate to each other. Going to work or school each morning would be like entering a room full of strangers. Each interpersonal experience would consume all our energies, as it sometimes does when we encounter a person who is one way one minute and another way another minute, or someone who says one thing and does another. Some people are so confusing that we begin to doubt ourselves. "Did I hear that right?" "Didn't you just say X?" "Didn't you just do Y?" When we invest energy in getting to know people, we rely on stability in their personalities. When it isn't there, we want them to change or just leave us alone!

CONSCIENCE: MORAL STABILIZER IN THE PERSONALITY

At a level only hinted at in those personality books, we want to know if people are trustworthy, responsible, just, and caring. We want to know if their intentions are honorable, if they mean well even when they do things that upset us. We want to know if they respect authority, rules, and the law; if they have self-respect; if they stop to help people in trouble. We want to get to the heart of their personalities, to understand their characters, to know their moral values. In a word, we want to know what kind of a conscience they have. Conscience stabilizes the moral aspects of our personality.

Conscience organizes the moral theme in our personality. It determines what we are likely to get serious about, what actions we are likely to consider imperative. The uniqueness of our individual personality determines how we express these valued imperatives. We may express them shyly or boldly, flexibly or doggedly, humorously or boringly, consistently or erratically. When we present ourselves to each other, we do it personality to personality, not conscience to conscience. That deeper part of ourselves, the heart of our personality, our conscience, is always a little bit of a mystery. Every life story must have its mystery to be interesting. Mystery makes the news *news*, gossip *gossip*, and tales *tales*.

MISCHIEF, HUMOR, AND THE IMP

When we say that someone has a good personality, we are usually not talking about "good" in the moral sense. We usually mean that this person is likeable, is fun to be around, and has a good sense of humor. Conscience does not function well without humor. A humorless person is likely to be overly fastidious, self-righteous, and boring to the core. Such a person tends to believe that if she and everyone else in the world will just follow her moral imperatives, life on the planet will survive. Otherwise, we are all doomed!

People who are "good" in both senses of the word have achieved a healthy balance between moral and mischievous impulses in their personalities. The morally minded mischief-maker is careful to separate the prankster in him- or herself from thoughtlessness or the desire to be intentionally evil. Such a person draws a line between fooling people and hurting their feelings; smashing an old jalopy for a quarter at a fair and watching a house burn down; seeing irony in someone's misfortune and actually enjoying that misfortune.

Nurturing conscience development in children becomes an over-righteous endeavor if parents do not appreciate the mischievous impulses in themselves and their offspring. A book about conscience development that does not honor the fun of mischief is in danger of being overbearing and boring! Therefore, we have contrived a little character we call the Imp to travel with us through these pages. The Imp is a personification of the mischievous impulses that we all have inside us (some more than others). The Imp represents human fallibility. It keeps us humble. We have made him male because of our cultural tendency to link mischief with boys. Nonetheless, we give full honor to mischievous, indeed naughty, impulses in girls.

We urge you to use your imagination with our Imp. As we envision him, he is sometimes located inside parents, making them do things like forget a rule at the same time their youngster is praying for a little inconsistency. At other times he is inside the children, advocating some kind of foolery. In some of this book's anecdotes, he is sitting on the sidelines — just watching. In other stories, he is cheering for a particular outcome. In still others, he goes into hiding to stay out of harm's way.

While attending a storytelling festival, Connie Regan-Blake, an Appalachian storyteller from Asheville, North Carolina, told a brief story that captures the spirit of the Imp. Listen in on the following telephone conversation with a little boy who speaks in whispered voice:

Little Boy: Hello.

Caller: Hello there, is your mother there?

Little Boy: Yes.

Caller: May I speak to her?

Little Boy: She's bis . . . sey.

Caller: Well, is your daddy there?

Little Boy: Yes.

Caller: May I speak to him?

Little Boy: (hesitates) He's bis . . . sey.

Caller: Well, is any other grownup there?

Little Boy: Yes.

Caller: Who is it?

Little Boy: The policeman.

Caller: What in the world is going on at your house?

Little Boy: (whispers more than ever) They're looking for me!

We need the Imp with us, not only when we are having fun, but as a companion when we are trying to crawl out of trouble, and definitely when we are trying to see both the good and the bad in a predicament at the same time.

THE SERIOUS SIDE OF THE IMP

In addition to being a symbol for fun, mischief, and humor, the Imp also has a serious side. He reminds us that fallibility is our most consistent human characteristic. No matter how lofty our parenting goals or how diligently we pursue them, we are always bungling something. The Imp helps us to find humor in our predicaments and to forgive ourselves. He helps us tolerate imperfection. He helps us turn humiliation into humor.

Another serious side of the Imp is his role in the integration of good and evil in our minds. The Imp, as well as the mischief he causes, lives in the sometimes innocent, sometimes knowing space between good and evil. As we envision him, he always leans toward the side of goodness. His shenanigans help us choose goodness, sooner or later. Older adolescents at the Integrating stage of conscience development often tell us that while there is good within evil and evil within good, goodness should prevail. The Imp helps draw us toward that conclusion. He is, at heart, in favor of humility, tolerance, forgiveness and, above all, humor.

A VERY SERIOUS SIDE OF THE IMP

Occasionally a life situation places the Imp closer to evil than to goodness. This is a situation in which the "moral" of a real life story is a tragic combination of humor, harm, and revenge—a story full of irony. We invite you to place yourselves in such a story. In this story, we as parents make a faulty assumption. We assume that if we keep our children in safe neighborhoods, in "good" schools, and in association with the "right" friends, they will develop good consciences and be protected from evil at the same time. We falsely believe that evil exists in other places—in "bad" neighborhoods, in "bad" schools, and among gangs of children of "bad" conscience.

Then something tragic happens to our children living in that good neighborhood, attending that good school, and avoiding those bad ac-quaintances. We are shocked into realizing that society is an intercon-nected moral network with holes in the net. When we don't concern ourselves with moral rights and needs of all children, our own children may fall through the holes.

Because we believe so strongly that, as parents and citizens, we all must be concerned about developing the conscience of the community as well as the conscience of all children, we will, from time to time, make an advocacy statement on behalf of all our children. Here is our first one.

THE ADVOCATE

While as parents we are intimately involved with our own children, we also have conscience-nurturing responsibilities toward the community of all children. Every time we focus on the moral rights and needs of all children, we contribute to the moral fiber of the community in which our children live. We each have the talent and opportunity to do something. Let's do it!

DELAYS AND DEVIANCIES IN CONSCIENCE DEVELOPMENT

Somewhere between fear and fascination are questions we all ask about conscience development gone awry. What about children who allegedly have no conscience? What about children who grow up to murder their parents, put babies in trash cans, shoot their classmates, or espouse Satan worship? What about the consciences of Napoleon, Hitler, Stalin, and Pol Pot? We have to admit that we too are fascinated and pained by what goes wrong in human development. We study development gone awry. And we'll write a book about handling delays and deviancies in conscience development—later. In this book we deal with the normal trajectory in conscience development, including its developmental crises.

DEVELOPMENTAL CRISES

Developmental crisis is part of normal conscience development. Some children are crisis-prone. Others sail into adulthood over velvet-smooth waters. Mid-adolescence is more likely to be punctuated by crisis than are other developmental periods. That fact will be evident in chapters to come. If children grew up without ever having a crisis of conscience, parents might become very smug about their parenting abilities. The Imp wouldn't like that. Developmental crises in children teach their parents how to be better parents.

CHILD-REARING AND PARENT-REARING

Rearing children is a two-way developmental process. Parents nurture children's development, while children nurture parents'. Children's growing-up experiences prompt memories of parents' own conscience-forming influences to rise to the surface. Let them rise. Those memories help us preserve the best of our moral heritage while adapting it to current reality. At the risk of making new mistakes, we dedicate ourselves to improving the flaws of the past. Life is moral lesson after moral lesson.

Developing the Moral Connection

2

Even before their birth, we have the capacity to form a deep psychological connection with our children. Bioevolutionary systems support our capacity to nurture. This capacity is general enough to make us respond to many forms of neediness. Thus, we also have a natural capacity to become psychologically connected as adoptive parents, foster parents, child-care workers, pet owners, and caretakers of all kinds.

Our nurturing capacity blossoms with stimulation. In parenting, stimulation comes from our children's neediness and our own conscience. Infants come to us innocent and lovable, and requiring constant supervision. Our conscience stimulates us to foster the rightful pursuit of goodness in them. How we do it is guided by care-receiving practices from our past. We modify those practices as we go along. We learn as our children develop.

In conscience formation, the psychological bond between parents and children becomes moralized—immediately for parents, and gradually for children. Parent moral responsibilities center around protection, empathic understanding, and gentle teaching. The gradually developing moral responsibilities for our children center around compliance and pleasing. We will explain the moralization process in more detail as we go along.

SECURITY

HIGH-QUALITY, HIGH-QUANTITY INVOLVEMENT

Peaches is a cat. In most ways, she acts like a cat. She purrs, licks her paws, scratches herself against rough surfaces, leaps from one piece of furniture to the next, and uses a litter box. In one important way, though, she is not cat-like: she has no air of indifference toward humans. She meets people at the door, not to slither by them to get to the outside, but to get acquainted. She jumps from lap to lap, begging for all the attention she can get. She is thought of by her human family as the best cat-dog they have ever known.

One week, Peaches was left alone while her human family went on vacation. A caretaker came every day to check her food, water, and litter box, as well as to pet and talk to her for about five minutes of "quality time." Then the caretaker went outside to work in the flower garden. The caretaker spent more time with the flowers than she did with Peaches. Peaches got mad. Or she went stir-crazy. Or something. She continued to use her litter box, but she expanded its borders to include the couches and the carpeting.

Our young children act like that, too, when they don't get enough affection, attention, playful interaction, or teaching. They may regress in toilet habits, too. On purpose? Well, not exactly. It happens at a deeper level—at the level of psychological security. Forget brief, intense, entertaining, "quality" time. Peaches got five minutes of undivided attention every day. She needed more, and so do human children. Need for high-quality interaction goes on hour after hour, day after day. High-quality, high-quantity involvement builds our sense of security.

Eventually, we parents don't have to be with our children all the time for them to feel psychologically secure. Don't ask how long that takes. Our teenagers' distancing cues will guide our common sense. The time simply comes when parent availability is more important than parent presence. By that time, our teenagers have internalized many moralizing experiences with us. We are there in the recesses of their minds. When moral choices or dilemmas arise, our teenagers speculate about what we parents would think mandatory, how we would reason it out, what we would do—if they take time to think about it. Internalized psychological security blends with moral influence.

INSECURITY

An attitude of parent entitlement corrupts psychological security. When we feel entitled, we believe that our children's compliance is our due rather than something that we induce through respectful management. We use authority over our children as though we are vanquishing an enemy. Our children cannot possibly feel psychologically secure if our child-rearing is a reign of terror.

Admittedly, we all get bossy when we are frazzled. Those episodes are far different from giving ourselves an all-season license to act meanly, punitively, tyrannically, or abusively. Our children will forgive frazzled episodes. In contrast, they will harbor long-standing grudges and disrespect for the despot.

Parenting despots may have a history of flawed attachments or bonding experiences. In fact, they may feel more psychologically connected to objects, social position, aloneness, or conscience-altering substances than to people. If these goals consume us—hiding our emotional neediness from ourselves—we may consider our children's needs a nuisance, an interference to more private pursuits. Fearful, rejected children find it hard to grasp their end of the moral connection. They have little motivation to comply or to please.

When disconnected from those who are vital to their well-being, people feel estranged, alienated, sickened, or lonely. If our children have these feelings, despair may slowly erode their desire or their energy to morally connect with us. They may not be able to articulate what is missing in their lives. They may misbehave because wrongdoing repeatedly grabs our attention. If we are salvageable parents—and mostly we are—the Imp may conspire with our children in humor-arousing shenanigans. Negative behavior gets attention, but negative funny behavior gets even more attention. Our children may use clowning to avoid punishment. When we get the point of the joke, we may wake up and connect more meaningfully.

Children are great hopers. If parents fade in and out of connectedness, children may cling to threads of hope. Even though worn to a frazzle by consuming work schedules, adults-only connectedness, or other diversions, we may wake up to what is most important in our lives—nurturing parent-child relationships. We and our children build society together. If we don't get that point or fade in and out of it, our children may find connection substitutes through media, the mall, substances, or emotionally and morally detached peers. They may be drawn to the same self-centered ambitiousness and busy diversions that distract their parents from human connection.

PROTECTING OUR CHILDREN FROM DANGER

Danger simply means that something bad may happen. Inevitably, danger becomes part of human consciousness. It may creep into our awareness slowly, unevenly, or abruptly. We may learn about it directly or through tales of other people's woes. Children's fairy tales are full of woe. Accidents, disease, pain, natural disaster, human-made harm, and war are always taking their toll somewhere. Human adversity pleads for moral meaning.

As parents we want to protect our children from danger—sometimes, from even knowing about danger. Yet we don't want to be so protective that they minimize, doubt, or scoff at its existence. Coming from the opposite direction, we don't want to be so protective that they fail to develop courage, shrink from worthy risks and challenges, or fail to aspire to occasional heroism. We want them to experience only as much danger as will guide their moral sensibilities. We want them to develop a sense of oughtness about protecting themselves and others from danger.

Parents want their children to know security. Security is a feeling state of sunshine, goodness, and grace—antithetical to danger and harm. We nurture security in our infants through regularly meeting their needs, showering them with affection, singing silly songs, clowning around, and soothing them in times of discomfort. We affirm their basic goodness with the natural but foolish-sounding, high-pitched language of parentese (baby-talk). We connect with our children in the mutual enjoyment of security.

EMPATHY

Empathy is the ability to enter into the feeling state of another person, to respond to the other's joy, distress, or sorrow. We nurture empathy in our infants when we mirror and remirror their emotional expressions. In contrast, mockery is an enemy to empathy. Mockery both imitates and demeans another person's emotional state. When we grow tired of our children's whininess, we sometimes mock them rather than help them alleviate the cause of their whininess.

Empathy guides *pleasing initiatives*—actions designed to bring out positive emotions in another. Empathy dovetails with the development of *perspective taking*—looking at a problem from someone else's point of view. Empathy promotes the practice of walking in another's shoes. Empathy knows when those shoes hurt.

We all have limits to our empathic capacity. Fatigue and personal adversity may slow its flow to a trickle. We have a hard time with bullies and those who lie, cheat, and steal. Bias and prejudice turn empathy to mockery; they devalue a specific social class, race, ethnicity, religion, age, physical condition, or gender. Teenagers are particularly vulnerable to narrowing their empathic vision to their own peer group. Temporary insecurity can send empathy underground when teenage group togetherness centers around nastiness toward an out-group or one of its members.

One day, a certain eighth-grade class cast empathy to the wind in front of their social studies teacher, Mrs. Brubacher. Mrs. Brubacher was a nervous woman. At times she became peculiarly shaky. Perhaps she had menopausal hot flashes. Perhaps she was hyperthyroid; her eyes did protrude a little. The class did not identify with her distress. They found her nervous habits curious and humorous. They mocked her when she wasn't looking. Furthermore, they were fascinated by the fact that they could intensify her trembling with their orneriness. Orneriness gave them a sense of group cohesiveness and power.

One day these eighth-graders went well beyond impishness. Impishness would have been dropping their pencils in unison at a certain tick of the clock. Mrs. Brubacher would have laughed at that, at least the first time they did it. Headless and heartless, the class decided they would all turn and stare at her at the same time. They did. Mrs. Brubacher started trembling. The class persisted with their stony stares. She ran out of the room in a state of panic! Mrs. Brubacher's flight brought the class back to moral sensibility. They suddenly realized that they were in trouble, the kind of trouble where you suddenly fear that your parents may be asked to come to school and you will be asked to give a public explanation of your behavior. Mrs. Brubacher might have gone to get the principal, or at least to Mr. Kramer, the math teacher down the hall. He didn't tolerate any shenanigans. The class awakened to their cruelty.

No negative consequences ensued. Mrs. Brubacher simply returned to her desk, gaze averted, while she pretended to grade papers. The students looked down at their desks, pretending to do their assignments. Not a word was said. There was no request for an explanation, no reprimand, and no apologies. No consequences were imposed. Nothing. No parent, fellow teacher, or principal was informed. Mrs. Brubacher was ashamed. The class was ashamed. They thought they were awful, and they were. The Imp grinned at their shame, but not at Mrs. Brubacher's. She had been victimized by the kids. They didn't do it again.

Cruelty is the antithesis of empathy. Empathy is a builder of oughtness, but lapses in empathy can also build oughtness. Weeks passed. Near Christmas break, Mrs. Brubacher announced that she was going to supply ice cream for the Christmas party. The class cheered. Eyes met. Appreciation reaffirmed the class's moral connection to Mrs. Brubacher.

OUGHTNESS

STAYING OUT OF TROUBLE

If someone asks a child why she refrains from doing something that might upset her parents, she may reply, "Because I don't want to get in trouble." At face value, parent stature, size of the voice box, or other indicators of punitive power may seem like *the* factors keeping our children in line. Some people believe that fear of punishment is the first and foremost factor moralizing children's behavior. We disagree. Punishment can control behavior, but it doesn't necessarily moralize it. In fact, too much punishment can have the opposite effect. We propose that oughtness, that sense of obligation that impels us toward refraining from some behaviors and pursuing others in behalf of goodness, is motivated by loftier goals than fear of getting punished—even in a young child.

Relationship trouble is the real motivator for developing oughtness. *Relationship trouble* means entering the danger zone for becoming emotionally disconnected from those near and dear to us. An occasional sharp word will not do it. An occasional slammed door will not do it. What will do it is a persistently negative or indifferent attitude from someone vital to our well-being. As parents we are vital to the security and emotional well-being of our children—as well as to each other. Chronically negative, dismissive attitudes on the part of someone vital create a hole in the heart, a feeling of badness or unworthiness, a feeling of being far removed from security and empathic understanding. Fear of being unlovable is real moral trouble. Being unlovable is license to do unlovable acts.

Situation by situation, we teach our children oughts and ought-nots for living. Psychological security and empathic understanding motivate that learning. Each lesson expands our children's understanding of the security-empathy-oughtness bond. Some oughtness lessons are hard to learn. Sometimes our children have a hard time reading us. We keep changing our expectations as they mature. What we may respond to as cute at one age, we define as an ought-not at another age. What may seem like a bad in our children's minds isn't always labeled as bad by parents. What to them seems like a good isn't always labeled as good. We'll explain these complexities in more detail in the chapters on moral valuation. Right now, we'll provide one example.

A certain first-grade boy got sick in school. Jeffrey vomited in reading group. He thought he was in trouble. Surely he would fail reading. While his classmates snickered or said, "Yuck," Jeffrey's teacher simply helped him clean up and sent him to the office. He thought the principal would spank him. Instead, the secretary said comforting things and called his home. Jeffrey thought the secretary was just being nice because that was her job. Surely he would be in trouble at home. When Jeffrey got home, nothing bad happened. His babysitter comforted him and called Mom at work. Mom told her to give him nothing more than a soda to drink. When she got home, she empathized with him about how terrible he must have felt in reading group. His teacher called to see how he was feeling. Security and empathy remained intact. Since he wasn't in trouble, Jeffrey reasoned that his oughts and ought-nots must be all right, too. The security-empathy-oughtness bond hadn't been broken. He just had more to learn about the criteria for getting a good grade in reading.

PLAYING WITH OUGHTNESS

Toddlers don't know much about oughtness. Parents are always retrieving their toddlers from danger zones and distracting them from trouble-in-the-making. It's an exhausting task. In one developmental study, mothers of ten-month-olds were noted to spend 90 percent of their time with their infants demonstrating affection, play, and caregiving. However, by the time the infants were thirteen to seventeen months old, the mothers were expressing a prohibition every nine minutes! Ought-not-to-touch is one of the first moral lessons we parents teach. We can leisurely pamper our way through toilet training, but there simply aren't enough locks, harnesses, and hard-to-open bottle caps to childproof a fast-toddling toddler. Teaching ought-not-to-touch and ought-not-to-go-there is the only solution.

Let's imagine trying to teach Nicole, a toddler daughter, to leave the knobs of the television set alone. Pretend the set is an old-fashioned one; the knobs are all in front rather than in a covered panel with a remote control. In contrast to stove knobs, there is no real danger with television knobs—no burning lesson to be learned. Of all the restraint issues we could have chosen, for unknown reasons we chose this one. Maybe the nuisance factor of having to readjust a set that's ready to go on the blink any minute influenced our decision. Resetting knobs upsets us. Nicole finds it fun. Since she can't understand the underlying economic issue, and since knobs are fun to turn, her sense of oughtness must be built out of "because Mom 'n' Dad said so." She has to agree to PG wisdom when she has no reasoning capacity for doing so. Oughtness linked to her own security and emotional well-being is the only thing that is going to make sense to Nicole.

Let's say that we believe Nicole to be beyond the stage when we should simply remove her from the set or distract her with another activity. We think she is ready to learn that we mean business when we say, "No." Nicole is a bold little girl. If she were one of those timid types who always burst into tears when looked at crossly, fear might be the immediate reason to obey. Then our story would be all over.

We initiate a series of teaching strategies with this fearless child. Whatever those strategies are—saying "No, no," taping the knobs, raising our voices, giving her a time-out, not letting her watch Barney, slapping her wrist—Nicole repeats in play. She makes a game out of the whole process. It goes like this: Nicole moves toward the TV set, and while looking engagingly and impishly toward us, she reaches out toward the knobs. We know that she knows she is not to turn those knobs. She knows that we will do something if she gets too close. She just doesn't know what it will be. It's a game. Will we do what we used to do—engage her in some other activity? Will we say "No, no"? Will we get angry and slap her wrist? It's a mystery game. Nicole giggles, keeping us engaged while we figure out our next move. What PG strategies will teach her the difference between play and seriousness? What will make ought-not-to-touch make sense?

Rules are play long before they are accepted as oughts. Playing or teasing with a rule implies some understanding of the rule, even when it is not taken seriously. The Imp loves this territory between knowledge and oughtness, between playfulness and seriousness. He enjoys our parenting consternation as we try to decide whether Nathan or Nicole is ready for a particular oughtness lesson. If parents find themselves getting all out of whack—losing control and slapping a wrist—it means that neither parent nor child is ready for the lesson. Expecting compliance before our children are developmentally ready to take a rule seriously is a waste of time and energy.

EMPATHIC OUGHTNESS

What determines acceptance of parent-guided wisdom before the age of reason? What turns on the oughtness knob? We propose that the development of our children's empathy is instrumental in their accepting parent wisdom. Compliance is forthcoming when our children realize that a particular demand is really important to us. That gives us license to show our distress—within limits. Our children gradually accept the viewpoint that what we believe is right. To illustrate, we will contrive two hypothetical conversations between a parent and a seven-year-old boy, the first of which never occurs and the second of which often occurs.

When John was three years old, his favorite ball bounced into the street in front of his house and was flattened by a passing car. His eyes grew wide as he looked toward his mom to rescue it. When innocent, spontaneous actions meet with painful results, a child's eyes ask, "What happened?" and plead, "Fix it, pleeeease!" Mom retrieved the flattened ball, tried to soothe John over the fact that it couldn't be fixed, told him he would be able to get another ball, but emphasized that they would play with the new ball in the safety of their backyard.

By the time John was seven, his love for balls had grown and grown. He loved basketballs, footballs, soccer balls, volleyballs, softballs, golf balls—even croquet balls. A golf ball had recently gone through his family's living room window, but it had been his friend Tim's accident, not his. One day he asked his mom, "Can I go out and play?" Mom replied, "Sure; where are you going to be?" John: "Out front with Tim." Mom: "OK, but if you're going to hit golf balls, I want you out back aiming toward the woodpile." John: "OK." Pretty soon, another ball went through the window of the living room, where John's sister was practicing the piano. Fortunately, she was not hit. Now comes the conversation that never occurs:

Mom: What happened?

John: I failed to listen to you, dear mother, and made an error.

Mom: What was your error, John?

John: I accidentally hit the ball through the window.

Mom: What are you going to do about it, John?

John: I'm going to pay for the window with my allowance.

Mom: What are you going to do next time, John?

John: I'm going to listen to you, dear mother, and always aim golf balls toward the woodpile in the backyard.

Mom: Yes, John, that's what you ought to do to be a good boy.

This sticky-sweet exchange of information, rules, consequences, and plans for reform never occurs. The more likely conversation sounds like this:

Mom: What happened?

John: Hmmm . . . (muffled voice; gaze averted) I don't know.

Mom: (with controlled anger) Where did I tell you that you could hit golf balls?

John: (very softly) In the backyard.

Mom: (continuation of controlled anger) Give me the clubs and go to your room. Tim, you go on home.

The second conversation demonstrates a big-time disruption in emotional harmony between mother and son. John's time in his room will give Mom an opportunity to design her next teaching strategy. It will give John the opportunity to deal with his shame and anticipate Mom's next move. Considering the history of their relationship and their previous experience with balls, few explanatory words will be necessary. Mom won't even need to mention that John could have harmed his sister. Besides, his sister will have reminded him of that herself. Exactly when and how John will moralize this incident —that is, accept the oughtness of Mom's rule about balls—is unknown, but the lesson is certainly getting ripe. Mom's messages are clear: "Read my emotions! What you did is dangerous. You are in trouble! Mind what I say! I know what I'm doing! I know what you ought to do!"

After a zillion such incidents—a finger cut by a do-not-touch knife, a toy rusted in the rain, a library book lost, a left-in-the-yard bicycle stolen, a candy-caused stomachache—we parents finally make some headway in shaping our children's sense of oughtness. Ever so slowly, children begin to get the thorny point that parents, magically or not, somehow know when danger and harm are coming. Once children catch on to our PG wisdom, they don't even ask us to prove it—until adolescence. So if our child happens to confuse natural consequences, like falling down and spraining a wrist, with parental clairvoyance ("I told you to walk, not run"), let's just not mention it. What matters is that our children accept their parents' good sense. When child sense finally tunes in to parent sense, oughtness begins to make good sense.

YOU'RE OLD ENOUGH TO KNOW BETTER!

Since oughtness is a slow-growing creature, we can get really frustrated by its two-steps-forward, one-step-backward progress in our youngsters. Amazing questions and comments fall out of us. We say things to children that we would never say to each other: "How many times am I going to have to tell you _____?" "Where was your head?" "Why don't you listen?" "When are you going to learn _____?" "You should be ashamed!" "You're old enough to know better!"

Do these shaming questions ever help? Since they all imply moral stupidity, they should have a demoralizing rather than a moralizing effect on the child. Many of them are humiliating. However, once in a while, at just the right moment—when parent frustration, disgust, and despair are matched by child frustration, disgust, and despair over some consequence that didn't need to happen—such a question may nudge our child toward oughtness. In that important moment, parent and child share the same feelings about the same event: "It's ruined!" Uncannily, though, it is at just such moments that silence is golden. Mutual feelings of frustration, disgust, and despair can seal an oughtness lesson without a word being spoken. Then, a hug seems more appropriate!

DANDELION KINDNESS

The moral of John's golf-ball story involves curtailment of energy. It represents all the times our child must put the brakes on behavior in order to be good. In this kind of situation, the moral lesson is to NOT do something dangerous or irksome. In contrast, moral meaning also flows from acts of spontaneous goodness. Think of the classic example of a child picking a bouquet of flowers for Mom. Now, this example could be another put-the-brakes-on-your-behavior story. The flowers could have come from the neighbor's yard. Instead, let's assume that the flowers are prize-winning dandelions from our own backyard.

An act of dandelion kindness has at least three possible motives in maintaining the moral connection. The first motive is the joy of presenting the dandelions as a gift—seeing Mom smile. A second motive is making a happy Mom smile even more—enhancing joy. A third motive is making a sad Mom happy—making joy return. We've purposely used the word *joy* three times. Moral motivation has as much to do with the positive emotions as the negatives ones. Shame and guilt don't get all the credit for being *the* moral emotions! Smiles as well as frowns strengthen the moral connection. As parents, we strengthen the moral connection when we acknowledge, appreciate, and cheer spontaneous goodness. And remember that spontaneous goodness should be play long before it is upgraded to demand.

SPONTANEITY AND OUGHTNESS

Spontaneity characterizes the energy of childhood. The zest of exploration—turning knobs, climbing on cabinets, playing with fire and water, creating artistic masterpieces—is an inherent part of childhood and, therefore, parenthood. Spontaneity interweaves with playfulness throughout our lives. It fosters inventiveness, cleverness, and genius in those who provide us with new gadgets, art forms, and theories. Spontaneity in human relationships keeps them from going sour. Good intentions bloom from spontaneity.

Spontaneity and oughtness may walk hand in hand as happy companions. Gift giving, sharing, politeness, or cheerfulness may be both fun and purposefully good. When acts of spontaneous goodness become expectations, propriety and oughtness start pinching and poking at us. Propriety formalizes niceness into manners and social protocols. Oughtness tugs at the heart to keep the niceness flowing consistently, even in situations where we have run out of energy.

If oughtness becomes a great big NAG, a joyless security-empathy-OUGHTNESS connection is created. Oughtness becomes so big that it overwhelms security and empathy. At other times oughtness is just a pin prick, asking us to balance our own interest with the interests of others. Think of the times our spontaneity and memory were out of sync with an anniversary or Secretary's Day. Think of a teenager looking sore and bored when ordered to attend his younger sister's piano recital. Think of a young child being coerced into making a halfway-false apology.

The Imp enjoys watching people struggle when spontaneity gets pinched and poked by oughts and ought-nots. He likes to sit at that fork in the road where playful, spontaneous goodness goes down one lane and mischievous spontaneity goes down the other. Danger and Trouble live in the woods by that second lane. The Imp watches for people who try to straddle both lanes at once—like the child who broke Mom's heirloom vase while putting a bouquet of dandelions in it. On such occasions, he doesn't watch the child. He watches Mom to see how she's going to deal with her conflicted feelings. Is she going to show pleasure over the child's joyful giving and hide her pain about the vase; show pain and spoil the child's pleasure; or muddle around somewhere in between?

DEVELOPMENTAL CONSIDERATIONS

DEVELOPING THE MORAL CONNECTION
AT THE EXTERNAL STAGE (0–6)

Cheering Development

Imagine a child's first memory of doing something good. Chances are that if the memory comes from before school age, it involves a normal biological function—something that is simply part of growing up. What is oughtness-motivating in these memories is the parent cheering—how pleased we show ourselves to be about the child's first steps, words, or potty aim. Connecting parent pride to growing up strengthens our child's end of moral connection. It affirms the basic goodness of growing up.

Interviewer: What is the very first thing you did that was called good?

Young child: I guess whenever I said "Mama." That was probably good for my Mom, made her happy.

Another YC: Walking. [My parents] tried to teach me to walk farther. They were happy.

Another YC: When I was potty trained. They made a big deal out of it.

Rescues from Danger

Cheering normal development is easy. All parents have to do is coax it along and clap. Helping our children to avoid danger is harder, especially if they are particularly adventuresome. Protecting them from harm requires more vigilant energy than cheering does. A sixteen-year-old boy, Josh, recalls how he came to know that playing with matches while watching cartoons in bed on a Saturday morning is wrong.

> Sixteen-year-old: When I was a kid, I burned my bed. I like fire. I got my parents. It was in the morning and I was sitting in bed watching cartoons. At that age, I didn't feel bad because I had done something wrong, but that my parents would get mad.

At the time of the incident, Josh had not yet learned that playing with matches in bed was an ought-not. However, he quickly became worried about how his parents would react to the flaming situation he had created. He was afraid that their relationship might be "on fire." Had he done something to char their emotional harmony? Not if he did some fast learning about the fierier aspects of his end of the moral connection!

Unfortunately, Josh was too young to use the match-lighting episode to predict all future dangerous events. At the age of eight, he put together a chemical experiment that blew up on him in the bathroom sink. And when interviewed at sixteen, he said he still liked fire! Fortunately, he added that he had learned to be more careful. Spontaneous, impulsive, experimental, and independent, but yet securely and empathically attached to his parents, Josh walked a pathway to oughtness filled with excitement and danger. For his parents, nurturing their son's sense of oughtness required an emphasis on survival, frequent smoke-detector checks, and a good homeowner's policy!

Oughtness Connected to a Coke!?!

The earlier our children discover their end of the moral connection, the sturdier their consciences will be. If a child happens to have come to our adoptive or foster-care home with a frayed moral connection, many applications of moral super-glue may be required. David, an eleven-year-old foster son, describes his resistance to making the moral connection:

> Interviewer: What is the first thing you can remember doing that was called good?

> David: About third grade. It was the first time I had actually asked if I could have a Coke. Usually I would steal it and drink it in my room. We were supposed to drink it in the kitchen, but I usually drank it in my room and didn't ask. I didn't even care. [That day] they didn't say "Drink it in the kitchen," but I actually stayed in there and drank it. After my parents found out I stayed in there, they were like, "WHAT!?!'" After that, I figured out that if you ask, you get just about everything. So now I ask!

This is not a typical first memory of goodness in an eleven-year-old. However, it is a very important one in the development of David's conscience. Expansive parental cheering is the crucial moralizer, the super-glue, in this story. What if his parents had flippantly or disgustedly said, "It's about time you started listening!"? Or what if their "WHAT!?!" was stated in mocking rather than enthusiastic tones? More stealing and hoarding would probably have followed.

THE ADVOCATE

Hats off to parents who adopt or foster hard-to-connect-with children. When adults take on the care of children who have mainly been raising themselves, the moral connection builds very slowly. These children's paths to oughtness are often thornbush after thornbush of danger and resistance. Unable to succumb to faith in parent-guided wisdom, they learn most things the hard way! However, a weak moral connection is better than no connection at all.

This Coke story raises an important question regarding making the moral connection. Did the parental cheering over David's spontaneous goodness teach him to want to please his foster parents? Or did it simply teach him how to get more Cokes and "just about everything" you want? Was his oughtness getting linked to security and empathy or to possessions? We suspect that at this point in David's foster-son development, his moral connection was 80 percent to Coke and 20 percent to parent security and empathy. Children, like David, whose needs for psychological security have gone unmet for years have a hard time believing that grownups' demands and limitations are in their best interests. Expansive parental cheering moved David a little bit closer to trusting them. Trust is a requirement for accepting parent oughts and ought-nots. A stable ability to trust may still be miles away for David.

From Security to Trust in Parental Guidance

Many young children buffer their fears about being physically separated from their parents' protection at bedtime by holding tightly to special blankets or stuffed animals. They seek these items in the daytime, too, when they feel in need of comfort. Psychologists call these security items *transitional objects*. They form a transitional bridge between security derived from the real live presence of parents and a representation of security in their minds. Once a mental representation of security is secure in their minds, transitional objects can be taken away without traumatizing our children—in spite of a few remaining protests from them.

David was beyond transitional objects. He created his own sense of security as he traveled from foster home to foster home. David needed a different kind of transitional object—a transitional trust object. He used a concrete reward (like the Coke) to succumb to trusting his parents' guidance. By accepting the Coke contingency—"Drink it in the kitchen"—David gave up a little bit of his premature autonomy. Other insightful breakthroughs may push him even further toward accepting parent-guided moral wisdom. "You can get about anything you want, if you _____" will, we can hope, change into "You can get what you need and what's good for you if you _____. Doing what's good for you feels good when your parents cheer you on." David's parents cheered any compliance in him vigorously, hoping that trust in their guidance would follow.

—— ADVICE TO PARENTS ——————————————————

Nurturing the Moral Connection at the External Stage (0–6)

- **Provide your children with protection, care, and gentle teaching. Remember their need for high-quality, high-quantity involvement.**

- **Mirror and remirror emotions, especially the positive ones. Empathize with the negative ones. Soothe distress.**

- **Cheer every aspect of your children's development.**

- **Rescue your children from danger without blaming them.**

- **Look for cues of readiness for oughtness learning.**

- **Tolerate impishness.**

DEVELOPING THE MORAL CONNECTION AT THE BRAIN-HEART STAGE (7–11)

Laddering Moral Learning

Teachers quickly identify children who have entered school unready to learn. Sometimes the unreadiness has to do with cognitive development. Other times it reflects delays in conscience development. Oughtness-prepared children can listen attentively, honor adult requests, and learn classroom rules. Their moral connection to their parents is ready to be extended to other adults—to the bus driver, traffic guard, teacher, and coach. Conscience-delayed children have a weak moral connection to authority figures.

They are poorly motivated to monitor their behavior in behalf of compliance and pleasing.

When conscience nurturance has progressed smoothly, our children enter first grade feeling basically good about themselves; well-cheered for natural development, self-care, and compliance with household routines; and ready to learn new rules. Their focus on compliance and pleasing adults is ready to transform into compliance with rules. When this transition occurs, honoring a rule of oughtness becomes as compelling as honoring the rule-maker. The rule itself carries moral weight. Conscience-delayed children have little motivation to accept rules when they have yet to accept the moral authority of the rule-maker.

Skill Development

Brain-Heart stage children often describe a particular skill when asked to recall their earliest memory of doing something good.

> Interviewer: What are your first memories of being told you had done something good?

> Older child: When I learned to write my name.

> Another OC: When I learned to ride a bike. My dad said he would hold on to the seat, but he let go. And I rode by myself!

> Another OC: I passed out ice cream to the other kids. [First memory of doing something bad?] I hit Jessica.

These children express pride in skill development—academic, physical, and social. Soon moral rules governing how a skill is practiced will be learned. "Always write your name in the right-hand corner of your paper." "Always wear your bicycle helmet." "Be kind to other children."

The Security of Structure and Rules

Imagine all of the skills that children master between the ages of seven and eleven. Thoughts about a certain seven-year-old granddaughter made the following list jump onto the page: sounding out new words, printing, adding and subtracting, drawing dinosaurs, slicing a kiwi with an egg slicer, playing soccer, riding a bike without training wheels, winning ribbons in a horse show, making up a softball game with five bases, staining woodwork for an art project, playing tricks on people, telling "knock, knock" jokes, playing with a friend for several hours without fighting, making a bed—the list could go on forever.

How do our school-age children fit so much play and learning into each day? It requires that we parents be very organized. We help our children (and ourselves) become neither frantic nor lazy by giving them chore and study routines balanced with free time; quiet time balanced with active and noisy times; alone time balanced with play-with-friends time; TV time balanced with family time. We promote security and emotional well-being by balancing help-you-do-it tasks with do-it-yourself tasks. Development-sensitive structure and rules help our Brain-Heart stage children expand their end of the moral connection. They learn to balance expected accomplishment with personal satisfaction.

The Market's Competing Connection

The moral connection we make with our children is not free of outside influences. The commercial establishment is very eager to use our children to influence parent values. While we are teaching them that pursuing goodness means skill development, the advertising industry is singing and tap-dancing a powerful parallel message—goodness is getting goods. When the market taps our children's demand center, we parents can easily confuse moral motivation with material motivation. Instead of offering our children psychological security and emotional understanding to motivate compliance and pleasing, we may offer them goods. Listen to the following child's story:

Interviewer: How do your parents show they care about your goodness?

Older child: They take privileges away from me, ground me. I have to stay in the house and can't play Sega or the pinball machine. They [parents] bought me a Sega and a pinball machine and a Coke machine—for getting along with my brother.

This example portrays a costly value mixture of materialism and brotherly love. Giving our children a bunch of stuff to be taken away when they don't behave may connect all of us more to materialism than to each other. We serve the promotion of brotherly love better when we take the time to model cooperative behavior, engage our children in moral discussions, and cheer fairness and caring decisions between them and their siblings.

"A" for Effort

As our children enter the years of rapid skill development, they gradually become aware of how their achievements compare with those of other children. They discover personal talents and love-to-do activities alongside can't-do's and hate-to-do's. They become aware of effort. Some children seemingly perform well with hardly any effort at all. For others, it's try, try, try. Making no effort can lead to shaming, bad grades, or even punishment; putting forth great effort can lead to praise, ribbons, and trophies. Our children learn that a certain amount of effort is required of them, whether they like it or not. They learn that effort is a value in and of itself; that others value them in terms of effort; that teachers tend to evaluate effort in written form about every six weeks. Effort becomes a moral issue, a way of pleasing.

Interviewer: How do your parents show that they care about your goodness?

Older child: A lot of times my Dad will say, "Whoa!" and sometimes he'll tell me a story of when he was little.

Another OC: They take me places. They congratulate me. If I don't try, they look at me in a mean way.

We parents support the moral connection by being neither oppressive nor permissive in our expectations of effort. With capital letters for emphasis—

- A security-empathy-OUGHTNESS connection destroys the desire to strive. Someone is expecting too much effort. Parents? Teachers? Our children themselves?
- A SECURITY-EMPATHY-oughtness connection produces an irresponsible child. Insufficient expectations for effort are being set.
- A balanced security-empathy-oughtness connection produces children who strive, tolerate mistakes, strive again, and know when to take a break.

As parents we empathize with our children's desire for success. Our empathy leads us to work with teachers and coaches to clearly define expectations that are within our children's developmental reach. Empathy leads us to listen attentively to tales of difficulty, defeat, and triumph; to balance lend-a-hand times with struggle-on-your-own times; and to encourage negotiation regarding effort expectations. We cheer successful achievement, effort, and limits on effort.

Achievement, effort, and limits on effort are important in our children's feelings of social success. Not every sibling, classmate, or playmate can be dealt with by just trying harder to get along. Sometimes parents need to help children with fairness-and-caring issues. The following mother gave sibling fairness a little boost:

Interviewer: What did your mother do when you took your brother's candy?

Older child: My mom, when she saw the candy wrapper, well, she tried to figure out something—and it was the opposite from the good things. And the next thing I wanted, she wouldn't give me it.

The Talented, Self-(Mis)guided Child

Now, a cautionary statement about children who never need prodding. Let's imagine that we are the parents of a child prodigy—a budding world-class pianist, gymnast, chess player, or quiz kid. When a talent like this first emerges, including the talent to pursue the talent, we are likely to show great pleasure, if not amazement, in the child's natural ability. For illustration, let's say the ability is in gymnastics. Given the opportunity for lessons and coaching, motivation to achieve seems to come entirely from the child. Success is followed by more success. No statement like "You ought to develop your God-given talents" is ever necessary. In fact, ought and ought-not statements seem totally irrelevant as the talented child efficiently strives to squeeze in all other developmental expectations in order to have plenty of time for further mastery of his or her talent.

Parenting a talented child is not as easy as it first seems. All kinds of moral issues crop up. Talented children may deny themselves normal childhood pleasures, including sleep, in pursuit of their talent. We may get caught up in our talented child's success to the point of inadvertently neglecting our other children's needs. A coach may be overly zealous, even punitive. Physical and emotional injuries may result. We seldom feel that we have "pushed" this kind of child. Talented children seldom need pushing. The moral question for us is whether or not we should "pull" in the reins and redirect the talented child's energies. There are no ready answers.

—— **ADVICE TO PARENTS** ————————————————————

Nurturing the Moral Connection at the Brain-Heart Stage (7–11)

- **Cheer skill development.**

- **Remember that security and emotional understanding are enhanced by structure and rules.**

- **Emphasize the goodness and burdens of effort.**

- **Intervene when your children's efforts are too little or too much.**

- **Beware of commercial competition to the moral connection you are building with your children.**

- **Protect your talented child from being exploited.**

DEVELOPING THE MORAL CONNECTION
AT THE PERSONIFIED STAGE (12–13)

Moral Identity: I Want to Be a Person Who Is _____

By the close of childhood, our youngsters' end of the moral connection is sharply defined. They consider compliant and pleasing behavior toward their parents and other adults to be morally impelling. Many rules of oughtness have been transformed into moral habits. Now, as they edge toward adolescence, the moral connection begins to weave its way into their personality. They begin to develop a *moral identity*. This means that in addition to feeling a sense of obligation toward real people in the real world, budding teenagers begin to feel connected to a moral guide within themselves. This guide is aptly described as a personified conscience—a metaphorical, internal someone who watches over, guides, judges, or chides. Sometimes, it seems to have human-like eyes or voice.

By the Personified stage, our teenagers know that moral perfection is impossible. How could it be otherwise when someone inside is always keeping a tally? Therefore, their oughts and ought-nots sound more like moral aspirations than rules. "I want [ought] to be a person who is friendly, kind, helpful, and generous." Their moral aspirations take on both the content of accepted rules and the attributes of the rule-makers. In this way, a rule of conscience, such as "Give part of your allowance to the poor," transforms into an aspiration to be a generous person. Moral identity gains definition through virtuous aspirations.

By the Personified stage, years of parent-modeled behavior begin to pay off. If our budding teenagers have admired our parenting behavior throughout childhood, they are likely to incorporate aspects of it into their own moral aspirations. If they don't admire it, they may consciously develop different aspirations. This is, of course, an overly simplified explanation of the complexities of moral identity. Many influences contribute to our teenagers' moral aspirations, including temperament, level of energy, style, opportunities, and challenges. Conscience functioning is as unique as a fingerprint. Nonetheless, we should not underplay our influence as parents in conscience development—whether we get standing ovations or not.

When teenagers begin to aspire to virtuous living, early memories reflecting such efforts come to mind.

Interviewer: What is the first thing you can remember doing that was called good?

Emerging teenager: My dad's back hurt. So I tried to get on the riding lawn mower [at age six or seven], but I couldn't even get the blade down, so no grass was cut.

Another ET: The first good deed I remember—when my grandmother's dentures fell on the floor and I picked them up. When you're young, your parents try to teach you to do things for other people.

Another ET: Thanking my friends for my birthday presents, when I was four. They probably wouldn't feel too good if you didn't like the present. Mom and Dad didn't say anything. They just smiled.

Another ET: The first good deed I remember—I used to give my clothes to Goodwill. We were talking about it at school one day, and I went home and told my mom I wanted to do this. I was so little. I was so happy. I was like jumping up and down. My mom was like, "You did something good." That made me feel really good.

Identifying with Others' Needs

Developing a moral identity—a self defined by virtuous strivings—goes hand in hand with empathizing with the needs of others. Oughtness stemming from the parent-child moral connection generalizes into a morality of obligation toward others. The tendrils of attachment reach outward beyond the family. Animals may get special priority as recipients of this altruistic reaching. We'll explain with a story.

A fifth-grade Sunday School class was given the opportunity and challenge to design a fund-raiser. Whatever money the children raised was to be donated to a charity of their choosing. The children were bursting with ideas about games for the fund-raiser. However, their opinions were divided over which charity should benefit from their efforts. An animal shelter and a human shelter were the two main contenders. The children were given the option of visiting different institutions to help them with their decision. No one expressed an interest in visiting a human shelter, but they all were eager to make a trip to the zoo or the humane society. The request was denied because every child had already been to the zoo and the humane society more than once.

After vigorous debate, the children voted. The animal shelter won. Some adult parishioners showed worried concern that the children were not being taught to place more value on relieving human suffering. The children voting for the animal shelter argued that it was the more worthy cause because animals in need were less able than humans to state their needs. The children appeared to identify with this limitation.

If the children had been a couple of years older, the human shelter probably would have won their vote. Altruism toward animals often predates altruism toward fellow humans. An unfortunate parallel is that children whose rearing has produced an impoverished or frayed moral connection often express cruelty to animals as a precursor or accompaniment to cruelty toward human beings.

Intentionality: Meaning Well

The gap between intention and action reflects human fallibility. Developing brain capacities in our emerging teenagers allow them increasing understanding of *intentionality*. They can differentiate the real effect of someone's actions from the intended effect—what that person meant to achieve. Mostly, our intentions are to do good, or at least to do no harm. Picking up on others' good intentions softens our judgment of them. It adds a dimension of flexibility to the moral connection. It motivates forgiveness of others when unintended harshness accompanies words or actions. It also allows room for excuse making: "I meant to do it; I just forgot!"

Our teenagers realize that the gap between moral intention and practice exists both in themselves and in their parents. Basically, they know that their parents want their teenage years to be spent in safe pursuit of fun, learning, and goodness. Understanding intentionality allows them to tolerate our long and boring lectures, our babyish restrictions, and our emotional outbursts when they misbehave. Not always, but sometimes.

Interviewer: How do your parents show that they are ashamed of you?

Emerging teenager: Usually what they tell me—like the rules and stuff— usually it's for my own good.

Another ET: They are showing me that they care when they punish me.

Another ET: They tell me I shouldn't have done that—tell me I'm a bad person. They can talk sometimes for a real long time and I can get very bored.

Another ET: My parents tell me what I've done wrong. They try to make me see what I've done wrong. We try to figure out why I would have done it. Depending on how bad it is, they usually punish me. They're really good about it. They're real nice about it, and it makes me not want to do it again.

Another ET: No matter what grade I get, if there's anything that I could have gotten better, it's always like "Wooh, why couldn't you have done that?" Fact is, they're never satisfied with anything. I think they just want the best for me. My dad always says, "Well, I always look back to my youth, and I just want you to have everything, you know."

Parent Moral Power

During our children's adolescence, we may find ourselves stretching our necks to look up at our teenagers. Many of them outgrow us. Looking up at them makes us think further about the moral connection. Without the power of mutual trust, respect, and understanding, we are powerless when looking up at someone bigger than us who is also upset. Not only are we vulnerable to losing physical fights, but we are vulnerable to humiliation. If our parenting power base is limited to fear induction, we do not do well under these circumstances. We must then threaten with power bigger than us—police, juvenile authorities, and so on. When our teenagers trust our good intentions in rearing them, they learn how to use their power benevolently. Mutual power in the parent-child relationship is very rewarding.

Interviewer: How do your parents show that they care about your goodness?

Emerging teenager: When I'm good, my mom praises me all the time. Every once in a while she'll buy me something. Me and her both feel like, if I do something good, she shouldn't have to buy me something. Her praise and her telling me is enough. I don't feel like I need anything.

Another ET: I can just tell that they're [parents] happy that I made the right decision about something—just their attitude.

Another ET: Of course, my sister, when she gets lectured, she always yells at my mom. That kind of makes me feel like why does she do that stuff?

─── **ADVICE TO PARENTS** ───────────────────────

Nurturing the Moral Connection at the Personified Stage (12–13)

- **Cheer virtuous aspirations.**

- **Provide opportunities for the moral connection to be extended outside the family.**

- **Enhance understanding of good intentions.**

- **Appreciate the power of a good relationship; note that material rewards are less and less beneficial.**

DEVELOPING THE MORAL CONNECTION
AT THE CONFUSED STAGE (14–15)

Out into the World

Appalachian folklore contains a series of stories known as the Jack Tales. The stories often begin with Jack leaving home to seek his fortune in the world. Sometimes leaving is his own idea. In other tales, his mother has to nudge him out the door because she can no longer support him. Jack's mother always sends him forth with a meager lunch but a mound of advice. Jack makes a lot of mistakes while away from home. Sometimes he gets so confused that he has to return home to reconnect with his mother and her advice. When he finally arrives home for good, he is ready to find a mate and till the soil on a plot of land nearby. His journey always seems to gain him more wisdom than wealth. Some of the wisdom he could have gotten from his mother—if he had only listened. Instead, he had to learn the hard way.

Psychological Emancipation

Unlike the Jack of old, who left home as a child and came back a man, today's Jack or Jill must go through adolescence. Adolescence is more than a chronologically confined number of growing-up years. Adolescence has become a very specific developmental passage in Western culture. Beginning around the age of fifteen and extending into young adulthood, today's youth go through a period of psychological emancipation from their childhood position in the family. Although adult-oriented compliance and pleasing are still vital to their moral well-being, an age-centered, collective, psychological, and moral identity also emerges.

Our modern-day Jack enters his decade of becoming an adult not alone, but with his peers. Each decade of youth has its own identifying characteristics: its dress, music, literature, inventions, politics, and problems. One teenager is no more experienced than the next one as they enter this confusing stage. Moral confusion loves company. Individually and together, these youths face the task of adapting moral wisdom learned from parents and conscience to their own time and place in history. Experimentation and mistakes can be expected.

Pseudo-Individuality

From a distance, mid-adolescents appear to look alike, talk alike, and act alike. Yet each one talks as though his or her thoughts, feelings, beliefs, and future plans are unique. Parents, quite appropriately, find this discrepancy confusing. To empathize with mid-adolescent confusion, we need to search our memories for the moral challenges of our own youth. What cloak of pseudo-individuality did we wear to cover insecurity during our psychological emancipation? What forces solidified the moral fiber of our coming-into-adulthood generation? Was it something greater than the mall, entertainment, and other offerings from the market-driven popular culture?

The marketplace can camouflage insecurity through the pseudo-individuality of dress, language, hairstyle, and music, but it cannot solidify moral identity. Mid-adolescents hunger for idols, ideals, and group ways to pursue goodness. Our mid-adolescents want to morally connect with persons greater than themselves. They want to make commitments to something really important, some virtue-seeking goal that will have an impact on the world. Having nothing to focus on besides social life can lead to despair and mischief. Sometimes parents can help teenagers find community opportunities to serve a purpose larger than self.

Pseudo-Conformity

Now, a cautionary statement about a different kind of teenager. Just as parents don't want to be fooled by pseudo-individuality, we don't want to be fooled by pseudo-conformity, either. In very stable cultures, a smooth transition from compliant child to conforming adult is the mark of maturation. In Western society, following that path may lead to pseudo-conformity. Pseudo-conformists are wimpy good kids who stay safely under our parenting wings. Because they never get in trouble, we may erroneously label them as mature. However, instead of making a direct transition to adulthood, they may simply be avoiding the moral challenges of adolescent emancipation.

As parents we promote wimpy goodness when we keep our teenagers so protected and occupied that they never join their peers in the decade-of-becoming-an-adult process. Teenage prodigies may fall into this category. They may be so dedicated to developing their talent that they forgo the social task of growing up. In contrast, however, they may override that risk by negotiating the adolescent passage vicariously or in an accelerated course. If they don't deal with it at all, they are vulnerable to experiencing delayed adolescence. A future spouse and children will be very displeased to find themselves living with an adult who is just discovering adolescent emancipation!

Pseudo-Distancing

The more our teenagers are in the community, the more actively connected to their consciences they need to be. They can turn conscience volume up and down at will. When they want to listen, rules of conscience are there for them to follow, expand, re-create, or declare obsolete. Private time, including sleep, allows them to figure out whether or not learned rules of conscience fit their current moral challenges.

How do we parents support our end of the moral connection with our mid-adolescents? What forms of psychological security and emotional understanding will not be rebuked during this period of psychological emancipation? Recall that Jack returned home periodically to reconnect with his mother. Our mid-adolescents do that, too. Much of the time, they are turned inward toward private thoughts, music, and friends. Every so often, however, they reach out to us parents to address their psychological and moral frustrations, challenges, and dilemmas. If we aren't available most of the time, we'll miss those important times of reconnecting. We'll also miss important cues telling us to temporarily set more limits or raise our expectations. Therefore, we must treat our adolescents with pseudo-distancing, always ready to reconnect at crucial times. We also need to be prepared for surprises.

WHAMO! Experiences

Deciding whether or not to leave our teenagers home alone with their consciences is a major trust-testing decision. Sixth and seventh senses are required of parents. Just when we believe that our teenagers and their consciences are mature enough to handle it, WHAMO, we may be in for a big surprise. A WHAMO! experience sometimes occurs on the phone. A particular mother received such a call one Friday evening, just as she and her husband were putting golf clubs into the car to head out for a weekend of adult pleasure. To be left behind were one fourteen-year-old and two seventeen-year-olds, each one carefully instructed. Chain-of-command arrangements had also been made with responsible stand-by adults. The polite voice on the phone said, "I'm Mrs. _____, calling to see what time the children are expected tonight. My daughter has signed me up to drive." WHAMO! a secretly planned, unsupervised party of fourteen-year-olds! And the seventeen-year-olds probably knew all about it. Oughtness times preempted tee times for these parents!

WHAMO! experiences come when parents least expect them. The household hums with emotional equilibrium; trust is high; responsibility seemingly reigns. And then, WHAMO! we can't believe what our beloved, carefully reared teenager just did! Among the possibilities are cheating in school; putting forth zero effort on a term paper; playing hooky; stealing something at the mall; slipping out of the house at night; having friends over when specifically told not to do so; borrowing the family car without permission, or maybe without a driver's license; getting drunk or high; having sex; staying out past curfew; or participating in an act of trespassing or vandalism. Not all of these things, just one or two of them! And what makes us really sore is when our trusted teenager skillfully lies to us about the transgression or refuses to own up to the obvious. At these demoralizing times, we feel that the moral connection we have worked so hard to build could fit under a toadstool.

Parent Self-Soothing

WHAMO! experiences call for parent self-soothing. We're not bad parents. We're just living through lapses in teenage conscience functioning. Mid-adolescence is peak season for lapses. Our teenagers may be full-grown, articulate, and bright, but their consciences may be just toddlers, able to pull only so hard at the internal moral connection.

Interviewer: How do your parents show they care when you have been bad?

Mid-adolescent: I always think I'm right, but when I do something wrong, it ends up screwing up something else. If I listen to them [elders], usually it turns out okay.

Another MA: I'm learning as I get older, your parents are right. It's sad but true.

Another MA: They let me learn for myself, after I've made a mess of things. But they're always there.

"Being there" is a nebulous job description. It involves being observant, but not being a spy; being available, but usually in the next room; being non-invasive, but ready to ask the right questions at just the right time; allowing space and time for learn-on-your-own experiences, but being ready to crack down when behavior gets out of hand. Being there means monitoring facial expressions and shifts in mood; sleep and eating habits; friends in and out of the house; phone calls that come and calls that don't come; music, books, movies, and videos selected; how the Internet is used; homework and grade cards; activities chosen or avoided. It means giving slack but never completely letting go of the rope holding the moral connection in place.

Sometimes parents have to do real detective work. If letters or diaries are left out in the open, they may signal a need for conversation. If we find ourselves listening to long accounts of *other* teenagers' problems, there may be a parallel concern in our own son or daughter. Morally related, problem-oriented topics chosen for school reports may clue us in to a need for personal or family counseling. At really critical times, our teenager may "make a mess of things." Moral-emotional distress may be obvious. Then we know why we are "there." We jump up and offer help. Sometimes we ask for professional help.

THE ADVOCATE

When our mid-adolescents are out in the community, we appreciate being informed whenever trouble is brewing. Having a good working relationship with a network of parents prevents WHAMO! experiences. Actually, parents need to become part of a community network that works in behalf of all teenagers. So let's be proudly tired every time we supervise a party, sponsor a spring break trip to a faraway city, coach a team, or become a Big Brother or Sister. Every time we serve on the PTA committee or school board, serve as a docent at the museum, or make a financial contribution to a youth agency, we are expanding the network. Every time we participate in a citizens' committee to protect the environment, monitor violence in media presentations, or set limits on commercial exploitation of youth, we are expanding the conscience of the community. When we smile and speak kindly to a teenager at the cash register—even one whose manners are underdeveloped—when we alert parents or other adults about teenagers in trouble, or we take time to listen to a distressed teenager anytime, anywhere, we are expanding the moral connection of the community.

Teenage readiness to talk comes at odd times. Scheduled, quality-time talks may produce nothing. Overtures to important topics may go absolutely nowhere. "Stop trying to analyze everything!" said one teenage boy to his mother. After WHAMO! incidents, confrontations and consequences are mandatory. Issuing consequences may be stormy. However, years of security and empathy emotionally buffer negative exchanges. Given a little time, our teenagers will remember that all the fuss is for their own good. We have their best interests at heart. Given a little time for internal processing, their ability to converse may improve.

> Interviewer: How do your parents show that they care when you have done something wrong?

> Mid-adolescent: They will just say, "Try better next time," and tell me what I should have done—a big lecture.

> Interviewer: Have these experiences had a lasting impact on you?

> Another MA: It's weird when you're growing up, 'cause it's like your mom don't grow up 'cause she's a grownup already. And you grow and catch up with her. I like that part a lot—think you can outsmart her, sometimes (laughter).

NURTURING THE MORAL CONNECTION
AT THE INTEGRATING STAGE (16–17+)

Moral Connections in the Peer Community

Sometime after mid-adolescence, our teenagers begin to find moral connections within their peer community. Their developing intellectual ability allows them to understand the moral complexity of good within bad and bad within good. They begin to choose friends, activities, and situations that are mostly good. Fortunate choices please them, their consciences, and their parents. With moral aspirations firmly identified in their peer community, they can be more open in dialogues with us. They don't need to defend themselves and their friends so vigorously. They can accept parent affirmations and suggestions, if we state them discreetly. Moral tension and confusion begin to subside in them and in us. We reach a new level of trust.

Older adolescents feel less pressured by peer opinion. They make decisions with increasing comfort as courage replaces anxiety. The cloaks of pseudo-individuality and pseudo-conformity are thrown off, or at least unbuttoned. An older teenager once described her thoughts as she sat in her room looking out the window. She lived near an airport. Her window provided a good view of the planes coming and going. She thought to herself, "If I'm going to get on those planes in the future, I'd better concentrate on this homework right now." A new level of academic seriousness emerged. She was gradually becoming her own authority.

Alone, but Connected

Independent moral decision-making need not be a lonely experience. Although oughtness may mean standing alone on important issues, it is firmly grounded in a lineage of connectedness. Within each of us is a storehouse of memories of important authority figures. Religious experience may expand that sense of connectedness to God. Standing beside us are others who have faced or are facing decisions similar to ours. Few of us face moral decisions that are truly unique. Generally, there have been like-minded people in history, or there are contemporary fellow strugglers standing nearby. Visions of the future are colored by how we believe those decisions will affect those who will follow us. In that way, we ready ourselves to extend the moral connection to the next generation. Our older adolescents are just beginning to picture the full cycle of moral connection. At moments, they may be filled with gratitude.

> Interviewer: What has been the lasting impact of these [growing-up] experiences?

> Older adolescent: Knowing that I only have one more year till I go away to college, it makes me respect people more because they're not gonna be there. I'm more thankful for them now.

The Cycle of Moral Connection

As parents we also feel gratitude when we hear our best words coming back to us or see behavior reminiscent of our best efforts. The Imp keeps us humble by arranging that we also hear our worst words and see reruns of our worst behavior.

> Interviewer: What has been the lasting impact of these experiences?

> Older adolescent: Whenever I'm babysitting, I sit down and say, "This is why we're leaving" or "This is why you're having a time-out." It's because of what you did. Now do you know what you did? If they say, "No," then you tell them [again].

> Another OA: My mom, she's ill, and I do a lot of household stuff. I do little things for her—just pick up a card—and it means so much to her. If she can't get out of bed, I do everything around the house—cook the meals, take care of my step-dad, and do the laundry.

The following teenager did not grow up in an ordinary family. Because of adversities in early childhood, Paul spent most of his life in out-of-home placements. His primary attachment figures were a series of child-care workers and foster parents. He was in a psychiatric hospital at the time. When he was around sixteen, a minor but nonetheless important medical emergency occurred on the unit. Paul became an immediate bundle of I-want-to-help energy. He demonstrated more knowledge than any staff member about the location of first-aid medical supplies—inflatable ice packs, splints, ace bandages, and the like. Sometime later during an interview, he explained the motivating experience behind his dedication:

> Interviewer: What is the first memory you have of doing something that was called "good"?

> Older adolescent: When I was at [another psychiatric hospital]. All of a sudden she [staff member] fell straight back on the concrete. The other staff member was in the bathroom, so I called 911. She had a tumor in the brain and she had something else. I knew I had done "good" by all the praise I got. I was eleven. I want to be a paramedic.

Although Paul had many disconnections in his life, he still made the moral connection.

—— ADVICE TO PARENTS ————————————————————

Nurturing the Moral Connection at the Integrating Stage (16–17+)

- **Anticipate increasing openness in communication.**

- **Anticipate processing of mistakes and wrongdoing.**

- **Cheer independent, courageous decision-making.**

- **Cheer moral leadership with younger children.**

- **Be grateful for gratitude.**

THE STORY SO FAR

Conscience is the mind's storehouse of moral meaning. Moral meaning first arises within the parent-child relationship. Nature provides us with a readiness to connect with each other in a relationship of obligation. We come to parenthood with our end of the moral connection in place. We are ready to nurture our children's pursuit of goodness in the way we have come to know it. Proceeding as well as we know how, we offer physical and psychological protection, emotional understanding, and gentle guidance to our children. In time, the security and understanding we provide will motivate our children to respond to our prohibitions and demands with compliance and pleasing. We teach our children a sense of oughtness.

By school age our children are ready to transfer their sense of oughtness with us to a wider range of adults. Furthermore, our children begin to center their sense of oughtness on the content of their teachings. They incorporate rules of conscience that, when practiced, develop into moral habits.

As adolescence approaches, our youngsters feel the presence of an internalized moral guide, conscience. They may describe it as having human-like characteristics. They now feel obligated to comply and please both real adults in their environment and the internalized conscience. Realizing that perfect rule-following is impossible, they transform rules of conscience into moral aspirations. They express moral connectedness in terms of virtuous goals.

By mid-adolescence, psychological emancipation from parents begins to occur. This process arouses moral anxiety and confusion. In time, our teenagers find friends with moral like-mindedness. Together, they reach out to connect to moral idols, ideals, and opportunities to pursue virtuous objectives together. By late adolescence, our teenagers feel more secure in their moral identity. They can tolerate good within bad and bad within good. They begin to speculate about how they will foster the moral connection with future progeny. In this way, the moral connection is made and remade, generation after generation.

Developing Moral-Emotional Responsiveness

3

Eight-year-old Dana and her dad had a very good relationship. Nonetheless, Dana would get really mad at him when he teased her too much or played with her too hard. At these times, she would sit apart from him, red in the face, huffing and puffing, announcing that she was never going to play with him again. After a few minutes, he would say, "Let's see if she's still sizzling." He would put a finger on her skin and make a pretend sizzling sound, like bacon frying in a pan. He would playfully repeat this test until she giggled. Then they would resume their play, but this time more gently.

Dana and her dad had a strong moral connection. Dad wanted to be protective, understanding, and instructive. Dana wanted to be compliant and pleasing. All in the midst of having fun. They wanted to have good feelings within themselves and between them. To do so, they each had to behave in certain ways. They used emotional cues, sometimes expressed through language and sometimes through behavior, to let each other know how they were getting along. Were they having fun? Were they hurting each other's feelings? Was one or the other of them getting mad? They adjusted their behavior according to the emotional cues they sensed in each other. In so doing, they kept their relationship in good moral-emotional equilibrium.

MORAL-EMOTIONAL EQUILIBRIUM

By the time we are grownups, we realize that we cannot always be compliant and pleasing. As parents we realize that we sometimes fail at being protective, understanding, and instructive. Nonetheless, we all want to feel morally good about ourselves. We want to feel that, generally speaking, we are good people trying to do the right thing. In this book the term *moral-emotional equilibrium* is used to describe this feeling state. It is a peaceful state. When we are in moral-emotional equilibrium, we feel in harmony with ourselves, each other, and the world.

Parents start nurturing moral-emotional equilibrium during their children's infancy. We begin by affirming the basic goodness of their existence. Long before they can understand anything about morality, we say, "Good boy!" "Good girl!" over every little move or utterance they make. We try to soothe away distress. Infants sense our affirmations. Positive feelings flow between us. In the process of generating and responding to positive emotional expressions, we help our infants build an "am good–feel good" way of knowing themselves in the world. Later, we gradually add criteria for transforming this primitive state of moral-emotional equilibrium into an "am good–feel good– *do good*" state. We teach and model the connection between emotional well-being, compliance, and pleasing. We guide our children in developing their own style of moral-emotional responsiveness.

MORAL-EMOTIONAL RESPONSIVENESS

Moral-emotional responsiveness is the domain of conscience that links our feelings about moral obligation to our body's physiology. Underlying brain-body mechanisms register those feelings throughout various body systems. The connections in some systems are consciously registered. Following a morally judged deed, we may tingle with excitement, shake with fear, feel sick to our stomach, flush with embarrassment, turn away in shame, or jump for joy. Other systems register impact more subtly.

Moral-emotional arousal is highly motivating. It signals us—indeed, prods us—to make corrections any time we veer away from our comfortable state of moral-emotional equilibrium. Negative feelings associated with wrongdoing mandate reparation and healing to restore our "am good–feel good–do good" state. We can push the "do good" business too hard, also. Excessive pride and feelings of self-righteousness also require correction—prodded by other people's feelings, if not our own.

In some ways nurturing the conscience is unique to a particular culture. We spoke in the last chapter about the special meaning of adolescence in Western culture. To understand conscience functioning, it is important to distinguish between the universal and the unique. Mind-body physiology governing moral-emotional responsiveness is universal. Human emotions and their underlying physiology are the same throughout the world. So is the existence of a moral connection. Everywhere, conscientious parents want their children to feel good about doing what they define as good, to feel bad about doing what they define as bad. What is different from culture to culture, and indeed within cultures, is the specifics of what one should feel good or bad about, as well as the rules for expressing emotion.

Let us now focus on the fundamental emotions. We will group them according to the way they seem to cluster in helping us regulate morality in our lives. Studying the universal nature of emotions as well as the ways that different cultures moralize them offers a tool for understanding people around the world.

FUNDAMENTAL EMOTIONS

FACE TO FACE AROUND THE WORLD

Charles Darwin is best known for his data collections supporting the theory of evolution. He is less well known for his scholarly observations of human emotions. On his five-year, around-the-world excursion on the *Beagle*, he did not limit his observations to rocks, plants, and animals. He also studied people's facial expressions in every culture that he encountered. Darwin was the first scientist to propose that people all over the world have the same fundamental emotions. Similarities are especially evident in children who have not yet learned how to mask their feelings. Darwin also pointed out similarities between emotional expression in humans and in other species. Think of a dog lowering its neck and pulling in its tail after being shamed.

Custom may direct us to mask or restrain the expression of emotion in some circumstances, but to be profusely emotive in other situations. To illustrate: Sisters Dee and Dee-Dee were a grandmother and great-aunt in a large German-American family. They had grown up during the economic depression that followed the 1929 stock market crash. A favorite memory in this family was watching them open presents on Christmas Eve.

The ceremony seemed to go on forever. Children worried that Santa would never get to come. Each package was turned, shaken, and guessed over for several minutes. Then, during the careful opening, no ribbon or scrap of paper could be torn. They would be used again the next year. When the treasured object came into view, exclamations knew no parallel. Surprise, pleasure, and appreciation were profusely shown over each trinket. These grand ladies had their own moral-emotional style for expressing gratitude.

SOCIAL REFERENCING

Young children's facial expressions are quite honest. We have no trouble telling when they are disappointed over a gift. On the other hand, when they don't know how to react to a situation, they "socially reference" their parents.

Social referencing is watching someone else's face and behavior very closely to judge what the proper reaction should be and to gauge how much emotion should be shown. Shy children do a lot of social referencing.

Controversy exists among scientists as to which emotions are fundamental and which are blends. Psychologist Carroll Izard's list of eleven emotions is very useful in understanding moral-emotional responsiveness. For each emotion on the list, save guilt, two-word descriptors are used to capture range and intensity. The list includes interest-excitement; enjoyment-joy; surprise-astonishment; shyness-embarrassment; fear-terror; dismell-disgust; anger-rage; contempt-hatred; sadness-anguish; shame-humiliation; and guilt. Perhaps guilt should be described as guilt and more guilt. Each of these emotions, again save guilt, has identifying facial characteristics. Brain scientists, using imaging techniques, have also begun to link expression of some of the fundamental emotions with activity in specific regions of the brain.

Emotions are connected to physiological arousal. Part of our response to that arousal is automatic. In response to danger, we may flee, prepare to fight, or freeze. Other aspects of emotional arousal affect the ways in which memories are stored. Still other aspects motivate us to think, to figure out what to do, to develop a strategy. Some emotions prompt us to go ahead — to pursue a goal. Others caution us or warn us of danger. Still others prompt us to stop what we are doing and to think long and hard about it. Let's speculate about our children's emotional expressions as well as our own while we review Izard's fundamental list.

The GO AHEAD Emotions

Interest-excitement is the most common emotion in everyday life. In our children, this emotion is involved in curiosity, mastery of new skills, and imaginative play. Interest is heightened by novelty. That should prompt us as parents to put some surprises into our family routines now and then. Interest-excitement is signaled in our faces by brows lifted or drawn together, visual tracking, softly opened mouth, or pursed lips. Interest may be invested in either goodness or badness. We have all experienced our children highly invested in doing secret good deeds. Sometimes we catch them similarly invested in a misdeed, alone or together.

Enjoyment-joy is expressed with smiles and laughter. We can see the smile of enjoyment in our three-week-old when we speak in those high-pitched tones known as *parentese* (baby-talk). In a four-to-five-week-old, just seeing our face may produce joy. Contagious joy can escalate into group ecstasy or degenerate into silliness. Although joy can be elicited by another, it is dangerous to make others responsible for our pleasure. Similarly, making enjoyment a life goal seldom works. Enjoyment is more likely to be experienced as a byproduct of another goal. If we continuously try to make our children happy, we may end up with bratty, demanding, never-satisfied children.

When we are joyful, we are more likely to be loving and giving toward others, playful, creative, and self-confident. We are more likely to see beauty and goodness in nature and in other human beings. When our children receive praise for hard-earned achievements, their joy often motivates them to work even harder. Conversely, if deception or wrongdoing meets with success in a person of bad conscience, enjoyment over the result may motivate more deception and wrongdoing.

The STOP, LOOK, LISTEN, and BE CAREFUL Emotions

Surprise-astonishment is a STOP signal for other emotions, thoughts, or activities. It is the emotion needing arousal when parents want to disrupt a child's mesmerized attention to a video game. We need to say or do something that will lift his brow, wrinkle his forehead, give his eyes that large, rounded appearance, and form his mouth into an oval shape. Child: "Huh?" Parent: "And now, before the Martians get here, _____." What is coming next may be pleasant or unpleasant, dreaded or desired; whatever it is, surprise alerts him to prepare for change—as when hearing the directive "Time to do your homework."

Shyness-embarrassment is the "somebody's watching me" emotion. It makes us lower our eyes and turn away from others, all the while remaining highly invested in the opinions of the persons whom we are seemingly avoiding. Shyness is associated with coyness and flirtation. Red-cheeked embarrassment is aroused when we are the recipient of a surprise party or an unexpected honor. Shyness-embarrassment makes us want to cling to familiar people, places, and situations while carefully evaluating newness. Embarrassment is an on-stage emotion, prompting us to check for undone buttons or zippers. Shyness invites sensitivity, modesty, tact, and ritual in social exchange. Shyness guides manners and propriety.

Fear-terror is the emotion signaling physical or psychological threat. Fear can immobilize our bodies, narrow the range of our perceptions and thoughts, or make us seek a place to run for protection. Uncamouflaged, fear is expressed with a frozen stare, a pale face, and cold and sweaty hands. Fear can be aroused by pain, aloneness, sudden changes in stimulation, strangeness, inconsistent treatment from caretakers, uncertainty about being loved, or natural disaster.

We can learn to be fearful by watching others who are fearful. We can fear not being able to do something that is expected of us, or we can fear that if we are successful, more will be expected than we can deliver. Fear is the main component of anxiety, a complex of emotions and thoughts that can immobilize us in states of chronic tension. Alternatively, fear can be overridden by courage and even transformed into excitement when pursuing a challenge. Fear is the friend of survival, but it can be the enemy of moral courage.

The DANGER ZONE Emotions

Disgust, anger, and contempt are a trio of emotions known as the hostility triad. Adults who consistently display this trio are said to have a hostile personality trait. Parents need to express these emotions parsimoniously when rearing children. We don't want to facilitate the development of a hostile conscience.

Dismell-disgust is considered to be the oldest emotion in evolutionary development, first serving survival by protecting us from food that was contaminated or poisonous (dismell). We seldom, if ever, use the word "dismell." However, we infer its emotional meaning when, suspecting some kind of foul play, we say, "There's something fishy about this" or "I smell a rat. Let's keep our noses to the ground." In an expression of disgust, the tongue is pulled forward as if ejecting revolting substances. Yuck! says our baby to some of the tastes we present to her palate. Yuck! thinks any one of us sitting next to someone who smells bad or does something crude.

Anger-rage is the "get ready to fire" emotion. It raises blood pressure and heart rate in readiness for defense. We boil with anger when we are restrained, our goals are blocked, others impose their will on us, we judge our own behavior to be wrong or stupid, or we are offended by what others do. Anger is part of righteous indignation. In a person facing the object of anger, the forehead skin is pulled tight to lower the brows, the eyes stare in an angular and narrow outline, and the mouth takes on a squarish or rectangular form.

Readiness to act requires us to think quickly and carefully so as not to overreact. While anger makes us want to move closer to the object of our hatred, the negative but cooler emotions, disgust and contempt, make us want to keep our distance. Careful parents are intuitively alert to this triad of emotions when engaged in a verbal exchange with a teenager whose anger is heating up. It is better that we allow the teenager to control his distance from us when engaged in a hostility-building conversation. Ordering him to "come here" can put both parent and teenager at risk for doing something harmful.

Contempt-hatred is the emotion we feel when we judge ourselves to be superior to others or when our conscience is so harshly critical that we feel self-contempt. A person who is contemptuous may cock the head to the side or pull one corner of the mouth back in a derisive smirk. Charles Darwin wrote of the sneer of contempt in bare-toothed animals. The coolness of contempt is operative in the expression of prejudice. Imagine how the hostility triad must operate within alienated street gangs.

The SLOW DOWN, GO INSIDE, and THINK ABOUT IT Emotions

Sadness-anguish is an emotion of depth. It immediately indicates that something is wrong. Our empathy is aroused when we see someone suffering. We vicariously hurt as we watch the inner corners of a person's brow draw obliquely upward and together, the eyes narrow, the corners of the mouth turn down. Posture and movement become slow and ponderous. Mind and body are slowed in the search for meaning after some disastrous event. For children, that event may be a lost pet; their parents' separation; the death of a grand-mother; a friend moving away; a failing grade; a personal act of meanness; an injustice from a classmate; frustration at being unable to please a parent or teacher; or a flood, hurricane, or earthquake.

Sadness motivates us to appreciate what we have, to move closer to loved ones, to accept responsibility for addressing a problem. Unremitting sadness can evolve into a clinical depression, a complex of distorted feelings and thoughts that demoralize and immobilize us until we dig our way out.

Shame-humiliation is the most tell-tale of the emotions—the *Scarlet Letter* emotion. Shame moves us beyond embarrassment toward humiliation. Shame is what we feel when we deem ourselves inadequate, wrong, or responsible for harm. We stand before others with evidence exposed, sphincter control lost, the memorized speech forgotten, having run the wrong way on the playing field, the stolen goods in our hands, and with no explanation for anything. We smile or stare meaninglessly, look away at nothing, stammer, or try to hide our faces or our whole bodies.

Shame may be reduced to embarrassment and humor when maturity allows us to see the Imp-inspired nature of youthful wrongdoing. However, when we are truly humiliated, we want to drop through the earth. We believe that others have judged us and found us wanting. If we agree with their judgment, we promise ourselves that if we can just get out of this situation, we will never, as long as we live, come anywhere near it again. On the other hand, as the child psychoanalyst Erik Erikson pointed out, if we override shame by deeming ourselves in the right or justified, we build our autonomy and individuality. Unmastered shame invites us to try to hide it from ourselves through denial or repression. "I never ____!" Mastering shame leads to courage and confidence.

Guilt-more guilt is the emotion of inner regret over wrongdoing. It is intimately connected to our ability to empathize with the distress of others. With no particular facial expression to identify it, guilt is a private emotion. If it is combined with shame, others may sense our dis-ease, but only our conscience knows what guilt looks like. Although accompanying sadness leads others to inquire, "What's wrong?" guilt often makes us ignore the question, leaving others guessing as we privately ponder our problems. The external judgment of "guilty" is far different from the internal feeling of guilt.

Guilt's power to quietly motivate us toward making reparations may be overpowered by the intensity of the more public emotion, shame. However, guilt is tenacious. It can go underground in our psyche, returning later, when we have more time or capacity to examine the wrongdoing that triggered it. Guilt motivates us to analyze wrongdoing. In privacy, we can peel off the layers of justifications we have designed to keep it underground. We can also examine the standards by which we are judging ourselves as having done wrong. Sometimes we decide that a particular standard is wrong. When we reach that conclusion, guilt motivates us to modify that moral standard. Guilt promotes moral maturation.

What do we do with this rich supply of emotions? How do we use emotions to enhance life's meaning? How do we teach our children to connect emotions to their sense of moral obligation? Emotions enrich every aspect of our relationships, including the moral aspect, by providing us with a special language. Emotional language helps us communicate what we believe to be intensely important. It also assists us in our pleas for understanding. Moral-emotional diplomacy becomes a skill of conscience—including the occasional need to grab an emotional fire extinguisher. Explanations appear just ahead.

COMMUNICATING WITH EMOTIONS

COMMUNICATING IMPORTANCE AND INTENSITY

Everyday conversation is colored with emotion. Feelings are evident in our faces, body postures, voices, and language. Emotional tones embolden how important we believe an issue to be, how passionately we feel about it, and how intensely we want others to understand—or adopt—our position. When we grasp the importance and intensity of what another person is telling us, we may not agree, but sensitivity to their emotional state helps us modulate how we express our own intensely important views. "I respectfully disagree with the senator from _____." Expressing differing views while respecting each other's feelings is an essential feature of moral-emotional responsiveness.

Parent relationships are models of moral-emotional communication. Our children see us sometimes being warm, affectionate, and cozy, at other times engaging in heated debates or icy silences. Children differ in their ability to understand or tolerate our heated conversations. While we may realize that "emphasizing importance" is moving us closer to resolving some problem, our children may realize only the tension and intensity of the words being exchanged. That's why some parents say with pride, "We made a point to never argue in front of the children."

In contrast, some scenes of parents noisily addressing problems may be stored in children's memories as sound examples of how to deal with conflict. Those memories may facilitate moral-emotional responsiveness when similar situations arise in their adulthood. If stormy family scenes do not take on problem-solving meaning, the memories may reemerge as painful emotional dramas that haunt and wound their psyches again and again.

Repetitious parent disagreements may amuse, shock, infuriate, or scare children. When scared, they may hide or get in the middle to distract us. Eight-year-old Alexa kept the Imp at her side as she watched her parents move closer and closer to divorce. To distract herself from emotional pain during their stormy arguments, she hid in the hallway, chalking up wins and losses on a make-believe scorecard.

Falling-apart or fallen-apart parent relationships are full of moral-emotional obligations to children. As individual adults, each of us has control over how much dissonance we add to the moral-emotional disharmony that everyone feels. Our contributions may be ongoing, entrenched hatred; cold condescension; indifference; or distant but cooperative respect. It is never easy. In the midst of our own pain, we need to listen to our children's intensely important communications.

BEING UNDERSTOOD

Being understood by others is intensely important to our emotional well-being. Business answering machines programmed with pleasant-sounding voices fail to temper our frustration over not being able to talk to a real person. "Your call is very important to us." Yeah, right! When we finally connect with a human being—double-checking to make sure the voice is real—our hearts jump for joy. "Maybe this person will understand my problem—and help me!"

Emotional expression helps us understand each other. When we don't "get it," we need to cultivate an empathic imagination. An *empathic imagination* invites us to project ourselves into another person's feeling state. One day, a man whose larynx had been removed was a guest on a radio talk show, giving his opinions about smoking. In contrast to the recorded message of robotized caring mentioned in the last paragraph, this man's mechanized tones, produced by regurgitating swallowed air, aroused real feeling. As he discussed the effects of smoking on his life, listeners with the slightest amount of empathic imagination had no trouble feeling connected to him and his suffering. Emotions could be inferred from his message.

Empathic imagination is especially important if we happen to have children born with communication problems. We may need special training, not just to exchange information with them, but to communicate emotional understanding. Hearing parents of deaf children have such an obligation. Parents of autistic children with limited speech or eye contact may require a great deal of empathic imagination to build meaningful communication with them.

Parents foster empathic imagination in everyday life when, after patiently listening to one child's side of a heated controversy, they ask how he or she thinks the other child would describe the same incident. Having that other child there to actually tell his or her story is even better training. Helping children listen—in emotionally calm states—to other people's emotionally laden stories builds two skills at once: empathic imagination and emotional self-regulation. Practicing the two skills together helps keep us in moral-emotional equilibrium.

MORAL-EMOTIONAL DIPLOMACY: EASING TENSION

Relationships get out of harmony. Sometimes, expressing emotions in highly charged ways helps to re-harmonize them. When it doesn't, learning to live with a certain amount of disharmony may be required. When we expect disharmony to be short-lived—for example, when a disliked house guest will soon be departing—we may deal with it best by masking our emotions. When the disharmony is prolonged—for example, when one child is convinced that an irritating sibling will never grow up—moral-emotional diplomacy must be carefully cultivated. Parents are responsible for cultivating that diplomacy, or at least planting the seeds.

In sibling strife, moral-emotional diplomacy is developed in that tiny space between overstated negative emotional feeling—"I hate you and I always will!"—and moments when the siblings are engaged in some mutually enjoyable activity and, although they won't admit it, actually seem to be enjoying each other. Ordinarily, we think of diplomacy in terms of thoughtful, problem-solving strategies. In this chapter we focus on the moral-emotional aspects of diplomacy.

Moral-emotional diplomacy is the pursuit of harmony within ourselves and our relationships *when it isn't easy*. It may not be easy for any number of reasons. As the chapters on moral valuation (Chapters 4, 5, and 6) will elaborate, respect for the rights and needs of authority, peers, and self is a three-pronged value system central to moral meaning. Duty and desire to respect three types of relationships simultaneously is invariably accompanied by some degree of tension. Tension exists among members of any family, neighborhood, or workplace—even when everyone is trying to do the right thing! Moral-emotional diplomacy in the family, then, is the process of quelling tension in parent-child, child-child, and person-to-self relationships while honoring the rights and needs of all members. Moral-emotional diplomacy keeps us at peace with ourselves and the world when we aren't totally happy about how things are going.

As parents we model and teach our children how to find peace within themselves. We do so by offering them private space, rest, soothing, and understanding. We provide them with breaks from difficult relationships. We teach them ways to relax and encourage the ways they discover to relax themselves. We expose them to the joys of nature, aesthetic pursuits, and the exploration of religious faith. We encourage them to find ways to detach from their worries. We affirm their basic goodness and the goodness of their moral striving.

Moral-emotional diplomacy is having enough sensitivity to know when to express emotions more fully, when to restrain expression, how to be receptive to others' feelings, and when to grab the emotional fire extinguisher. Moral-emotional maturation is learning when, how, and with whom to be open, as well as when, how, and with whom to be merely quietly attentive. Sometimes emotional preparation is necessary for us to even listen to certain facts. Do you have memories of thinking or saying, "Don't tell me! I'm not ready to hear what I think I'm going to hear"? When one mother wanted to talk about sex with an emerging teenager, the girl replied, "Could you wait until I'm about . . . twenty-five?" Compromise was in order.

GRABBING THE EMOTIONAL FIRE EXTINGUISHER

Excessive emotional expression can distort reality. When we get overwrought, we may express emotions senselessly or totally misinterpret others' intentions. Chronic sleeplessness or stress can unglue emotional sensitivity from sensibility. Some days, parenthood can do this. Some days, having to be a kid can do it. "Why am I the one who always has to _____? who never gets to _____?"

During emotional crises, we really need to help each other out. We need to become moral-emotionally responsive. When a child is emotionally "wigged out," we parents are morally obligated to remain calm. When one of us is in the same predicament, we hope there is another adult around to slip into the role of the calm one. Remaining calm is only half of the moral-emotional obligation. The other half is deciding when to continue listening patiently and when to put the kibosh on further emotional expression. Every family needs an emotional fire extinguisher on every floor. "Get yourself together. We'll talk about this tomorrow."

We now turn to a discussion of how moral-emotional regulation goes on inside each of us. How do we regulate our emotions in response to some sensible life plan? in response to a moral plan? in response to moral issues in our relationships? How do we live in a moral-emotionally responsive and responsible way?

MORAL-EMOTIONAL REGULATION

BASIC GOODNESS

An earlier section of this chapter described how natural it is for parents to nurture a sense of personal worth in their newborns. The immediate moral response of parenthood is to provide infants with copious amounts of physical and emotional protection, comfort, and stimulation. And then some more. By responding to every need and most signals of distress, we let our children know that, just by existing, they are good and have the right to feel good about it. We do everything we can to chase away negative emotions. We want them to experience an "am good–feel good" state of being. Later, we moralize that state by adding ought-to-do and ought-not-to-do contingencies to their sense of well-being. Those contingencies build the moral-emotional connection in their lives. The am good–feel good state transforms into one in which *do good* is connected to feelings associated with basic goodness.

Awareness of oughtness does not guarantee compliance. Human fallibility provides us with a variety of ways to express our moral failings. "I didn't know I was supposed to ____" merges into "I forgot I was supposed to ____" or " I knew I shouldn't have ____, but ____." The "am good–feel good–do good" state may stay in place for only a minute before we get in trouble, or at least into some kind of mischief. The space between mischief and trouble can be very small, especially when we are young. When we get in trouble—fail to meet first parental, then personal standards of right and wrong—we feel bad. There's a break in that chain of am, feel, and do good links. Then, we have to fix things to get back into moral-emotional equilibrium.

THE MORAL-EMOTIONAL CYCLE OF REPARATION AND HEALING

Infants and toddlers have no knowledge of moral rules. Yet they are emotionally responsive when they hear each other cry or see someone get hurt. They shy away from things and people that appear dangerous to them. They sense when things aren't right—hurt fingers, broken toys, spilled milk, torn clothing. They try to comfort others who are distressed. They solicit adult help to fix broken and spoiled things, to make hurts feel better. When satisfied with the results, they show contentment.

Under the surface of the skin, physiological mechanisms reflect a similar cycle in response to wounding. An infectious agent attacks the body. Symptoms and signs of illness appear. The immune system responds, maybe aided by medication. Wounded tissues repair and return to normal. We feel better.

The moral-emotional domain of conscience links conscious awareness of good and bad, right and wrong, to this underlying cycle of emotional and physiological responsiveness. As parents we nurture its development by teaching our children what they ought to feel good about, what they ought to feel bad about. We show our own feelings of pleasure and approval, anger and disappointment when they obey or disobey, try to please or put forth no effort. After hurtful words and actions, we encourage them to apologize and repair what they can, to compensate in some way when repair or replacement is impossible. When we think they are just going through the motions, we may ground them from pleasurable activities for more "processing time." We hope that their internal feelings match the compensatory actions that we require of them. We want them to feel good about making amends, about planning self-reform. We want them to learn to be moral-emotionally responsive. We rejoice with them when their baseline state of "am good–feel good–do good" returns, when they are back in moral-emotional equilibrium with themselves and the world around them.

Not all infections are curable. Even before adulthood, we also realize that some wrongs cannot be righted, forgiven, or forgotten. Those wrongs may be ours or others' wrongs that we feel must be avenged. Whether in response to our own deeds or to those of others, surging emotions may refuse to be quiet. When reparation and healing cannot be completed, we may direct those disquieting energies toward a moral cause larger than ourselves. We may become excellent moral advocates for legislative change, memorials, relief organizations, and so forth. When healing seems impossible, we may feel drawn toward religious or philosophical healing beliefs. We may reach for a moral-emotional harmony that goes beyond human understanding. All major religions of the world present avenues for reaching for this type of harmony.

DEVELOPMENTAL CONSIDERATIONS

The moral-emotional cycle of reparation and healing is understood in simple form from an early age. The basic process can be explained by kindergartners. "I shouldn't have ____. I'm sorry. I won't do it again." Changes that occur through development involve the intensity and duration of moral-emotional distress, the number and type of strategies employed for reparation and healing, and the depth of moral meaning achieved. As we go through the five developmental stages, note the following emotional dimensions in the words of the children and adolescents quoted as well as our discussions of them:

(1) *Moral Enthusiasm:* how the GO AHEAD emotions (interest-excitement; enjoyment-joy) are incorporated into a zestful pursuit of moral goodness. These emotions are also present, although more quietly expressed, in the baseline state of moral-emotional equilibrium.

(2) *Moral Anxiety:* how the STOP, LOOK, LISTEN, and BE CAREFUL emotions (surprise-astonishment; shyness-embarrassment; fear-terror) are incorporated into signals of moral distress.

(3) *Moral Moodiness:* how the SLOW DOWN, GO INSIDE, AND THINK ABOUT IT emotions (sadness-anguish; shame-humiliation; guilt-more guilt) motivate moral reparation and change.

(4) *Moral Outrage:* how the DANGER ZONE emotions (dismell-disgust; anger-rage; contempt-hatred) are incorporated into pleas for moral reform. These emotions are seldom used in teaching moral-emotional responsiveness EXCEPT by parents who have "lost it" or who are clearly abusive.

(5) *Moral Reparation:* how various ways of "making things right after wrongdoing" are employed in restoring moral-emotional equilibrium.

(6) *Moral Healing:* how various ways of "making oneself feel better after wrongdoing" are employed in restoring moral-emotional equilibrium.

DEVELOPING MORAL-EMOTIONAL RESPONSIVENESS AT THE EXTERNAL STAGE (0 TO 6 YEARS)

Moral Anxiety: Realizing I'm in Trouble

Sometime before the age of six, children begin to "really" understand the moral concept of "getting in trouble." The physiological registration of trouble—shaking hands, butterflies in the stomach—accentuates the message. Those who have less physiological arousal get the message more slowly.

Interviewer: What happens to you, inside and out, after you have done something wrong?

Young child: I feel really nervous. Just what kind of punishment am I gonna get? I get really shaky, just in my hands.

Another YC: When I get in trouble, I feel scared. I get butterflies in my stomach, I shake, and I look down. My parents are yelling. I'm afraid of what they're going to do.

Another YC: My heart beats faster; no, it beats slower.

Young children do not mask emotions very well, even when they try to do so.

Interviewer: Would I be able to tell by looking at you if you had done something wrong?

Young child: No, you wouldn't know if I did something good or bad unless I told you, but you might see the chocolate on my face.

Moral Moodiness: Brief Grumpy Times

Young children's moral moodiness can be expressed in three ways. They may feel grumpy over their misdeeds (what we parents hope they will feel), feel grumpy that they have been caught, or feel grumpy about the punishment or other consequences that are imposed on them to teach them a lesson. Or all three. Fortunately or unfortunately, grumpy times do not stay for long in young children's minds. Keeping those pouts and frowns in place takes too much effort.

Interviewer: What happens after you have done something wrong?

Young child: When my mom says go to my room and think it over, I feel sad—for about half an hour, or ten minutes.

Another YC: [When my mom wouldn't let me play], I was playing with someone, but it wasn't anyone someone could see. It's more than one person, it's a hundred people.

When we parents overdo punishment, thinking that we're going to drive home a particular moral lesson once and forever, we're fooling ourselves. Inducing prolonged looks of shame and anger on our children's faces does not ensure that they feel guilty about the wrongdoing or that their behavior will be different in the future. If they are bold enough to get impudent with us during one of our stormy lectures, giving them "something to be sorry about" (such as a beating) simply does not improve their moral-emotional responsiveness.

Young children's minds scamper with ease from thoughts about wrongdoing to their mental worlds of mischievous or innocent playfulness. The Imp even lures them in that direction when parents overdo discipline. He can help children find fun ways of enduring almost any punishment that grownups can dream up. Attention and memory are mostly short-term at the external stage of conscience development. Adults need to move quickly through their moral lesson plans.

Interviewer: What do you do while you're sitting there [in your time-out]?

Young child: I just sit there and think about what I did.

Interviewer: What are your thoughts?

YC: I don't know.

Interviewer: Does it make you feel better to sit there?

YC: . . . Yeah [spoken in an unconvincing way].

Moral Reparation: Quick Fixes

In young children's minds, wrongdoing is over when it's over: "I quit _____. What more do you want?" Their minds do not focus for very long on regret.

Interviewer: What do you do to make things right after you have done something wrong?

Young child: I wish it had not have happened! I should have known better!

Another YC: [I say] I'm sorry, I won't do it again. [Then I ask] Can I go play?

Another YC: I'm going to tell and get the punishment over with.

Giving young children prolonged time to think about bad deeds may center their thoughts on the "badness" of their demanding and punishing parents. Retaliatory feelings may set in, leading them to engage in more wrongdoing. They may scream, kick furniture, spit, or write all over the walls. Then we parents may feel that we have to discipline the wrongdoings that have resulted from our wrongful approach. A stubborn parent and a stubborn child, locked in repairing a never-ending list of wrongdoings, may never get to the healing step. Moral-emotional disequilibrium may reign far too long to be productive.

For young children, repairing a wrongdoing means a quick fix. They can be taught to apologize and, at least sometimes, to actually fix something. If another child's toy has been broken, we can ask them to give up one of their own. They may honor our admonishment to be nicer or to let the other child choose the next activity. Whatever reparative measures are taught should be ones that can be quickly executed. The best "fixes" are ones that children think of themselves.

Moral Healing: Lots of Hugs

Young children are quick to heal when the way is paved for them. Making things right often means feeling better instantaneously. They are able to forget negative feelings very quickly. However, it never hurts to play, take a nap, have something good to eat, or hug a teddy bear. The way we parents show forgiveness is important. Hugs and attention are very good ways to restore harmony.

Interviewer: What do you do to make yourself feel better after doing something bad?

Young child: I've lied to my mom before and I keep on lying to her, and then I tell her the truth and then it's OK. It makes me feel better if I tell her the truth. I still get in trouble, but I feel better.

Another YC: I just go off and have some fun that won't get me in more trouble.

Another YC: I just go in my room and play without anybody else. I run from my brother because I don't want to hear him talking anymore.

Another YC: I forget about it. I just say, "Go away, go away."

Nurturing Moral-Emotional Responsiveness at the External Stage (0 to 6 years)

- Affirm the "am good–feel good" moral-emotional connection.

- Teach the "am good–feel good–*do good*" connection slowly. Keep demands and prohibitions simple and few.

- Become aware of your child's moral anxiety and moodiness.

- Keep confinement, punishment, and other consequences brief.

- Teach your child ways to "fix things." Show appreciation for effort and originality.

- Don't stay mad. Be forgiving. Give hugs and attention.

DEVELOPING MORAL-EMOTIONAL RESPONSIVENESS AT THE BRAIN-HEART STAGE (7–11)

Moral Anxiety: Empathic Anticipation

When younger children worry about getting in trouble, they usually think only in terms of what will happen to them. "Just what kind of punishment am I gonna get?" After the age of seven, moral anxiety begins to broaden its focus. Anticipating how breaking rules may hurt someone else adds an empathic dimension. Older children can anticipate that if they break a rule, parents may be disappointed, friends may not get to come over, and other people may not like them as much. We parents accentuate the empathic dimension in moral anxiety when we refer to how disappointed we will feel if _____ happens or ask children how they think their friends will feel if _____ happens. We need to be clever. There is a fine line between eliciting moral imagination and eliciting boredom.

The intensity of physiological arousal accompanying emotions differs from child to child, with genetics making a strong contribution. Children with high levels of arousal learn to anticipate, and thereby stay out of "trouble" more readily than those with lower levels of arousal. Empathic anticipation is using one's physiological arousal as a cue in pleasing others. Rule-following comes easily to children with high levels of empathic anticipation. When such children do break rules, they may not be bold enough to own up to their mistakes right away. Fortunate for their moral development, their high levels of physiological arousal may not come down until they own up to their mistakes.

Children with very low levels of physiological arousal have a harder time learning to follow rules by anticipating "trouble." Low arousal may even set them up for "double trouble," because they find it so easy to mask emotions, hide the evidence (or themselves), or construct alibis. Children of this type have to make more conscious choices about being good because they have less physiological prompting leading them in the direction of compliance.

The following children hint that they are on the edge of developing empathic anticipation.

> Interviewer: What happened on the inside or outside of you when no one knew about your bad deed?

> Older child: I felt really uneasy, but I didn't know why.

> Interviewer: What happens on the inside or outside of you after you tell a lie?

> OC: I quit lying because my mom could always tell by the look on my face.

Some children naturally want to take the focus off themselves, even when they are being good, and particularly when they are being spectacular. They are the children who turn red in the face every time the focus is on them. They are naturally self-effacing whenever they get praise or appreciation, win awards, or do something especially nice for others. The following comments anticipate the development of modesty or humility:

> Interviewer: What happens inside or outside of you when you have done something good?

> Older child: [When doing something good] I turn red.

> Another OC: I get goose bumps when I do something good.

> Another OC: You feel a little bit ticklish when you feel proud.

> Another OC: Sometimes, when you do right things, it can get you embarrassed or you feel like an oddball and everybody looks at you kind of funny.

Moral Moodiness: Long Moments of Sadness and a Little Self-Contempt

Using their own vocabulary, school-age children generally tell us that they feel sad, ashamed, and guilty after wrongdoing. Sometimes they describe a little self-contempt. In contrast to children at the External stage, these Brain-Heart stage children tolerate these emotions a little longer before wanting to chase them away. If briefly confined to their rooms, they may actually use the time to think about what they have done wrong. Time alone gives both child and parent time to plan an "appropriate" punishment or other consequence.

Interviewer: What happens inside or outside of you when you have done something bad or wrong?

Older child: I don't like myself when I'm mean to my sister; Mom doesn't either.

Interviewer: Do you act differently when your parents don't know about what you did that was bad?

OC: I might not act normal or talk as much until Mom and Dad find out. When they find out, then we talk it over and I have to fix it and say I'll never do it again. And then it's over.

Interviewer: What happens inside or outside of you when you have done something wrong?

OC: I feel guilty. I look and act embarrassed. My parents yell or talk forever. They just don't shut up about what I did [broke glasses]—and my bad mood. My sister teases me when I do something wrong.

Another OC: [After buying baseball cards with money meant for Christmas presents] I felt gloomy. I didn't feel well and my heart was pounding.

Moral Reparation: Planned Restitution

When our children sense that their actions have disappointed us, they feel emotionally distant or separated from us. In turn, our feelings of frustration, anger, disappointment, even outrage, distance us from them. This distancing should be used wisely. It is very important that we parents ourselves be in a state of moral-emotional equilibrium when helping our children restore theirs. If we send them to their rooms during this cooling-off period, we ought to clarify that the separation is not punishment. We may choose to punish later, but not now. Separation becomes punishment if we go into an angry sulk, treat our children contemptuously for a few days, and then gradually forget about the incident without ever processing it with them. If we act that way, moral learning may not occur. Bad feelings may start characterizing our relationship.

Processing wrongdoing requires that we listen attentively, question wisely, act benevolently, and be ready to forgive. If we choose to punish, mutual consensus between us and our children is often possible over the nature of the punishment. The following children describe their thoughts and actions in the reparation process:

Interviewer: What did you think about what your parents said?

Older child: I thought it over and it [the child's misdeed] was wrong.

Interviewer: What did you do to make things right?

OC: I make myself come in early one night if I've been late [coming in from play] another night.

Another OC: When my mom lets me out of my room, I show that I'm sorry and I can get along with the group.

Another OC: I asked her [my friend], "Do you want to do something [special] tomorrow?"

Another OC: I should think first next time.

Another OC: I don't want to face Mom if I ever do that again!

Self-clarification of wrongness, compensatory actions, display of sorrow, improved interpersonal behavior, social generosity, and plans for reform make an impressive list of ways to restore moral-emotional equilibrium. Simply asking the question "What do you think you should do about this [wrongdoing]?" may stimulate reparative creativity in children. Self-generated repair is more likely to enhance moral-emotional responsiveness than any passively endured punishment.

Moral Healing: Relaxed and Energized

Wrongdoing causes a break in the moral connection. Bad feelings upset moral-emotional equilibrium. Restoration of the "am good–feel good–do good" state relaxes and energizes body, mind, and spirit. The following children express these feelings in a variety of ways:

Interviewer: Would I know by looking at you that you were feeling better?

Older child: You could tell that I was feeling better because of the way I was walking.

Another OC: [You could tell I was feeling good] by the action in my hands.

Interviewer: What do you do to make yourself feel better after you have done something wrong?

Older Child: I scream a lot to make myself feel better.

Another OC: I go to my room and read or listen to my radio.

Another OC: [I feel better] after I listen to a song or read a chapter of the Hardy Boys.

Another OC: I eat ice cream.

—— **ADVICE TO PARENTS** ————————————————

Nurturing Moral-Emotional Responsiveness at the Brain-Heart Stage (7–11)

- **Appreciate your child's development of empathic anticipation.**

- **Appreciate your child's feelings of sadness, shame, guilt, and a little self-contempt after wrongdoing.**

- **After wrongdoing, allow a cooling-off period for moral-emotional responsiveness to do its own self-teaching.**

- **Listen attentively, ask questions wisely, act benevolently, and be ready to forgive.**

- **Encourage self-initiated reparation.**

- **Enjoy the restoration of moral-emotional equilibrium in your child after reparation.**

- **Enjoy the renewed relaxation and energy.**

DEVELOPING MORAL-EMOTIONAL RESPONSIVENESS AT THE PERSONIFIED STAGE (12–13)

Moral Anxiety: Responding to That Internal Moral Presence

At the dawn of adolescence, young teenagers begin to describe conscience in terms of an internal moral presence, a someone who guides and judges their moral lives. This moral presence we call the personified conscience. In addition to having internalized rules for judging behavior as right or wrong, feeling the presence of the personified conscience brings forth all of the psychological dynamics that govern real relationships. Imagine a conversation a young teenager might have with his or her personified conscience. "Are you pleased with me, Conscience? Are you mad? disappointed? Are you going to punish me? I think you're just being mean. I'm going to ignore you. Why didn't you keep me out of trouble? Why didn't you shout a little louder?"

At the Personified stage, moral anxiety is aroused in response to judgments of external authority as well as to those of conscience. With pressure coming from both directions, emerging teenagers may experience moral anxiety with greater intensity than in their younger years:

Interviewer: What happens to your body when you have these feelings?

Emerging teenager: [If you saw me after doing something wrong] I might be pale and sweating and benched over and shaking.

Another ET: I get sick to my stomach and I feel really bad.

If a teenager happens to have a "bad" conscience, one that does not govern by rules of respect, strong emotions may still be aroused after wrongdoing. Anticipatory anxiety registers fear of punishment by real authority rather than fear of displeasing an internal judge. Law-breaking teenagers may show increasing anxiety because they know that if they get caught, the law will punish them more harshly than when they were younger.

Interviewer: What happened after you stole that stuff?

Law-breaking teenager: I had butterflies in my stomach, and I got really nervous because it was really late. I was just really sweaty and I was shaking and we hid from all the cars we saw. Then we got back to Jeff's garage. Whew!

This teenager's words sound like he is physiologically aroused because he has gone against his conscience. In actuality, this troubled and troubling boy had no compunction about stealing, even though he knew that other people disapproved. He simply wanted to avoid getting caught and punished. His physiological arousal was related to the excitement of escaping undetected rather than anticipation of being caught for something he valued as wrongful. We include this example to illustrate that anxiety can be amoralized as well as moralized.

Moral Moodiness: The Goodness of Guilt

A private moral life allows the emotion of guilt to come into full power. Although guilt is often portrayed as something we should get rid of—like extra weight or zits—we can also see it as a private moral resource. Guilt maintains moral focus and motivation without the prodding of external authorities. Learning to manage it actively and wisely is a moral fitness skill. The skill involves learning how to let it take us to the depths of self-questioning and moral problem-solving without burying us in despair.

Guilt in Parents

When our teenagers repeatedly get into trouble, we are likely to feel guilty—perhaps more so than our teenagers. Let's think about how guilt works in parents. That is our best clue for guessing how this emotion works in our teenagers.

Parents can respond to guilt disastrously or wisely. To illustrate a disastrous response, imagine being the parents of a very errant teenage daughter. She has [make a nightmarish list of misdeeds]. In response to these misdeeds, we can become very sensitive about our parenting, especially when others shame and blame us for her delinquent behavior. Even when they don't actually do this, we imagine them doing it. Shame and self-contempt rise in us.

Instead of letting guilt carry us deeply into introspection and solution-seeking, we fight it as hard as we can. We allow shame, blame, and anger to rise in us until we fire rageful reactions toward this errant daughter. We threaten her with all the powers we can conjure up—juvenile authorities, revered and deceased grandparents, a furious God. We blame the environment—our teenager's companions, the school, an absent parent, the advertising industry, the Internet, and the media. We threaten to sever our moral connection with her. We devalue our own child to spare ourselves from going inside and using guilt wisely.

The wise use of parent guilt means taking ourselves slowly and deliberately through the steps of moral reparation and healing—the same ones we have been teaching our children and adolescents. We do it alone or with an adult counselor. We are interested in our teenagers' opinions, but we do not place them in the role of counselors—it isn't their appropriate role to be our counselors. Our repeatedly asking, "Where did we go wrong?" only opens the door for them to manipulate us through our guilt feelings. This mournful question may also further demoralize our errant teenagers.

Instead, we ask ourselves privately: What parenting mistakes have I made?

How can I make amends? What can I do to strengthen my parent-teenager moral connection? How can I let my most private emotion, guilt, motivate change in me? (Or forgiveness, if change is impossible.)

The wise management of guilt guides us not only toward improved child-rearing, but toward benevolent attitudes as well. Imagine that the errant teenager mentioned above has behavioral problems completely beyond parent control. Imagine that they are more or less beyond her control, also. Let's say that she has one or more of these biologically based characteristics: low physiological arousal, impulsivity, high novelty-seeking, high risk-taking, poor judgment, or any number of learning disabilities. Add a few bad companions for environmental stimulation.

> **THE ADVOCATE**
> There are children and teenagers whose biological makeup interferes greatly with conscience development. They have problems staying out of trouble and learning from their mistakes after they are in trouble. Personality traits interfere with the wise use of guilt. Along with receiving help from their parents, they need to be treated in environments that provide them with ongoing external motivations to be good. They do not need rageful reactions and punishment. Their weak moral-emotional responsiveness needs daily support.

If we parents have carefully reviewed and repaired what we can to facilitate her conscience development, this wise use of guilt frees us from shame, blame, and anger. We will always feel bad about this child's difficulties, but we can freely have a positive attitude toward getting her professional help, letting her find her own way, and protecting ourselves and our other children from her problems.

Guilt in Teenagers

Physiologically normal children begin to use guilt productively during early adolescence. During the first ten to twelve years of our children's lives, we have had numerous moral dialogues with them. When we felt their moral-emotional responsiveness was insufficient, we acted in ways that we hoped would increase the intensity of their arousal. We still do that. What is different during the teenage years is that we now have a child-rearing buddy—our teenager's personified conscience. That makes private time as vital as parent-teenager time for moral processing. Guilt, aroused by conscience, demands its own form of accountability.

The following teenager makes promising statements about how personal guilt is working hand in hand with past and present parent influence to support her pursuit of goodness:

> Interviewer: How did you feel after you tried pot?

> Emerging teenager: I felt so stupid smoking pot, but I did it anyway—to impress my friends. Then, I said, "No, you guys go ahead," and I left. I could already hear what my parents would say. And I didn't feel so good about it myself, either. I know it's not good for you. I'm just going to have to listen to my conscience more.

Moral Reparation: Doing Something with Those Guilty Feelings

Guilt is a persistent motivator of reparation. Listen to these teenagers:

> Interviewer: What do you do with your guilt feeling?

> Emerging teenager: It lasts longer if I don't do something about it.

> Another ET: I moped around until I finally apologized; after that, I felt like my old self.

> Another ET: I feel bad and I don't really want to be around people. I feel like I'm in this little cage and I just want to be alone. I feel bad in my heart. I just stay hidden. I stole candy from my sister on Halloween and she told me if I did she'd smack me. She smacks hard. I stole some and I didn't feel too good inside so I just put it back. She's 18—a freshman in college.

> Another ET: I feel like somebody just punched me, and I feel really bad and I want to go back and do it the right way.

> Another ET: I just feel guilty [after misdeed] so I'm sure I look like it. If I volunteer to do my chores days before Friday, my mom usually knows something is going on.

Now we present a turning-point response in a law-breaking teenager. Conversations with law-breaking teenagers are often characterized by entrenched negative attitudes about authority. But not always. In the following conversation, guilt and empathy motivate reparative action.

> Interviewer: What happens inside or outside of you when you have done something wrong?

> Law-breaking teenager: I came back laughing [after stealing the cartons of cigarettes]. I felt sneaky and guilty—guilty because the cops could have

had an important call to go to instead of just sitting there waiting for a suspect that's already in a group home.

Although this boy's first response to wrongdoing was amoral excitement, guilt feelings were aroused through his ability to identify with the policeman's role. This combination immensely improved his prognosis for becoming a good citizen.

More Reparation: Reconnecting with Others

Wrongdoing wounds the moral connection we have with each other. The following teenagers discuss repairing broken moral connections with others:

Interviewer: After displeasing your conscience by doing something wrong, what do you do to make it right?

Emerging teenager: I got to talk to my mom and talk things out with her and then that usually—like—helps me with my decision.

Another ET: Just do something to relax myself and not be so tense about it. My bestest friend in the whole wide world, I know I can say anything to and she won't tell anybody. She really knows how to help me. I'd probably call her up and start talking about it. She usually helps me out.

Another ET: [After a fight] You would maybe help them do something— help them with something they can't do.

Another ET: I stay around the house—do something for them [parents].

Another ET: I try to do a good deed and help someone that needs help— try to be kind of friendly. I might do an extra chore that I don't really have to do to get my allowance, just to help you. It makes me feel better knowing that I'm helping someone and that somehow they might return the favor.

Moral Healing: Letting the Sun Shine In

The longer it rains, the more we appreciate sunshine. The longer it takes to resolve a moral issue, the better we feel when the task is done. When reparation and healing are completed, positive emotions flow like rays of sunshine. The good feelings laugh and skip while we hunt for good things to do. Note the evidence in these teenagers:

Interviewer: What do you do to make yourself feel better after wrongdoing?

Emerging teenager: I pray to God and ask him to help me make things right.

Interviewer: Does that make you feel better?

ET: Yeah, it always does.

Interviewer: What happens inside or outside of you when you have done something good?

ET: Feeling good in your heart makes you want to do more good things because people might be happy with you for doing that.

Another ET: I did the dishes and cleaned the car for no reason at all; I just felt good.

Another ET: If I did something right, I'd be "mess around happy."

—— ADVICE TO PARENTS ————————————————————

Nurturing Moral-Emotional Responsiveness at the Personified Stage (12–13)

- **Appreciate how our teenagers' consciences become co-parents.**

- **Appreciate the usefulness of guilt in ourselves and our teenagers.**

- **Be aware of amoralized excitement.**

- **Appreciate that time alone is moral processing time in our teenagers' lives.**

- **Expect longer and more meaningful conversations, when they come.**

- **Enjoy moral-emotional exuberance. It flows from moral-emotional healing.**

DEVELOPING MORAL-EMOTIONAL RESPONSIVENESS AT THE CONFUSED STAGE (14–15)

Moral Anxiety: Loyalty Conflicts

During childhood, youngsters are generally content making friendships wherever their families happen to live. Emotional bonds stay mostly family-centered. By the time our children become mid-adolescents—around fourteen or fifteen—specific friendships, specific groups of friends, and specific social communities become very important to them. Moral-emotional connections to friends come to dominate their private thoughts, conversations, and activities. Mom and Dad are placed at a respectful distance in their minds.

In the last chapter, we described how psychological emancipation from parents, along with the formation of a strong sense of individuality, is valued in American culture. Adolescence becomes a moral-emotional zone of its own where teenagers work on issues of right and wrong among themselves within the context of the society in which they are being reared. In Chapter 5, "Developing the Golden Rule of Conscience," we will talk about value formation among peers. Here we will focus on the moral-emotional feelings that get aroused when teenagers first realize that they are, at the same time, a son or daughter, an individual, a friend, a boyfriend or girlfriend, a peer group member, and a citizen.

Loyalty conflicts become particularly distressing issues of conscience in mid-adolescence. How does one remain faithful and true to parents, oneself, friends, and the group all at the same time? How does one remain true to conscience? Loyalty conflicts arise for mid-adolescents when they find themselves attracted to different people with differing values in different situations. A simple example: A student learns that her friend cheated on a test. She has no trouble defining cheating as wrong. That has been a rule in her conscience for years. Her problem is figuring out what her moral-emotional response to her friend should be, taking into consideration all of the factors she knows to be present. We'll return to this example further on, when we discuss *empathic processing.*

Mid-adolescents have a general desire to please and to be accepted. However, there are times when they feel caught in the middle between the wishes of one friend and another, a friend and the group, or the peer group and the authority of the adult community. Furthermore, mid-adolescence is usually the first time teenagers even think about questioning rules within their own consciences. Moral anxiety may rise to the point of confusion. Hard choices must be made. "How can I maintain a friendship while refusing to participate in certain activities?" "Is it possible to not go along with the crowd while still remaining a member of the group?"

Fortunately, confusion is episodic during the Confused conscience stage. Much of the time, our teenagers' lives run smoothly. They are distressed and confused only when they are distressed and confused. While parents may look at teenage moral dilemmas with undistressed clarity, teenagers do not. To help out, we stand patiently by, waiting to be asked for our sage advice. That is, unless harm is imminent—then we don't wait to be asked. Our protective duty moves us to action, whether our teenagers like our rescue efforts or not. But mostly, we wait to be asked. We can't do our teenagers' moral learning for them.

This teenage girl reviews how she felt in the midst of a conflict with her parents over her boyfriend. We can imagine how anxious her parents were feeling at the same time.

Interviewer: How do you feel after doing something wrong?

Mid-adolescent: I'm worried about it. I feel uptight—like when people talk to me, I'm like, "Why are you talking to me?" I'm like all confused inside, and I feel uptight about what I just did. On the outside, I'm snappy and mean and I don't really know why I'm doing that. It's one of those things where I know I'm doing it, but I don't know why, so I just keep doing it. I used to date somebody my mom and dad didn't want me to date. We dated a long, long time. I didn't ever try and hide it from them. That year I was so mean to everyone around me and I didn't know why.

Moral-emotional development is in process. The girl obviously has a strong moral connection to her parents. She values their opinions and wants to please them. Nonetheless, she wants to choose her own friends, especially her boyfriend. Moral-emotional disequilibrium is manifested in terms of both anxiety and moodiness. She doesn't want to be a mean and snappy girl. Her distress is crying out for a decision that will restore moral-emotional harmony in her, between her and her parents, and perhaps between her and her boyfriend.

Moral Moodiness: Figuring Out What to Do

Assistance from Parents and Friends

In the last section (Personified stage), we spoke about the value of private time for young teenagers to process thoughts, feelings, and plans for repairing particular misdeeds. Within the loyalty conflicts and value clashes of mid-adolescence, wrongdoing is sometimes a matter more of relative harm or potential harm than of a specific wrong deed. "Going with that guy will do you no good!" There are no concrete conscience-stored rules for the girl in the example above to assess this judgment. Going inside herself may not help her understand "no good" better. Learning more about the boyfriend, looking at the relationship from different angles, seeing other people's relationships, and talking about it with her friends and family are more likely to help.

When teenagers offer us the opportunity to join the dialogue—or when a dangerous situation requires that we mandate a dialogue—the following questions may be helpful: What is your distress telling you? What is your anxiety or moodiness saying? What moral conflicts are churning inside of you? What about the relative good or relative harm of what you are doing now? What about your future? What do your friends think? What decisions will relieve your distress?

Some teenagers are quick to justify less than satisfactory choices by claiming that "a little ____" isn't going to hurt (let's define "a little ____" as any risk-taking or submissive behavior that goes beyond mischief). As parents we generally recognize these behaviors very easily because we've "been there." When harm is imminent, we are duty-bound to move from allowing our teenagers to "learn from experience" to stating explicit opinions and setting limits —even if the dialogue gets a little stormy and the limits are resisted. If we do not act courageously at critical times, we are not modeling good moral-emotional responsiveness. Memories of stormy family clashes over defining and protecting goodness are better than memories of raw or deadly experiences devoid of adult input and rescue efforts.

Sometimes teenagers wrestle with moral dilemmas better when talking with a favorite teacher or school counselor, a best friend's mom, an older brother's friend, or a youth leader. At other times, physical exertion restores emotional equilibrium whether a solution is reached or not.

Interviewer: What do you do to make yourself feel better?

Mid-adolescent: When I'm mad I go play a sport to take my aggression out on instead of on somebody.

Another MA: If we [a friend and I] are arguing, and I get stressed out, I just don't call her. I just go work out or something. It relieves stress, you know.

Empathic Processing

Moral-emotional disharmony is not confined to personal moral dilemmas in teenagers' lives. Mid-adolescents also become acutely involved in their friends' issues. Let's return to the example of the girl whose best friend cheated in class.

Interviewer: What happened inside of you when your friend got caught cheating?

Mid-adolescent: When Mr. B. asked for her paper, I knew S. was in trouble. My face felt hot so I kept looking down. S. hadn't been studying because she and her boyfriend were in the process of breaking up. They were fighting on the phone all the time. I know she shouldn't have done it, but, oh, I don't know what I would have done in the same situation. Her parents will really be mad.

The empathic responsiveness in this teenager is remarkable. Her friend's problems have definitely become her problems. Although she doesn't approve of cheating, she is totally caught up in her friend's situational conflict. She infers that making up or breaking up with a boyfriend is just as important as passing a test. But does it justify cheating? She infers that studying and making good grades the honest way are also very important. Those values, established much earlier in development, have currently become invaded by the pangs of a teenage love problem. Studying and getting along are right; cheating and useless fighting are wrong. She is so empathic when pondering the problem that it might as well be her own.

Alongside moral dilemmas, plain, straight-out wrongdoing continues throughout adolescence (and life). Guilt continues to prompt repair under these circumstances. Note how sadness and guilt have a "SLOW DOWN, GO INSIDE, AND THINK ABOUT IT" effect on this teenager:

Interviewer: What happens on the inside of you after you have done something wrong?

Mid-adolescent: [After I snuck out of the house one time] I got kind of an empty feeling. It just keeps bugging me until I do something about it. I kind of get, not depressed, but don't have as much energy. I just sit there and mope. People ask what's wrong, but I try to keep to myself. I really don't want to talk about it.

Interviewer: What did you do about it?

MA: I finally told on myself.

Moral Healing: Moments of Moral Euphoria

Resolving a conflict or repairing a wrong can be healing in its own right. Teenagers tell us that moral-emotional equilibrium is also restored by the soothing effects of listening to music, reading, talking to friends about "other" things, showing kindness toward an unpopular or mistreated person, or prayer.

Interviewer: What do you do to make yourself feel better after wrongdoing?

Mid-adolescent: I pray to God and he forgives me—helps me do the right things and not the wrong.

Healing may send positive emotions skyward—toward euphoria. Euphoria means energy for action, which, without the wisdom of moral anticipation, may lead to more trouble.

Interviewer: How do you feel after [reparation] is over?

Mid-adolescent: You feel fulfilled or free of guilt in any way. Life's a little easier for some reason. Everything is free off your mind. Nothing to worry about. It lasts until the next time I do something wrong.

Another MA: I'm getting along with Mom and Dad; I'm making good grades; I'm getting along with my friends; nobody is mad at me.

Another MA: I feel happy. I feel like I just want to keep doing it and doing it again so that way I'll never mess up my life again.

───── **ADVICE TO PARENTS** ─────────────────────────

Nurturing Moral-Emotional Responsiveness at the Confused Stage (14–15)

- **Expect a variety of loyalty conflicts in mid-adolescence.**

- **Expect moral anxiety to occasionally escalate to confusion.**

- **Help your teenager process moral dilemmas. Look for an association between moodiness and moral issues.**

- **Appreciate the value of teenagers' processing problems with friends and other trusted adults.**

- **Intervene with opinions and limit-setting when harm is imminent.**

- **Set limits on over-involvement in other people's problems.**

- **Enjoy teenagers' euphoric moral moments.**

DEVELOPING MORAL-EMOTIONAL RESPONSIVENESS
AT THE INTEGRATING STAGE (16–17+)

Moral Anxiety: Subsides with the Growth of Conviction and Courage

Episodes of moral anxiety begin to decrease in number and intensity as our teenagers pass their sixteenth birthdays. They begin to have more of a sense of self within their peer community. Discovering personal moral convictions, including the courage to act on them, becomes more appealing than following the enticements of the crowd or trying to please everyone. These changes do not occur all at once—just now and then, situation by situation.

One day, a situation will arise that prompts an individual teenager to express a self-derived moral conviction: "This is what I believe is right." (More about self-derived values in Chapter 6.) Another day, he or she will take a stab in the direction of courage: "I'm going to [start doing ____ or quit doing ____] no matter what anyone else says." Active and prolonged moral-emotional processing may precede these defining moral moments.

Alternatively, a change in behavior may just happen, surprising everyone—friends, parents, and teenager alike. Some teenagers just start acting more grown-up without being able to explain the change. We parents may think, for a moment, that maturation is magical. Unknown to us and unacknowledged by these less articulate teenagers, the change may coincidentally follow right on the heels of a morally important discussion in school, in a youth group, or in a conversation with a friend. Furthermore, ideas that we seeded long ago may have found their way into these discussions.

When teenagers come to new moral truths, those truths are truly new and truly theirs. They may mirror our convictions, but they have been self-derived. The truths are consolidations of moral-emotional processing. Resist all urges to say, "I told you so," but wink at the Imp.

What reinforces self-derived convictions more than anything else is release from emotional turmoil. When our teenagers' moral-emotional processing leads them to compelling convictions, a state of calm confidence develops in them. Decision-making and courage flow from this state. Note the words of calm in the next two examples:

Interviewer: How do you feel when you have done something morally good?

Older teenager: Comfortable. Everyone else at the party was drinking, but I chose not to. It didn't bother me.

Another OT: Everyone there was pro-choice; I am not. They have a right to their opinions and I have a right to mine. I feel good when I express mine.

To summarize, children and young teenagers find moral-emotional satisfaction in compliance and pleasing. Older teenagers discover moral-emotional satisfaction in personal conviction. Mid-adolescence is that stormy period in between. Personal conviction allows our teenagers to override moral anxiety about displeasing others, to transform it into a state of moral calm. Calm conviction strengthens the am good–feel good–do good connection. Courage emerges from a state of relaxed moral alertness.

Moral Alertness

Performers of all kinds—athletes, musicians, public speakers—tell us that a certain amount of anxiety is good, even necessary, for peak performance. Many tell us that even though they spend many hours under the scrutiny of the public eye, they are basically shy people. They have learned to refocus their self-consciousness and anxiety on accomplishing chosen tasks. Hours of practice are necessary before they achieve a state of confident performance readiness. Moral performances, acts of conscience, also require peak alertness and practice.

Moral alertness is any preventive strategy that a person consciously uses to resist temptation and to pursue goodness. Beckoning temptations for teenagers include deception; cheating; stealing; smoking, drinking, or using drugs; driving recklessly; vandalism; sexual indiscretion; and friendships with people of "bad" conscience. Preventive strategies include using self-derived convictions—keeping them posted on an internal bulletin board; practicing moral-emotional diplomacy—remembering how to say "NO" nicely; and sensing when Imp-inspired mischief may turn into harmful trouble.

A "lock-in" is a special kind of preventive strategy used by youth leaders of church groups and other teen organizations. Teenagers "locked in" a safe environment (adult protection and guidance) for a whole weekend have plenty of time to explore self-derived convictions and to affirm such development in others. They also have the opportunity to practice moral-emotional diplomacy in a setting that usually allows a little mischief but guards against the emergence of harm. An older teenager describes the effect of such a weekend on herself:

Interviewer: What happens on the inside of you when you have done something good?

Older teenager: Doing good makes you feel good. You have a feeling of inner peace within yourself. You kind of glow. I went to a church retreat for a weekend—a lock-in. I didn't know anybody there. It was my dad's church. I guess I did a lot of good there just by talking to people and listening and trying to help them a little bit—and also good for me on the inside, spiritually.

In the next two examples, teenagers express how the calm pursuit of goodness may help others as well as themselves.

Interviewer: How do you feel after you have done something good?

Older teenager: After doing something good, I feel reassured—feel warm inside. I look more comfortable. Maybe it makes others think twice and think that if they, maybe, follow my example and do what I did, or be happy that I did what I did, maybe, will be more friendly to me.

Another OT: [speaking about competition] You've got to be happy with yourself so you'll be happy with others. If you know you have the ability and you disadvantage yourself and don't do it, then you should be unhappy with yourself. Sometimes it's good to put pressure on yourself. Sometimes it's good to accept yourself as you are—and others.

Moral Moodiness: Diminishing Episodes

Older teenagers who follow personal moral convictions have many fewer episodes of moral moodiness than they experienced during mid-adolescence. The calm pursuit of goodness in a state of moral alertness sustains a happy, even zestful, moral mood in them.

Interviewer: How do you feel now that you've made your decision?

Older adolescent: My friends said, "What are you—a little Jesus girl now?" And I said, "Maybe I am!"

Interview: How do you feel when you make good choices?

OA: I stick to my morals because they are morals that I set. If I just stick to my morals and my priorities that are set, you know when you need to take a risk and when you don't. 'Cause you have that feeling inside. You know it's okay to go where you want to go if you stick with your morals. In the past I got in so much trouble, and it's taken me all this time to build up all this trust with my mom, and I don't want it to go away. I like the way I am now.

Moral Reparation: Learning to Live with Unresolvable Wrongs

In spite of increased moral alertness, wrongdoing does occur. A new realization at this stage is that not every wrong deed can be repaired. When repair is not possible, learning to seek forgiveness and to forgive oneself is necessary for the return of moral-emotional equilibrium. Patience, tolerance, and forgiveness of self and others must be integrated into the moral-emotional system.

> Interviewer: What do you do to make things right after you have displeased your conscience?

> Older teenager: If you say something that hurts someone's feelings, you can't really erase that. You can apologize but you can't really correct it. You have to live with it.

Thoughts about the potential effects of wrongdoing on mood feed moral alertness.

> Interviewer: If you did something wrong and no one knew about it, how would you feel?

> Another OT: I would probably wear myself down because it would always be on my mind, and I'd probably become tired and maybe sick. I'd be tearing myself up inside thinking of it all the time and not getting it out.

Moral Healing: Moral Enthusiasm

Earlier in the chapter, we defined moral enthusiasm as the incorporation of the GO AHEAD emotions (interest-excitement; enjoyment-joy) into the pursuit of goodness. Now we'll explore reasons why some teenagers—let's generalize to people—develop moral enthusiasm while others are more prone to sinking into moral despair.

Similar moral-emotional experiences may characterize both groups. Both may develop strong personal convictions. Both may develop moral alertness. Both may have courageous moments. Both may realize that not all wrongdoing can be repaired. Perhaps morally enthusiastic people are simply more "turned on" or "revved up" by goodness. Perhaps it is a matter of choice: What attitude am I going to adopt toward morality through life? In Chapter 6, we will discuss moral choice in more detail. We close this chapter with an example of an adolescent who experiences moral enthusiasm, who gets "tingly" over the pursuit of goodness.

Interviewer: What happens, inside and outside, when you have done something good?

Older teenager: When I do something good, I just go on and not worry about things. If it's something really good, I get like cold chills or something—kind of tingly because I know I did something right. Like when, behind our neighborhood, we built a little shelter for the homeless—it was kind of neat.

—— ADVICE TO PARENTS ————————————————————

Nurturing Moral-Emotional Responsiveness at the Integrating Stage (16–17+)

• **Admire the emergence of personal moral convictions.**

• **Appreciate the emergence of moral calm and courage.**

• **Never say, "I told you so."**

• **Admire the development of moral alertness.**

• **Talk and listen. Listen and talk.**

• **Empathize with episodes of moral despair.**

• **Affirm patience, tolerance, and forgiveness.**

• **Affirm moral enthusiasm.**

SUMMARY

In this chapter we described how the developing conscience incorporates the emotional system to express moral-emotional responsiveness. All fundamental emotions and blends of emotion are recruited to express moral concerns: interest-excitement; enjoyment-joy; surprise-astonishment; shyness-embarrassment; fear-terror; dismell-disgust; anger-rage; contempt-hatred; sadness-anguish; shame-humiliation; and guilt. Each of these emotions has physiological ties to the brain and body. Emotions link the consciousness of conscience to bodily sensations.

Parents influence children's moral-emotional development from infancy onward. We do so by expressing and mirroring satisfaction in our children's very existence. Gradually, we teach them right from wrong through demands and prohibitions, through affirmation and disapproval, through constant caring and moral alertness. Moral-emotional equilibrium comes to mean an "am good–feel good–do good" state of existence. Wrongdoing disturbs that state. The disequilibrium is signaled by increases in moral anxiety and the development of moral moodiness. Reparation and healing restore moral-emotional equilibrium. As parents we guide our children through these processes.

Children and young adolescents gain most of their moral-emotional satisfaction from compliance and pleasing. Mid-adolescents struggle to add satisfaction from more personalized convictions. Their moral-emotional equilibrium can become very changeable in response to influences outside our homes, mainly peers and the popular culture. As older adolescents consolidate personal convictions, episodes of moral anxiety and moodiness diminish. They are replaced by episodes of moral courage and moral enthusiasm.

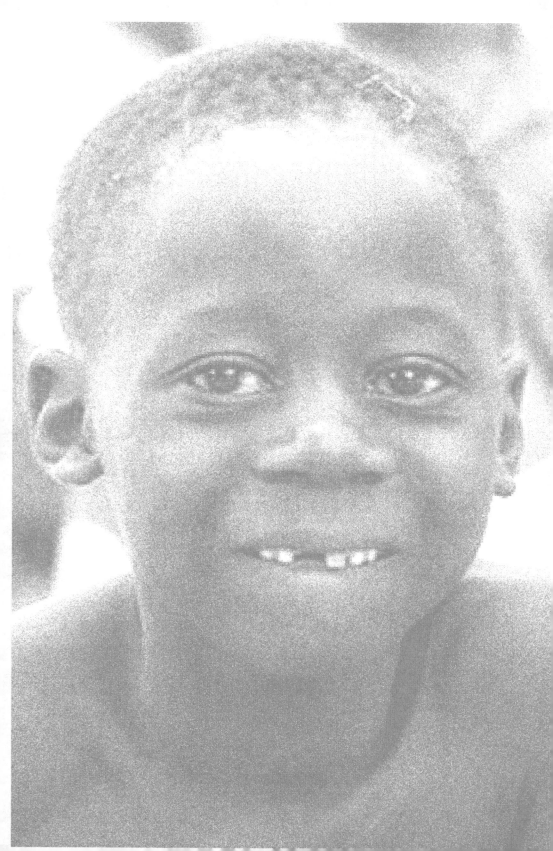

4

Developing the Authority of Conscience

The moral obligation to honor authority is fundamental to civilization. During periods of rapid social change, rules of authority, as well as persons in authority, are challenged, or at least doubted. When change progresses to social disintegration, the foundations of moral meaning begin to crack. At those times, people cry out for new moral authority. If change is so overwhelming that people do not know how to articulate their distress, their behavior cries out for authorization of new meaning. Children bringing guns to school may be making that kind of behavioral cry.

Although we parents would like our children's future to come with warranties for environmental, economic, and social stability, we know that it will more likely come with guarantees of change. Changes as simple as style or as complex as scientific breakthroughs require ongoing assessment of their moral meaning. We cannot give our children advance directives as to how to assess those changes. We *can* teach them rules for judging change.

Parents contribute greatly to the authority of children's consciences. Both our moral teachings and our teaching style are reflected. We model strong but flexible authority through the ways we protect, instruct, admonish, exemplify, and encourage. We authorize values of conscience through the routines, rules, customs, laws, and commandments that we honor. Each interaction contributes to the authority of our children's consciences.

AUTHORITY

THE NATURE OF AUTHORITY

Grownups generally admire the child who "listens." What we really mean, however, involves much more than listening. We admire the (imaginary) child who agrees with what we have to say, who acts in accordance with what we have said, and who thanks us for such wise guidance. As a matter of fact, we admire these listening characteristics in spouses, students, pets, team members, employees, parishioners, voters, consumers, and anyone else whom we might summon to our command! Fortunately or unfortunately, value for authority is always balanced by value for autonomy. Nonetheless, most adults enjoy the fantasy of pure authority—being in total control of the world around us. So do children. Just listen in on the roles they assume when they play.

Young child: [keeps turning pages of book]

Slightly older child: You not s'pose to turn the pages till I tell you to. If you don't stop, I won't [pretend] read to you!

Psychologists make a distinction between authoritarian and authoritative parenting. Authoritarian parents' main concern is the power of their position: "Do it because I said so!" Authoritative parents know what they are talking about. Children like to make a point of the difference: "Why are you making me do that? It doesn't make any sense!" When "it" makes sense to us but not to our children, our need to protect may place us in the position of having to be authoritatively authoritarian. The child in the example above is pretending to be very authoritarian. Since she doesn't know how to read, she and her playmate have to do a lot of pretending to consider her authoritative. The Imp loves to find us parents in the same position—not exactly knowing what we are doing, but trying to do it anyway.

THE GOODNESS OF AUTHORITY

Young children readily build an image of a good and powerful super-parent. A grandmother sat with her two-and-a-half-year-old granddaughter watching a man descend in an air balloon at an art festival. The child said matter-of-factly from her stroller, "My daddy can do that!" In a conversation about sleep she said, "God helps me go to sleep. That's what Mommy says." To the young child, an authority figure is big, strong, and protective; knows the answers; fixes things; makes good things happen; and knows the right thing to do.

The ballooned-out respect we receive from our very young children gradually deflates to realistic size. During adolescence it may shrivel like a pin-poked balloon. Teenage self-consciousness may bring comments like this one delivered to a mom driving to soccer practice: "Mom, when you drive us to soccer practice, would you just not say anything!?!" As our children reach different developmental stages, we learn that there are times to express our authority vigorously and times to just let it rest.

REALMS OF AUTHORITY

Dictionary definitions of authority speak of the power to influence or command thought, opinion, or behavior. Our young children's needs and expectations define realms of authority just as well as a dictionary. The bonds that our children form with us define the realm of kinship authority. The size and strength of our muscles and vocal cords define the realm of physical command. Questions answered and explanations offered define the realm of authoritative knowledge. Watching how things get fixed defines the realm of practical know-how. Answers to queries about God define the realm of religious conviction. Rescuing a bird fallen from a nest exemplifies the realm of virtue. Modeling "do's" and "don'ts" defines the realm of moral restraint and mandatory action. In other words, living with our young children's needs and expectations defines the realms in which we must learn to be authoritative.

EXPECTATIONS OF MORAL AUTHORITY

Our young children expect more than practical answers and solutions from adults. They expect explanations of good and bad. They want to know not only how to open the peanut butter jar, but who decided that peanuts were good in the first place, and why can't all children have peanut butter whenever they want it. Questions have a way of moving toward the moral realm, and children are receptive to value-laden explanations.

Moral authority, therefore, is the power to influence or command thought, opinion, or behavior about good and bad. As moral authorities, we parents protect, govern, and educate our children in line with values we have come to honor. The responsibility can make us feel a little shaky. Feelings of uncertainty direct us to Grandma, the doctor, the pastor, the teacher, or the child-development expert for additional support and guidance. These resources support and guide, but do not substitute for, parent authority.

Seeking support for her authority as a parent, Mrs. Johnson insisted on placing her three children in the parochial school that she had attended, in spite of the considerable expense. This mother had periodic emotional breakdowns. "I want to know that when I'm having one of my problem times, my children will continue to receive the guidance they need." Mrs. Johnson knew how to use support and guidance. Unfortunately, some parents are unable to use the support and guidance of outside authorities. They feel squelched or devalued. In turn, their children feel distressed and confused. Children like to see their parents in authority.

THE ADVOCATE

When the community must substitute its moral authority for the moral authority of parents who have abdicated it, issues arise as to who is most in need of support: the parents, the children, or the family unit. We ally with children, who want to have their own parents in authority. Teaching parents how to be authoritative in each of the realms—protection, power, knowledge, experience, religious belief, and moral conviction—is the best way to support respect for authority in the community. Yes, this is an idealistic statement. Getting some parents to come in for guidance is akin to trying to lasso the moon. There are many other complications. Nonetheless, we hold to this principle.

Children cast great moral responsibility our way when they ask us parents to be protective, strong, knowledgeable, experienced, virtuous, and morally right. We generally take to the honor, but struggle with the performance. No matter how well we convey our moral lessons, whether through well-thought-out pearls of wisdom or through bungling, self-conscious half-statements and wishy-washy actions, our children are likely to decipher our good intentions as they mature. A rule as concrete as "Don't grab the rolls; ask politely that they be passed to you" will be assessed for its worthiness in different ways at different ages. Those rules our children find valuable will remain as part of their consciences. Others will be cast aside, except when somebody else is watching. Still others will be filed in a mental box labeled "Oh well, they meant well." Yet others will be dug out of that box years later: "You know, that wasn't a bad idea after all."

When we adults get really lofty, we link day-to-day moral lessons with dreams of a future moral paradise. Lofty expectations in long speeches are always being directed toward graduates: "You are the hope of our future. The world is in your hands." Graduates usually forget these anxiety-provoking invocations to responsibility; they are deep into celebrating. Celebrating is a way of anxiously coping with the next step in life. Laying the responsibilities of the future and the world on our graduates may satisfy parents' and teachers' desires to delegate, but the graduates hear only what they can handle. Do you remember what was said at your various graduations? Do you remember the anxieties expressed in the movie *The Graduate*? We graduate to figuring out what to do next. The moral aspirations of that next step may be no more lofty than reinterpreting the rule "Don't grab the rolls."

One May evening, a certain grandmother attended an eighth-grade graduation at a small parochial school. There were only twenty-six graduates, sixteen
of whom had been together since kindergarten. As the parish priest talked with
the youngsters, he told them that they probably wouldn't remember what was
said at their eighth-grade graduation—he didn't remember what was said at
his. However, he hoped out loud that they would remember one message: that
they had been loved. His message brought tears to the grandmother's eyes as
she thought about the authority of protectiveness in a world of family disruption, guns, drugs, and media invasion. She could take time for lofty thoughts
because she was not a grade-school graduate nervously wondering what high
school would be like. Days later, her granddaughter was asked if she remembered what the priest had said. She didn't—yet. Memories have a way of
incubating when they contain worthy messages.

AUTHORITY CHECKED AND BALANCED

We Americans have complex layers of authority in our society. Because we
honor individual freedom so much, we check and balance authority every step
of the way. Layers of municipal, state, and federal authority alternately extend
and constrict power, alternately protect and curtail individual freedom. As
authority figures in our children's lives, we parents operate within this hierarchy of government power. Sometimes we feel empowered by it; other times we
feel disenfranchised. Our children absorb our attitudes and gradually learn
that parent authority is set within a larger authority. As the next two stories will
demonstrate, our children's understanding of authority may include political
features.

PLAYING POLITICS WITH AUTHORITY

The Imp likes the politics of authority, especially when it involves dynamic
complexities within the family. He is right there when our children decide to
check the balance of power between their parents. He is right there when they
work on the easy parent. One school night, Jennifer, a fifteen-year-old, ma-
nipulated her way out of the house. The ongoing rule was "stay home on
school nights." With the Imp at her side in the form of a freshman brother,
Jennifer caught her father alone and pleaded to be allowed to go to a
Wednesday night football game. Her brother, Sam, stated with moral conviction that students ought to show more support for the football team. Homework could be done in the afternoon. The father found this exception to the
rule worthy. He gave it his stamp of approval.

Jennifer's mother, listening in the next room, was convinced that the father had just been "had." He later confided that he suspected the same, but "you know how it is when two super salesmen work you over while your wits are only propped up by a La-Z-Boy chair." The mother knew that their daughter had little interest in football and that this surge of school patriotism had to be a signal of something else. Some weeks later, Jennifer admitted that a boy she had recently met at the drugstore attended the school that their high school was playing that night. She just had to go to the game to see whether he was there, who he was with, and whether she could get him to notice her.

Jennifer's manipulations were clever and harmless. The Imp enjoyed it. In contrast, moral alarms go off when our children's mischief veers off into wrongdoing. Mrs. Baker spent all Monday afternoon discussing the wrongness of stealing with her second-grade son, Ben, after he arrived home from school with a watch that wasn't his. Ben had been adopted late in his fifth year after several foster home placements, and oughtness did not come naturally to him. Mrs. Baker worked Ben over with just the right amounts of shaming, reasoning, and adverse consequences. She complimented herself for her performance.

The next morning she enthusiastically stirred pancake batter, confident that she would be sending a well-fed, morally improved son to school that day. She lost her confidence and cool when Ben casually stated that he liked stealing and intended to do it again. A wooden spoon full of pancake batter went flying across the room as she forcefully mandated, "YOU ARE NOT GOING TO STEAL AGAIN!" With a little pancake batter still behind his ear, Ben took but one step onto the school bus before announcing to the driver that he had been physically abused that morning. Duty to pursue the allegation led to a full investigation and, fortunately, full exoneration of this exasperated but generally conscientious mother.

A conscientious parent is one who tries to do the right thing most of the time. All conscientious parents either "blow it" or get "blown away" from time to time. At these times, children are adept at seizing opportunities to take command, to authorize their own desires. In the first illustration above, Jennifer had internalized much of her parents' authority; manipulating them was a surprising event. Hence, the mother's antennae went up. In contrast, Ben's deficits in early nurturance led to his resistance to internalizing parent authority and its values. Many additional conscience-building sessions would be required (minus the wooden spoon).

ENDORSING AUTHORITY IN OTHERS

When our community is functioning at its best, our children are surrounded by an alliance of protective authority. In one schoolchild's life, for example, parent authority interlinks with the authority of the bus driver, one or more teachers, school security personnel, after-school caretakers, one or more coaches, Officer Friendly, a piano teacher, a Sunday School teacher, the neighbor next door, and probably others. That is what is meant by a village. Exercising parent authority includes endorsing and seeking endorsement from other authority figures. And it certainly means communicating. The more links in the protective chain of authority, the more likely that breaks in the chain will occur. When communication breaks down, homework doesn't get done, messages get lost, misbehavior isn't handled consistently, and disrespect for authority does not get corrected.

> **THE ADVOCATE**
> Divorced parents must communicate about child-rearing. Teachers and parents must communicate about children's learning. It's the only way to build and maintain respect for authority and its knowledge.

Endorsing other authority figures in our children's lives can strengthen our own authority. A certain think-ahead, consequence-oriented mother told a story of endorsing legal authority with her six-year-old daughter, Tasha. The mother had gotten a traffic ticket. Instead of just paying the fine, she went to traffic court, taking Tasha with her. The judge asked the mother, "If you were going to pay the fine anyway, why did you come to traffic court?" The mother replied, "Because I wanted Tasha to know that adults make mistakes, too, and are held accountable for them." The judge and mom shared, endorsed, and enhanced each other's authority.

AUTHORITY THROUGH THE AGES

THE LINGERING POWER OF AUTHORITY

Many of us adults carry memories of childhood lessons that we no longer endorse. Such memories may involve religious practice, gender and occupational roles, sexual expression, or attitudes toward wealth and status, differentness, or parenting. Specific rules may come to mind—never do this; always do that. We may also remember stories with strongly implied morals. The moral punch lines in the stories may now be considered scientifically invalid, unworkable in a changed world, built on faulty premises, counter to our adult rationality, or just plain unimportant. Children label the unimportant "stupid."

Reassessment of moral lessons may lead to thought-provoking intergenerational discussions, heated arguments, new mutually shared insights, or icy silence at holiday gatherings. An older teenager once said that the only thing she and her father could agree on at the dinner table was the nature of salt and pepper. Regardless of shifts in our belief system, childhood attitudes about authority maintain lingering power. The advertising industry takes advantage of this knowledge every day. For example, does any mother in her right mind really assess her grown-up daughter's character by whether or not the daughter's house is spotless? Yet how many adult daughters pick up the mop, the vacuum, the duster, the sponge, and a bottle of the latest miracle cleaning product the minute that phone call announces that Mom is on her way? Authority is powerful irrespective of the content of its lessons. It makes us feel that we ought to come clean.

Disengaging from particular lessons is not the same thing as disengaging from our baseline respect for, fear of, or awe of authority. The power of authority lingers on in thoughts like "What would Mom or Dad think if they knew _____? How do I tell them that I'm going to _____? What will they think when I introduce _____? How do I show respect and assert my beliefs at the same time?" Internalization of the presence of authority stays with us no matter how much we modify the substance of its teachings. Furthermore, that's good, because moral heritage is essential to cultural preservation.

CULTURE: CHAINS OF AUTHORITY-DERIVED WISDOM

In the midst of intergenerational spats, basic agreements operate without notice. We become conscious of those agreements when culture conflicts with culture. It is then that loyalty to common values solidifies the moral meaning of the culture.

Preservation of culture mandates respect for the chain of elder wisdom. One generation cannot possibly figure out the complexities of right and wrong as well as chains of generations can. A single generation cannot create all the stories necessary to dramatize universal truths. Any one generation has limited moral energy and vision. It can focus on only a finite number of issues in one developmental period of life. Traditional ways must suffice until we become passionately awakened to moral flaws within our cultural practices.

DISCOVERING ENCULTURED MORAL FLAWS

Naturally, we recognize flaws in someone else's culture before seeing our own. For example, we Westerners affirm without hesitation that female genital mutilation is wrong. However, while outsiders may seethe with moral outrage, insider mothers are much more aware of the complications of protest. A morally awakened mother must examine the range of possible effects on her daughter if she resists the practice. Resistance means destabilizing power in the culture. She and her daughter will be in danger. The mother must decide whether the indignity is severe enough to risk dangerous and unknown consequences.

Eliminating a well-ingrained cultural practice after moral awakening invites danger and chaos. The protective realm of our parent authority is challenged. Some of us will find the change so necessary that we will fight for it at all costs. Others will acknowledge the need for change with equal clarity, but focus on political strategy, timing, and alliance. Most of us parents will weigh change versus the status quo in terms of the safety and well-being of our children and their future. Can we support change without hurting our children in the process?

Mandatory school segregation is wrong. However, the one-way busing solution placed most of the burden of dealing with change on the shoulders of children. Some children thrived. Robert Coles described Ruby Bridges, at the age of six, forgiving her jeering New Orleans enemies with the compassion of a morally full-grown adult. Integrating school teaching staffs shifted some responsibility to adults, but teachers are only one link in the chain of interconnected authority necessary to rear a moral child. It's a long way, physically and psychologically, from the teacher in a distant township to the parents and culture of the local neighborhood. In time, arguments for local control of schools logically evolved.

Did a shortcut to goodness—delegating responsibility to the next generation—combine with other social stressors—for example, changes in family structure, gender roles, and the growing culture of consumerism—to engender a lessening of respect for authority throughout the larger community? Maybe.

THE ADVOCATE

When responsibility for solving problems is delegated to children while adults are not engaged in the front line of solving the problems ourselves, we invite our children to disrespect authority. When community authority is not an extension of parent authority, we as a community invite our children to disrespect authority. When multiple authorities compete for our children's loyalty—for example, when the authority of the advertising industry is pitted against parent values—we as a culture invite our children to disrespect authority.

The lasting effect of a moral lesson resides in the authority of the people who believe it, teach it, and practice it. If lessons separated from their authority were all that mattered, moral guidance could be delivered through encyclopedias and CD-ROMs. Parents are what make heard-it-here-first moral lessons important and enduring. When we extend our authority to others, the base of our authority should be broadened and strengthened. When substitutes take over parent authority, the base is weakened. If we send our children to school but are not involved in the educational process ourselves, or if we bus our children to church without being on a religious quest ourselves, the moral impact of the lessons presented has questionable authority. When we use institutions as substitutes for authority rather than being part of the authority of those institutions, we weaken our authority. In short, we parents are the bedrock of authority in our children's conscience, our communities, and our culture.

GENERATIONAL PRUNING

When we parents internalized the teachings of our forebears and those they legitimized as extenders of their authority, we acquired a stockpile of moral truths. We then examined the fit and applicability of these truths to our current life at different stages of development, gradually building an agenda of personal commitments. These commitments are further authorized by the way they fit the time and circumstances in which we live. We pass on oughts and ought-nots to our children, who, in turn, prune—keep, discard, or adjust—them to fit their own time and circumstances. In time, they reauthorize moral truths regarding protection, benevolent power, knowledge, religious conviction, virtue, and restraint. The more stable the truths, the more credibly they fit life's circumstances time and time again.

BAD AUTHORITY

Bad authority is selfish, power-hungry, and insensitive. If as parents we show these characteristics, our children will internalize them into the authority of their consciences. As they prune, they may cast aside these characteristics or carry them forth into their generation. Sexual and physical abuse are rooted in bad authority. So are other behaviors that seduce or coerce children into crossing generational boundaries. One term for such behaviors is *generational trespassing*. Examples of generational trespassing include appealing to a child to become the parent's "best friend," burdening a child with adult mental or marital problems, and holding a child responsible for keeping a family together. Children who are allowed to overrule parental authority are being taught to be generational trespassers. These family boundary problems confuse children's understanding of authority.

Power assertion for the sake of power alone is wrong; it squelches our children's autonomy. Power assertion in behalf of protection may be a little noisy in expression, but our children will eventually understand the goodness of our intentions. As parents, let's imagine ourselves as compressed and wizened authority figures inside our grownup children's heads fifty years from now. When the memory tapes roll, which actions do we want to see replayed? Such imagining can help us strive to improve our parenting.

VALUING AUTHORITY

TRAUMATIC LEARNING

"GET OUT OF MY HOUSE!" ten-year-old Abby yelled at two sisters who lived on the next street as they ransacked Abby's absent parents' dresser drawers. Abby's mother had repeatedly told her, "Never have anyone in the house while we are gone." Abby didn't know that whatever good authority these girls' consciences had incorporated would be left on the sidewalk outside. Fortunately, they left in time for Abby to bring some order back to the house before her parents came home. When she told them about her misadventure, her parents were empathically gentle with their admonitions. They knew that learning was in process.

Abby's experience with these strangely intrusive sisters expedited her moral learning. Traumatic experiences can do that. She learned that her parents' rule about house guests was a wise one. She learned that not all children are taught to respect authority or property in the same way. We parents do not wish traumatic experiences on our children. However, when they occur, they may affirm that parent warnings are worth heeding.

DISCOVERING HOUSEHOLD RULES

Children first experience rules as behavioral sequences. One action is predictably followed by another. In a certain home, the playroom was just below the kitchen. By the time the children were four-to-six-year-olds, a parent's calling downstairs "Dinner is almost ready" was followed by children's picking up toys, washing hands, and coming to the table. A regular, and then an occasional, check reinforced the steps in the sequence. The sequence was laden with moral values: compliance, order, cleanliness. In early development, values are embedded in the routines we establish for our children. Simply reinforcing the routine is sufficient teaching for the young child. Moralizing with words is unnecessary.

Predicting what is going to happen next has a feeling of goodness about it—the goodness of order. When a psychologist says that children benefit from consistency and structure, it means that routines help children feel secure. When children can predict what is going to be expected of them, feel that they can do the job, gain personal satisfaction from it, and anticipate approval, they begin to see the worthiness of the activity itself: "Before bedtime, I brush my teeth. See, I have no cavities. If I don't brush them, I might get big cavities." Value-sensitive rules flow from predictable routines.

Unpredictability engenders anxiety and self-doubt. Children growing up in chaotic households may not be able to articulate their distress with words. However, their anxious behavior may boldly state, "I never know what I'm supposed to do or when I'm supposed to do it. I don't know if I'm good. I never know if I'm right. I don't know what's happening next." At the other end of chaos, overly rigid routines also engender anxiety and self-doubt. Somewhere between chaos and military barracks are more or less predictable and comfortable family routines. We are spared from oppression and boring precision through the bound-to-happen foolery of human infallibility. The Imp is in charge of foolery. He calls for fire drills just before spelling tests, makes the lawn mower break down on perfect go-to-the-pool days, and sometimes makes us parents forget about the groundings we impose.

The Imp giggles over the ways we sometimes execute behavioral routines. Our child may dilly-dally with our requests because the Imp has taught her the *real* behavioral routine in the household. For example, raised voices and tones of anger may be integral to the routine. If crescendos of anger are integral to parenting routines, a child's retelling of the sequence may go something like this: "The first time Mom calls down the stairs with 'Time to pick up toys,' keep playing or watching television (SHE'S NOT SERIOUS). The second time she calls down—when her voice is louder—turn off the TV but keep on playing (SHE'S JUST STARTING TO GET SERIOUS). The third time—when she starts threatening us with whatever—start picking up; trouble is near (NOW SHE IS SERIOUS)."

PLAYING WITH POWER

The Cryders had four daughters. Mrs. Cryder was alarmed when she saw the girls yelling and spanking their dolls for being bad. Since the parents seldom yelled or spanked, and watching violence-tinged TV was not allowed, perhaps the girls' play was an overzealous investment in the power of pretend authority.

Seriousness and play are side-by-side influences in our children's development of respect for authority. Pretending to be the ruler, making rules, and ruling by them are all empowering. Pretending deadly seriousness is a great form of play, especially when accentuated by a magic wand. When our children rule, they may playfully imitate our parenting styles or they may completely outdo us. Playing at being ruler develops understanding of authority and, we hope, respect for it. Pets are more likely to be recipients of kindly authority than are siblings.

Keshia, a third-grader, had a charismatic teacher. Miss Ringley's curriculum and style of delivery had been fine-tuned to the third-grade mind through years of practice. Although Keshia didn't always like her, especially when Miss Ringley made fun of her in front of the class for not knowing the difference between a Pilgrim and a pioneer, she identified with Miss Ringley's power, knowledge, and other teaching skills. She especially appreciated getting to use Miss Ringley's very special silver and gold crayons on an art project. Like a sponge taking in nutrients from the sea, Keshia internalized Miss Ringley's teaching style. When third grade was over, she was convinced that she could teach next year's class—if the principal would just ask her. She came out of Miss Ringley's classroom valuing the authority of teachers, teaching, knowledge, and Caddie Woodlawn, her favorite pioneer character. Miss Ringley had become a model of authority for her conscience. Keshia pruned out the part about making fun of students who confused pioneers with Pilgrims.

As parents and teachers, we never know exactly what kind of a power impact we are having on our children. We hope our power is seen as caring. With that end in mind, we keep routines simple and consistent, wink at playfulness, maintain good will, exude enthusiasm, and show approval and gratitude for approximate compliance. Praising a more or less made bed is better parenting than damning an unmade one. Imitation and internalization of our manners occur when we least expect them. Seven-year-old Mia was helping her grandmother make a bed. While pulling the bedspread up over the pillows, Mia said that Grandmother wasn't doing it correctly. Pillows were supposed to be karate-chopped into place "like we do it," meaning Mia and her dad. The Imp was obviously involved in that procedure. Rigidity and over-seriousness produce sour attitudes toward authority. They can produce a sour conscience, also.

FROM ROUTINES TO MORAL RULES

When our children begin to differentiate the important from the unimportant in our family routines, rules begin to form in their minds: When such and such happens, the next thing that should happen is _____. Once our children are rule-ready, we parents reinforce the routine-to-rule process with verbal restatements, emotional reactions, and behavioral consistency. The rules then go to an Imp-inspired child rule laboratory. In this laboratory, rules are tested by being put through various fun-factor analyses: "What will happen if I just _____?" Creative rule manipulations can be fun for children and their parents—if disrespect of authority is not the goal. Outright rule avoidance may mean only that a lesson is about to be learned the hard way. Remember Abby's experiment with letting the two naughty sisters into her house: first she let them in; then she figured out why her parents had warned her against having unsupervised guests.

Serious rule-testing asks these questions: If I don't follow this rule, what harm will result? What negative emotions will be aroused in my parents or me? What consequences will follow? What sense does this rule make? What good will come from following it? Through this kind of questioning, or a shortcut of it, our children assess the value of a family rule. In general, a family rule acquires moral value when it strengthens the moral connection—the security-empathy-oughtness bond—between us and our children; when it supports moral-emotional harmony between us; and when it makes sense within our children's level of moral reasoning. The assessment results in our children's *internalizing authority-derived, value-sensitive rules.*

RULES AND RESPONSIBILITY

Internalizing moral rules introduces our children to the land of responsibility. Arriving at this destination usually makes them feel rather grown-up. Alternatively, it may only make them nostalgic for carefree younger years when parents were responsible for all the rules. We need to be sensitive to our children's ambivalence about responsibility.

Sometimes we get ahead of our children's developmental trajectory by becoming overly ambitious about their academic, sports, or social achievements. We can become overly ambitious about their moral trajectory, also. If pressure from our own consciences causes us to anxiously hurry our children through a naturally deliberate, and maybe dawdling, value-seeking process, our impatience may distract rather than focus their efforts. Resistance to internalization may outweigh value acceptance. Alternatively, anxious attitudes may be internalized right along with the value-sensitive rules. Conscience may take on the characteristics of a pressure cooker.

Family rules percolate in our children's consciences for many years. We want them to have the authority of a comforting but guiding companion. When eighty-five-year-old African-American photojournalist Gordon Parks had a retrospective exhibit of his work at the Corcoran Gallery in January 1998, Jim Leher interviewed him for public television. Parks described his mother, who died when he was fifteen, as being the most important person in his life: "She taught me right from wrong." He recalled that whenever he was about to make an important decision, he always looked at the pictures of his parents that he kept on the mantel. We can assume that they had much to do with building the authority of his conscience.

MORAL JUSTIFICATION

VARYING LEVELS OF VALUE PENETRATION

Value-sensitive rules have different levels of penetration into the conscience. Some values are firmly established through well-habituated behavioral routines: "I always get my homework done." Some values just sit in the conscience like treasures in a museum, admired, but not to be touched: "My sister is the type who always gets her homework done. That's admirable, but me, I just _____!" Some values lie dormant until moments of red-faced embarrassment or ashen-pallored shame make them obvious choices: "I quit stealing after I got caught coming out of my sister's room with her allowance." Some values come to consciousness only in situation- or person-cued circumstances: "When I'm with _____, I never forget to _____." Values sometimes conflict with each other. Thomas Jefferson's practice of slavery has forever been a historian's moral puzzle. Scientific and technological advances bring "can do's" faster than "ought to do's" can be figured out. We may daringly proceed with actions that ought to be labeled "value undetermined."

PLEADING WITH CONSCIENCE: MORAL JUSTIFICATIONS

Sooner or later, the authority in our conscience holds us accountable for some clumsy mistake. That makes us want to defend ourselves. This process can be called *moral justification*. We morally justify ourselves when we concoct reasonable explanations for our moral failings and procrastination. We don't like to think of ourselves as bad people. We don't like to think of ourselves as irrational, stupid jerks. After a moral failing, we want to explain ourselves in ways that will make us not just forgivable, but understandably forgivable. We want our conscience and all other observers to identify with our plight. We want others to think that if they had been in the same circumstances, they would have done the same stupid thing. Justifications are pleas for clemency from whoever may be judging us, including our conscience.

Katie, a 21-year-old sober college senior, drove her boyfriend's car in an unfamiliar city while he was getting a medical evaluation. She went downtown shopping while he waited for tests to be completed. She got a parking ticket. It was the first parking ticket she had ever received. She tore it up and threw it in the trashcan. Then she came to her senses. How was she going to explain this irrational behavior? With great shame, she reported her stupid action to her boyfriend. Paternalistically, he took her to the courthouse, provided justifications—excuses—for her, and paid the ticket. On the way back to their college campus, he kept pondering out loud, "I just don't understand why you tore it up." "I don't know," she muttered. A moral justification just didn't come to mind.

FACE-SAVING

How many times do we ask our children for an explanation of misbehavior and receive the reply "I don't know"? Should we prefer silence, justification, or truth? That's easy; we want truth—the bare facts plus all motivational factors. However, between silence and truth is an enormous space called face-saving. When a child is in moral trouble, there is often more than one face to be saved. We are likely to feel that we have failed at parenting. Both generations feel ashamed. We desperately plead for a single justification that we can comprehend: "How could you possibly have done that? Were you sick? Did you lose your mind? Did someone force you into it? Haven't your mom and I gotten through to you?" When we hear this barrage of questions coming out of our mouths, it's time for us to take a deep breath, remember our own youth, or go to a face-saving support group.

EXTRACTING TRUTH

When we parents feel patient enough, meaning that we have our negative emotions under control, gentle probing combined with a faintly suspicious attitude will probably produce bits of value-sensitive, albeit face-saving, information. Silence may give way to lame excuses, which later may give way to more believable cover-ups, which still later may give way to plausible explanations touching at the skirts of truth. This certainly won't happen in one all-night marathon session, but in little blurbs of spontaneity spoken when we least expect it. A veteran foster child once reported that when something was missing in her foster home, the kids would all be made to sit in the family room until a confession was forthcoming. Under that reign of terror, the foster siblings bonded in an impenetrable wall of silence. Nobody ever told.

Often we must wade through many moral justifications on the road to truth. Listening through our children's justifications can lead us to understanding, tolerance, compassion, and, eventually, improvement in our sense of humor. If we keep asking "Why?" in thunderous roars, it may scare truth away while leaving the young wrongdoer feeling humiliated, thoughtless, and devalued, and leaving us feeling morally righteous but alienated. If we keep asking "Why?" gently, persistently, and with genuine curiosity, the trek toward truth will proceed a little faster.

When children's moral justifications become ponderous, parents may rightfully suspect that psychological conflicts have driven a wedge between conscience and behavior. When children believe their own lies, they definitely have a problem. Helping them work their way through a wedge of denial may require professional assistance. On the other hand, if the wrongdoing is short of serious harm, the Imp may ease them through the wedge. "The reason I'm in this closet is because _____," stammers the red-faced child found in hiding with chocolate on his chin. The more fumbling the excuse, the funnier the Imp finds it. Impish teasing by parents, short of mockery, sometimes closes in on the truth. So does offering a range of possible truths, including some ridiculous ones. Sometimes humor can rebond us while it also helps us get to the truth!

THREE KINDS OF MORAL INSIGHT

Moral insight is the final destination on the road to truth. Moral insight can be divided into three types: hindsight, foresight, and blind sight.

Moral Hindsight

Moral hindsight is the sadder-but-wiser learning that comes from examining past omissions and commissions. Its wisdom is often the result of the humiliating experiences we would love to bypass. If moral learning could just be processed as quickly as one-hour photos, we wouldn't even have to define hindsight. No such learn-as-you-go luck! The following story shows an adult trying to keep one step ahead of humiliation.

Ms. Pang, a mother of three children under eight, was driving her children home from the library. Suddenly, a car from a side street failed to heed the stop sign and swerved into the right rear of Ms. Pang's car. She whirled around to see if the children were injured. They weren't. As she turned back around, she thought she saw the driver who had just hit her speeding away. She sped right after that car. At the next stop light, the chased driver, looking perplexed, said, "Do you want something?"

"You're not supposed to leave the scene of an accident!" barked Ms. Pang.

"I'm not the one who hit you. She's parked back there, at the scene of the accident."

By this time, Ms. Pang had completely lost trust in her judgment. She decided she had no business driving a car. She parked it. With her three children tagging silently behind her, she retraced her way to the scene of the accident. The person who had hit her car had left by this time, undoubtedly thinking, "If she's not going to stay at the scene, I'm not going to, either," A policeman arrived. No one knows who called him. The fact that he was the father of one of her children's friends added to Ms. Pang's frenzy. She tried to tell the story in as logical a fashion as possible, emphasizing justification for her faulty decisions. The police officer shook his head and said, "Bizarre." When her husband listened to the story that evening, he said, tolerantly, "I'm glad you're all okay." Still concerned about justifying herself, Ms. Pang said, "At least I had sense enough to know that I wasn't making sense."

Ms. Pang had perfectly good rules in her conscience about how to behave after a car accident, including knowing that she wasn't supposed to leave the scene of an accident. Confusion got in the way of obeying the law. If a grown woman can get into this much trouble driving to the library and back, think of how much trouble our adolescents can get into during their first years of driving. On-site justifications often sound a bit crazy. After the painful memory of a humiliating experience has faded a bit, processing the bare facts of the experience builds hindsight.

Moral Foresight

Moral foresight is prevention based on value-sensitive predictions. It involves taking lessons from the past, possibly testing them under new circumstances, and then constructing cautionary mental statements for the future. Sometimes we can efficiently gain foresight from other people's mistakes. Gossip is a voyeuristic tool that can build moral foresight. "Can you believe what _____ did? Why, I wouldn't do that in a million years." Reasoning our way through hypothetical dilemmas is an efficient intellectual path to moral foresight, but gossip is much more entertaining!

It's possible to overuse foresight. Chronic worriers do that. They need to relax and make a few real mistakes.

Blind Moral Insight

Blind sight is a neurological condition in which a person cannot see what is before him, yet can act on the provided information as though he has seen it. We're going to use the term *blind moral insight* to describe a particular kind of "blind" moral learning. Blind moral insight involves learning from our mistakes without submitting them to moral-emotional processing.

The wrongdoing involves an experience that the person originally didn't even think of as containing a moral issue. When the morality of the situation hits home, a rule of conscience immediately forms without the whole process of acknowledgement of the wrongdoing, arousal of guilt feelings, efforts at repair, and making of reform statements. Humiliation is spared. The college student who tore up the traffic ticket never did it again. Moral-emotional processing was bypassed. Humiliation was held at bay until she could tell the story with humor. The Imp helped her find the humor.

Adults' stories of their own teenage wrongdoing often contain evidence of blind moral insight. As they sit at the holiday dinner table recalling and telling these stories, adults usually add, "I can't believe we did those things! We were terrible!" While listening to these stories, the adults' parents think, "I can't believe we didn't know anything about this. Where were we? How did we slip up?" The following true holiday dinner story illustrates this situation:

Steve carried a blind moral insight around with him for years. When he was eleven, he received a BB gun for Christmas. A practice range was set up behind the garage, and another in a corridor in the basement. Steve's father gave him careful instructions and warnings about how the BB gun should be used. During a holiday family gathering, Steve and a similar-aged male cousin, both under the influence of mutually reinforcing, fun-seeking thoughtlessness, slipped out of the house with the BB gun. They chose easy targets, street lights. No one missed the boys, no police officer appeared at the door, and no one suspected their activity. The Imp stayed inside with their other cousins. The boys may have felt some guilt. At least, they didn't go back to school bragging about how many street lights they had shot out over vacation.

Soon Steve lost interest in the BB gun. His parents thought he just wasn't a born hunter. Steve didn't explain the situation until he was a man of thirty-three, at which time he said to his mother, "I never could figure out why you

and Dad got me a BB gun." It took more than twenty years for Steve to see—
to realize how cousinly camaraderie and poor child (as well as parent)
judgment had led to blind moral insight. If his parents had been informed
earlier, maybe they would have learned something, too.

CYCLIC FALLIBILITY

We want our parenting to be completely morally foresighted. However, no
matter how forward-planning our efforts, value transmission is an exercise in
cyclic fallibility. We criticize the last generation for teaching us values that we
consider unimportant today. We push our parenting act forward by vowing
never to follow those old-fashioned ideas. That clears the space for new errors. New errors are inevitable, because the world is always changing. Then
our children not only confront us with our despicable mistakes, but regenerate
lessons of oughtness from two generations back. Strictness and permissive-
ness come and go. The Imp winks at the irony. The endless process of recognizing faults, purging, and renewing leads to generation-specific pro-
nouncements about how children ought to be reared. Dr. Spock is likely to be
reincarnated every other generation.

In sharp contrast to the way in which cyclic fallibility governs the ebb
and flow of some values, other *bedrock values* are perennial. Bedrock values
never become old-fashioned. Valuing connectedness to others, moral-emotional harmony, intergenerational responsibility, and the pursuit of goodness
never goes out of style. Other bedrock values will be identified in chapters to
come.

THE ATTITUDE OF AUTHORITY

Our legal right to parent authority comes with the birth certificate. Real
authority is earned through solidifying the moral connection. Parents provide protection, empathic understanding, and gentle moral guidance in
exchange for restraint and pleasing. In the process, our children absorb and
construct values from many encounters with us. Authority-derived values
and attitudes about authority are learned simultaneously. "Don't hit your
brother or I'll hit you" provides a confusing message about authority. The
tone of its delivery adds an additional message. The sensory impact of our
voice and movements teaches our child much about attitudes that go with
authority. Fortunately, children become able to separate our routine messages and attitudes from those that erupt from us when we are overwrought.

DEVELOPMENTAL CONSIDERATIONS

DEVELOPING THE AUTHORITY OF CONSCIENCE AT THE EXTERNAL STAGE (0–6)

Authority in Action

A typical morning routine in a young child's life, on a morning when parents go to work and older siblings go to school, includes getting up on time, dressing, eating breakfast, brushing teeth, and gathering up whatever needs to be taken to daycare. It may also include small household chores that, if completed quickly, allow time for play or television. A number of value-sensitive rules are embedded within this routine: "Get up and get going when you're called. Always eat breakfast. Brush your teeth after meals. Don't fuss with your brother in the morning. Remember where you put things. See that the cat has food and water."

Within the hustle and bustle of family routines are values about which activities have more or less importance, how they should be pursued, who should be in charge, and what role each member in the family should play. Awareness of family dynamics adds up to values about authority itself. Parents can model authority in an organized way with thoughtfulness, kindness, and fairness, or we can model it in a grumpy, hurried, bossy, and disorganized manner. We can be active or passive in our attitudes toward responsibility. The sum of what our children experience will be reflected in their attitudes toward authority, including the authority of their consciences. Their developing judgment of the rightness or wrongness of our parenting ways will modify their authority-derived values.

Authority's Rules

When a backpack goes back and forth to preschool day after day after day, why does it get lost at least one morning a week? Although young brains soak up information like sponges, ought-to-do rules appear to squeeze their way back out through the holes in the sponge. It's like helping a child learn spelling words that are beyond his capacity for retention. With extreme effort on the part of child and parent, the words may be spelled with dictionary-perfect accuracy before bedtime. The next morning, the letters are all in a jumble again. Moral learning is like this. Before the age of seven, rule-following must be constantly cued. Note these examples:

Interviewer: Why do you do your chores?

Young child: If I don't do my chores, I have to sit in my room for an hour.

Interviewer: Is it ever OK to say bad things?

Young child: When my mom doesn't know about it.

—— ADVICE TO PARENTS ——————————————————

Nurturing the Authority of Conscience at the External Stage (0–6)

- **Develop consistent family routines.**

- **Assess the values being taught in family routines.**

- **Assess the manner in which you execute family routines. Are you proud of those memory tapes that are being formed?**

- **Begin pointing out the rules in the routines.**

- **Don't expect rules to be followed without your active participation.**

DEVELOPING THE AUTHORITY OF CONSCIENCE AT THE BRAIN-HEART STAGE (7–11)

Rule-Based Authority Comes of Age

Ask a child between the ages of seven and eleven to enumerate the "do's and don'ts" that she lives by. Rules concretized from family and school routines will fill the list: "Take care of your things; don't let strangers in the house; recycle cans and papers; turn out the lights; do your homework; don't scream at your brother." When asked why she follows such rules, the child will explain—in her own language, of course—that rule-following maintains the harmony of her moral connection to parents, teachers, and other persons in authority in her daily life: "I don't like being in trouble; I like smiling faces." From routines of doing come rules for how things ought to be done. These rules of oughtness, stored in our children's consciences, begin to supplement our parent supervisory role. Note the word "supplement" rather than "substitute for." We parents aren't off the moral teaching hook yet.

A Resource Team of Moral Authorities

Parents are not alone in authorizing rules for living. Authorization also comes from those to whom we extend our parenting authority. Important members of this moral resource team include teachers, relatives, religious instructors, daycare workers, older siblings, and older playmates. Rules jelled from routines make their best memory traces in children's consciences when we and our care-extenders make the messages and style of our authority consistent. The authority of conscience is developed best when guidance from adults outside the home "fits" with parental guidance. Competing directives may undermine parental authority or leave a child confused. On the other hand, directives that a child realizes to be "totally wrong" may strengthen allegiance to parental authority.

Intrusive and disruptive sources of authority include unauthorized television, certain advertising, and exposure to older persons of bad conscience. When these invasions occur, parents must override their effects with protective caring, empathic listening, and value-sensitive dialogue. Again, the style of our interaction adds greatly to the authority of our position.

Conscience: The Brain's Moral Rule Organizer

Advances in neurological development during the Brain-Heart stage help children deduce value-sensitive rules from life experiences and remember them. To highlight the brain's development, think of all the advances in children's learning during the grade-school years. The ability to symbolize with letters, shapes, and numbers comes with ease. Drawings become detailed and realistic in presenting life experiences. Memory capacities grow by leaps and bounds. Children remember people in terms of their characteristic actions, voices, and emotional demeanor and the content of their messages.

Conscience development moves forward as children learn to code experience by the moral lesson learned. They then file, retrieve, use, lose, or revise those lessons at will. In the meantime, out in the real world, they may rule over games of Monopoly with an authoritarian style that amazes us. We wonder who schooled them. Probably the style came partly from parents, partly from other images of authority, partly from playmates, and partly from the children's own sense of authority.

Our seven-to-eleven-year-old children are, therefore, budding moralists. They can differentiate the important from the unimportant, the silly from the serious, the mischievous from the harmful. They understand conscience to be the part of the mind that organizes, stores, and accesses rules of oughtness. They can grade new experience in terms of moral meaning, but just how the moral process works is a mystery to them. The following children attempt explanations.

Interviewer: Where do your "do's and don'ts" come from?

Eight-year-old child: My mom, she has rules, and we copy off them and we know what to do. Your brain tells it to yourself and you say, "You better not do that or else you are going to get in trouble."

Interviewer: How might it work?

Child: It falls out of your head, maybe.

Interviewer: Does your conscience grow or change as you get older?

Child: The older you get, the more rules you know, so your conscience gets bigger as you get older.

Posting Rules

Posting a rule can prompt rule-following if it summarizes or concretizes our children's moralizing experiences. Moralizing experiences include both routine and fresh experiences with authority figures—hearing their voices, seeing them in action, feeling their emotional communications, examining the content of the interaction, and deriving a moral rule from it

Suppose the school library has posted a big sign saying "Don't write in library books." Will children follow a rule simply because it has been posted? Maybe. More likely, they will follow the rule because it summarizes their own interpersonal experience or that of other children whom they have watched closely. The following children's words portray personal, vicarious, and hypothetical experiences that reinforce rule-following.

Interviewer: Why shouldn't you write in library books?

Older child: The lady in the library said not to.

Another OC: I did it once, and I had to stay in at recess and erase it.

Another OC: This boy in my class—he scribbled all over this big, important book and he got in big trouble.

Interviewer: Why do you follow these rules?

Older child: You should follow rules because you'll learn more. If you're talking when your teacher's trying to show you something, you won't be able to know it.

Interviewer: Tell me about these "don't" rules.

Older child: "Don't speak to strangers." Well, if you tell them where you live, they might break into your house. If you're going on a trip in the summer, they might rob your house while you're gone.

Cultural Undermining in the Rule of Authority

Certain cultural trends in our society may undermine the respect for authority that we try to engender in our children. One undermining trend is a pervasive negative attitude toward anything that is old, worn, or wrinkled—in other words, aging. A second undermining trend is an overwhelmingly positive attitude toward anything that is new, bigger, faster, or more immediately gratifying. In our ever-moving market economy, sustaining loyalty between employer and employee has become an obsolete value. At home, sustaining commitment to the "for better, for worse, for richer, for poorer" marriage vow has also become an endangered value. These trends support youthful disrespect for the old and fascination with the new. They give our children reason to doubt the authenticity or timelessness of authority before they can even formulate these abstract concepts. At the concrete level, they may live every day with authority split into competing units.

Children at the Brain-Heart stage of conscience development enjoy the safety and dependability of rule-governed living. Our seven-to-eleven-year-olds may even entertain the idea of living at home forever. Changes in the rules of authority or the authority of rules stress that comfort. The stress of change may create a more flexible, reality-oriented child. On the other hand, multiple changes may produce a child full of doubt and disappointment. Regressive (babyish) behaviors may reappear.

Whenever school-age children have to endure change in residence, school, companions, or family composition, they have to adjust to changes in routines and rules. Their respect for authority and its rules may destabilize. Some days they will hold themselves accountable for the distress of change, and some days they will hold their parents accountable. In response to their gloom, parent frustrations and justifications for "how things are" may soar. In these circumstances, children need help in restabilizing the meaning of authority in their lives—the authority of rules and the rule of authority. Parents must take more time to re-attach or strengthen the moral connection, listen empathically, and re-authorize moral meaning in routines, rules, and relationships. Life under new management generally re-stabilizes if all adults involved make respectful, loving efforts.

Playing with Rules

On the lighter side, the Imp is always ready to guarantee fun in our children's lives. Playing with rules is one form of fun. Playing with changing rules may be even more fun.

Interviewer: What are your best reasons to lie, to not mind your parents, and other things like that?

Older child: There is never a reason to lie or not mind your parents, but sometimes it's fun.

───── **ADVICE TO PARENTS** ─────────────────────────

Nurturing the Authority of Conscience at the Brain-Heart Stage (7–11)

- **Applaud your child's ability to deduce moral rules from family routines.**

- **Applaud your child's ability to deduce moral rules at school and in the community.**

- **Applaud your child for being a rule-follower.**

- **Appreciate the stress of change in your child's life.**

- **Appreciate how change may involve new moral rule building experiences.**

- **Enjoy playfulness with rules at any age.**

DEVELOPING THE AUTHORITY OF CONSCIENCE AT THE PERSONIFIED STAGE (12–13)

The Voice of Conscience

We all like to talk privately about important aspects of our lives. Young children use dolls and stuffed animals. In the British comedy *Shirley Valentine*, Shirley talks regularly to her kitchen wall. When she finds herself alone on vacation in Greece, she talks to a rock on the beach. She confides to the audience that it doesn't understand her very well because, after all, it's a Greek rock!

Dolls, stuffed animals, kitchen walls, and rocks do not talk back. Although they are very patient listeners, they provide no moral guidance. Sometimes we need someone to guide us, privately. Around the age of twelve or thirteen, teenagers begin to feel that they have a private relationship with their consciences. Emerging teenagers may well describe their consciences as having human-like characteristics: "My conscience is like someone watching over me. It's like a voice talking to me." This characterization means that they can have a moral dialogue within themselves. Therefore, when we want to prompt our teenagers to behave conscientiously away from home, we can change our former admonition, "Remember what you've been taught," to "Remember to consult your conscience."

Many of us grew up being taught how to ask for guidance from God. The quest for religious authority reaches beyond human comprehension. The quest for moral authority reaches inward to decipher the wisdom of our cumulative learning. Quakers bring these quests together, envisioning both God and conscience as voices within. Emerging adolescents are just beginning to appreciate conscience as a private authority. Have you ever wondered what your teenager's dialogues with conscience might sound like? We can't go there, because it's private. However, we can positively affect those dialogues in two ways.

First, we can model real-life moral dialogues with them that gently support their search for goodness, repair, forgiveness, and moral growth. We can model a moral voice that is well-centered between demand and encouragement, firmness and kindness. Secondly, we can share memories of how we used—or wish we had used—our own conscience to make moral decisions when we were their age. At times, these confessions may lead to revealing wrongdoing that was more foolish than harmful. Every moral dialogue should be sensitive to the Imp's presence.

Intentionality and Forgivability

While running errands in the car one day, twelve-year-old Emily suddenly said to her mother, "I know what you want us [three children] to be, Mom. You want us to be independent." The mother was shocked, pleased, and impressed: shocked because she had never consciously shaped this goal in her own mind, let alone articulated it; pleased because "being independent" did ring true with respect to her parenting goals; and impressed because her daughter had distilled an underlying intention across many mother-daughter interactions. When our emerging teenagers reach for deeper meaning within our parenting routines and rules, they find something very special in our authority—our goodness of intention. They may also find an occasional streak of meanness or some other character flaw. Parents' moral growth is stimulated when our teenagers see through us.

When parents and teenagers begin to see through each other, we find much to admire, tolerate, and forgive. In special moments, we see each other's goodness of intention and fallibility at the same time. Our parenting authority is strengthened through this growing sensitivity. Growing tolerance influences our young teenagers to follow rules that they consider absolutely old-fashioned. Respect for our good intentions motivates their compliance. Listen to the tone of benevolence in these dialogues:

> Interviewer: Why do your parents have you clean up your room, help with the dishes, feed the cat—all those things?
>
> Young teenager: They give us chores to teach us responsibility.
>
> Another YT: They want me to be organized, responsible, helpful.
>
> Interviewer: Why do you follow your parents' advice?
>
> Young teenager: They have lived longer and know what is best for me.
>
> Interviewer: What is your best reason for respecting your parents?
>
> Young adolescent: Parents listen and help.

Moral Self-Esteem

Moral self-esteem is a very private matter. It is the conscience appreciating one's own moral goodness. Conscience scoffs at moral justifications—those lame excuses that we make up to save ourselves from public humiliation. We may hide from conscience for a time. But when we come out of hiding, we must be courageous enough to admit facts and motives to a conscience that already knows them anyway. To spare self-mortification, we must acknowledge fallibility, forgivability, and potential for moral growth. When facts, intentions, fallibility, forgivability, and willingness to learn are in balance, we can consider ourselves morally responsible and trustworthy.

Our young teenagers are just beginning to comprehend the meaning of the inner dynamics of moral self-esteem. Out in the public arena of real life, we often hear them protesting loudly about being responsible and trustworthy. Knowing that they will be spending more and more time in the community in years to come, we also protest loudly about responsibility and trustworthiness. We generally develop a formula for handing out small increments of freedom so that we can test the growth of these moral qualities in our youngsters. When our teenagers don't think we have handed out enough freedom, they protest madly. When we hand out the right amount, we are all pleased with the results. When we hand out too much freedom, trouble is ready to pounce. Balancing parent authority with the fledgling authority of a teenager's inner conscience makes adolescent-rearing a fascinating adventure in risk-taking. Think of all the dynamics involved in these snippets of conversation about trust:

Interviewer: Why is it important to be "on time"?

Young teenager: Uhh, trust. It develops a lot of trust whenever you're on time or told to be somewhere at a certain time. My parents are very impatient people.

Interviewer: What do people admire in you?

Older teenager: I'm very trustworthy. I can be trusted with my boss's keys, and her car keys are on there!

—— **ADVICE TO PARENTS** ————————————————————————

Nurturing the Authority of Conscience at the Personified Stage (12–13)

• **Appreciate the inner personalization of conscience in your emerging teenager.**

• **Model moral dialogue that emphasizes facts, intentions, repair, fallibility, forgivability, and moral learning. Tell personal moral stories from when you were the same age.**

• **Appreciate the growing understanding of intentionality.**

• **Appreciate the meaning of moral self-esteem.**

• **Link trust and responsibility to increasing amounts of freedom in the community.**

DEVELOPING THE AUTHORITY OF CONSCIENCE AT THE CONFUSED STAGE (14–15)

The Search for *REAL* Authority

If progressive change and individualism were not such enticing values in our culture, our offspring might progress from compliant child to conforming adult without interruption. The defining of self that begins in mid-adolescence and consumes much of young adulthood starts with unavoidable episodes of distress about authority. Although we are eager to help our teenagers sort out their moral confusion, they may resist our invitations for dialogue during mid-adolescence. Furthermore, they may engage in some troublesome behavior that makes us fear that our conscience-nurturing efforts are imperiled. The foundation of respect that has been built between us and our children—our moral connection; the regulation of moral-emotional harmony; the internalization of value-sensitive rules, including an appreciation of good intentions; in short, all domains of conscience described so far—may seem to be suffering. Do not despair! The disruption is a prelude to development in moral autonomy. Resistance signals teenagers' desire to privately re-authorize their consciences. The re-authorization process in conscience development involves transforming what we have learned from others into personal convictions. Chapter 6 will provide more details. Right now, we will focus on the confusion.

> Interviewer: Describe your conscience.

> Mid-adolescent: It's just my thoughts. I don't think much. My thoughts just all tumble out at once. I don't know what I think. I think too much.

The moral goal of all teenagers in our culture is to make up their own minds about what is important in life—what is good and what is the right way to pursue it. The moral goal of parenting is to support the process. Acknowledging that goal allows us to be more tolerant of taunting questions and assertions: "How would you know? Back in your day, you never _____." Along with their peers, our teenagers are examining new sources of authority. Together, they are looking for *real* authority. We parents should patiently exchange winks with the Imp during the search—unless danger lurks. Then we must conscientiously intervene!

Where do our teenagers search for *real* authority? Among their peers, in any adult other than their own parents, in the media, in the marketplace, and in entertainment and sports arenas. Their hearts beat in rhythm with the words of charismatic idols and ideals—especially those words that are set to music. While taking this in, we parents experience an odd mixture of admiration, distress, abhorrence, and humor. We patiently listen to our adolescents tout their friends' parents as being more open-minded, more lenient, and generally more "with it." We hear that our teenagers' friends are more knowledgeable about life than most adults. We smile approvingly when they idolize teachers, ministers, coaches, or historical figures, and we relax when our private research proves them to be persons of good conscience. When evidence is to the contrary, we issue warnings or prohibit contact. We hope for maximal learning and minimal hurt. We feel anxious when our teenagers' idols are celebrities from the entertainment world. We study videos and lyrics for moral content; some of it is tolerable, occasionally inspiring, and some of it is abhorrent.

> Interviewer: Why do you admire [singer]?

> Mid-adolescent: If you want to know what I believe, listen to his music.

We did. The lyrics questioned authority, idealized love and peace, expressed concern for the future of the planet, and placed hope in youth. What more could parents desire? In contrast, other lyrics, using the most offensive language possible, condemn rather than question authority; idealize anarchy, violence, and self-destruction; promote nihilistic attitudes; and place hope in no one. Idols and idealism strengthen the authority of conscience when they honor universal values. The following teenager idolized Martin Luther King.

> THE ADVOCATE
> We can be among those "other" adults who inspire and influence teenagers outside our family. We can be part of *real* authority!

Interviewer: Why is it important to be a good person?

Mid-adolescent: To be known for what you have accomplished—like, for instance, Martin Luther King. Look at him. When you die, people think more of you by what you did.

Freedom and Re-authorization of the Conscience

Our adolescents' search for *real* authority goes on in three arenas: in their minds, in negotiations with parents and other authority figures, and in the activities of the peer world. In each arena, authority and freedom require balance. Concepts of freedom are very appealing to teenagers. They may be very attentive when learning about the constitutionally guaranteed freedoms of adulthood. Education, entertainment, and advertising expose them to our cultural romance with freedom and individuality as well as romantic ideas about adolescence itself. Compliance with adult authority may be overridden by courageous loyalty to friends and even siblings. When we ask, they may justify these actions in terms of rights that they associate with freedom.

In the real world of interacting with authority, our mid-adolescents have been negotiating with us for a long time—as they measure time—to gain increasing freedom in the community by providing evidence of trustworthiness and responsibility. In purest form, freedom is experienced as a giddy, exciting state completely outside the world of oughtness. Pure freedom is associated with risk, speed, altered consciousness, and zero responsibility. We might call this form "fool's gold" freedom. That pure freedom is not the goal we have in mind when negotiating with our teenagers. We are not interested in their showing us responsible behavior in order to earn freedom from responsibility. We want to give them freedom to choose right ways of behaving on their own. Moral reality carefully balances pure freedom with consequences, other people's rights, and the demands of real authority—like the flashing lights of a police car. We want our teenagers to be free to learn.

By mid-adolescence, teenagers have gathered enough experiences—real, vicarious, or hypothetical—to feed an internal dialogue with conscience about moral freedom. They are ready to work out an equation balancing freedom with responsibility. That equation re-authorizes the conscience. Teenagers give conscience permission to guide them in how much risk they should take, to whom they should listen, as well as to whom and to what they should be true. In the process of re-authorizing their consciences, teenagers may seek outside reinforcement:

Interviewer: How does going to church help you?

Mid-adolescent: I go to church 'cause they help keep your morals in. It's just something about church that helps keep everything together. When I work out and stuff—it helps me keep everything focused in staying in church.

Evidence of Re-authorization

When fifteen-year-old Aaron went to bed, he usually wore whatever T-shirt or sweat pants were handy. That day's clothing would be piled on top of many days' clothing. Homework would be scattered everywhere. Only his CDs were in any semblance of order. This same boy also owned a pair of tan pajamas with white ribbing. He had purchased them the previous summer when he got his first clothing allowance. They were exactly the style that his father wore. No one ever mentioned that.

Periodically, Aaron would go through a ritual that looked like he had just returned from reform school. He would take a shower, put on those tan pajamas, comb his hair, assume a serious demeanor, clean up his room, do homework, and go to bed early. Music muffled the words, but his parents were sure that they could hear him having a moral dialogue with his conscience. The next morning he would be particularly cheerful, the way he had been at younger ages.

Aaron's parents suspected that this ritual followed forays into the land of freedom. Sometimes they had hard evidence. Other times Aaron's attitude was their only clue. Whenever teenagers go through a reform ritual, we can suspect that re-authorization of conscience is in process. Freedom and responsibility are being re-balanced.

—— ADVICE TO PARENTS ————————————————————

Nurturing the Authority of Conscience at the Confused Stage (14–15)

- **Expect confusion over authority. Expect a search for *real* authority.**

- **Expect episodic resistance to moral dialogue. Be patient.**

- **Honor the privacy of your teenager's thoughts, moods, and possessions.**

- **Intervene when behavior may be harmful to self or others.**

- **Expect your teenager to develop idols and ideals that honor individual freedom and peer responsibility.**

- **Be on the lookout for adults and peers of bad conscience.**

- **Affirm inspiring teachers, religious leaders, coaches, and all others who work with youth.**

- **Be an admired authority for someone else's teenager.**

DEVELOPING THE AUTHORITY OF CONSCIENCE AT THE INTEGRATING STAGE (16–17+)

Integrating Moral Lessons

Imagine being Elisa's parent. Sometime after Elisa's sixteenth birthday, you start to notice an occasional change in her. Her bedroom door isn't always closed. She seems to be less sensitive, defensive, and emotional. She is more selective in her choice of friends, activities, and use of time. Her attitude is more cooperative. She doesn't resent going to family events as much as before. She seems to work harder at school assignments, even though she has a job, is on the volleyball team, and does volunteer work at a preschool. She seems more trustworthy, more goal-oriented, more responsible. We hand her the keys to the car with more ease. Freedom and responsibility seem to be in balance. Elisa seems to be integrating the moral lessons she has been taught with others of her own design.

In contrast to Elisa's development, many of us have known a teenager in crisis on the road to moral maturity—if not our own teenager, then one or more classmates. A teenager in moral-developmental crisis takes many flights into freedom. Some flights land in mere mischief; others land in serious trouble, possibly including academic failure, theft, drug or alcohol use, sexual indiscretion, vandalism, truancy, curfew violation, or runaway behavior. One of the consequences may even be a little time in the juvenile detention center.

Teenagers in moral-developmental crisis linger at the Confused stage of conscience development. They spend more time searching for *real* authority. They have a harder time balancing freedom with responsibility. They are more resistant to re-authorizing moral lessons. These teenagers may need some therapeutic assistance. When they get over the hump, alone or with the help of others, they are much more relaxed and mature. They take on the characteristics of Elisa, described above. They have achieved a state of moral freedom.

Moral Freedom

Pure freedom is making any decision that we want to make. Moral freedom is making any decision that satisfies the authority of conscience. Moral freedom requires that our free will take into consideration the oughtness of our moral connections, our moral-emotional responsiveness, and values we have learned. We're comfortable with moral freedom when we realize that no decision is absolutely right or wrong. In the example above, Elisa appears to have reached that understanding. Her behavior indicates that she is currently at the Integrated stage of conscience functioning.

In contrast, moral freedom is stressful when life's complexities reach new levels. It is stressful when we cannot draw on former experiences to help us out. At those times, we may feel like screaming, "Will someone just tell me what to do?" Stress is reduced when we figure out that the right answer is the one we have the courage to make, taking everything we value into consideration. Our older adolescent, at the Integrating stage, is just beginning to learn how to assume individual responsibility in the midst of moral complexity.

─── **ADVICE TO PARENTS** ───────────────────────

Nurturing Authority of Conscience at the Integrating Stage (16–17+)

- **Encourage as much complex moral thinking as your teenager can tolerate.**

- **Give your teenager room to make as many independent moral decisions as you believe he or she can handle.**

- **Congratulate courageous moral decision making.**

SUMMARY

The authority of our children's consciences is rooted in the moral connection we form with them. Compliance and pleasing are reinforced through moral-emotional responsiveness. The authority of conscience is also influenced by experiences with other authority figures and authorizing experiences. Authorizing experiences include routines, rules, and unique solutions that provide moral satisfaction.

The pathway from compliant child to conforming adult is not smooth in a culture that honors progressive change and individuality. These influences motivate our teenagers to challenge, test, and re-authorize authority. They search for *real* authority in their minds, among their peers, in adults outside their own homes, and in the culture. Along with their peers, they judge noteworthy adults who are acting in bad conscience. They integrate new learning with old lessons. In the process, they come to understand moral freedom as the freedom to choose the oughtness path that best satisfies the authority of their consciences. They learn the value of internal authority.

Developing the Golden
5
Rule of Conscience

LIMITATIONS TO AN AUTHORITY-CENTERED CONSCIENCE

We parents often use our authority to settle children's squabbles. We do so in good conscience, wanting to show fairness and caring toward each child. The power of our authority-centered solutions may produce submissive but not heartfelt cooperation. When one of our decisions fails to please one member of a squabbling duo, the "winner" may be heard derisively humming, "Na-na-na-nah-nah," while the "loser" goes into a super-pout. A sense of injustice may run so high in the "loser" that he or she looks for any maneuver possible that will get authority "on my side" and the other child in trouble. Manipulating authority to settle a peer-centered dispute is far less effective than learning skills of cooperation and conflict resolution — except, occasionally, when the Imp makes a manipulation backfire.

Two families met at Yellowstone National Park to do some joint vacationing. One family was traveling in a recreational vehicle (RV). The other family was traveling by car and staying in motels. The two children traveling in the car, middle-school-aged Chris and Chelsea, asked to ride in the RV with the three children in that family. The mother in the RV had noted that Chris and Chelsea were constantly being mean to each other. Therefore, she told them that they were welcome to ride in the RV, provided that they did not put each other down — not even once! Chris and Chelsea were model siblings all day long. Back in their motel room that night, however, they lit into each other with more than the usual vengeance. Power-mandated goodness lasts only as long as power entraps it!

When adults squabble with each other, they too may ask a higher authority to settle their disputes. We may call the police, cite laws and commandments, hire lawyers, and threaten court actions. We may regress to a Cain and Abel level of conflict resolution. Unless we learn to value others as we do ourselves. Unless our consciences incorporate and apply the Golden Rule.

Some people's consciences are very authoritarian. Duty to follow authority and the letter of its law dominates internal guidance in their moral lives. Other people's consciences, while dutifully respecting authority, also urge them to seek solutions to human moral problems at the person-to-person, group-to-group, or total-group level. "What is the fairest or most caring thing to do in this situation?" Sometimes, no authority-derived rule of conscience covers the circumstances. Incorporating the Golden Rule gives a conscience flexibility. We want our children to develop a flexible conscience—one that will help them think through moral issues in uncharted waters according to a general principle of fairness and caring.

KINDERGARTEN UNDERSTANDING OF
PEER-CENTERED VALUES

In a classroom of eighteen kindergartners, a volunteer—a person of weak authority when the teacher is absent—came to read stories. The teacher instructed the volunteer to help these inattentive children develop their listening skills. When the volunteer was reading, the children often were bothered by a dozen or more peer-centered issues involving cooperation or conflict. Issues spontaneously emerging in this five-year-old group included: How could they keep their sit-on-the-floor circle large enough so that everyone could see? Who would get to sit next to the reader? Who would get to hold up the pictures? Who would get to sit next to her best friend? Was it OK for a boy to braid the hair of the girl next to him? How could the group convince one person to stop getting in the way, another to not answer all the questions, a third to keep her dress down?

Sometimes the volunteer combined her authority with that of the teacher to stifle the issues. She told the children that they would "lose stickers" if they didn't listen quietly. At other times she explored the problem-solving potential within the group. The simple statement "That's a problem; how can we solve it?" often generated a worthy idea. For example, Rosa frequently distracted others in the reading group. Physical complaints were her attention-seeking specialty. One day, she complained of a pain "in my armpit." The volunteer asked the group what they thought Rosa should do. A frustrated but caring classmate said, "Well, Rosa, you could try to be brave like the girl in the story!" Thereafter, Rosa said, "I guess I'll be brave" when distracted by her own bodily complaints. Accepting advice from a peer was a major step forward in Rosa's ability to problem-solve without whining to authority. When two children can see a problem in the same way and accept advice from each other, they are inching their way toward grasping an aspect of the Golden Rule.

Adults and children are often focused on different values in the same situation. In this kindergarten group, the volunteer was focused on her obligation to help the children develop listening skills. The children, although interested in the story, were primarily focused on fairness and caring issues among themselves. Both the authority-centered goal and the peer-centered goals had moral value. Both needed to be respected. By giving the children an opportunity to find a solution to a disturbance within their group, the volunteer strengthened the power of her authority and the children's authority simultaneously. Rosa accepted peer advice, and the group returned to listening to the story.

Peer-centered values are rules of conscience governing fairness and caring between peers, people of equal rank. Although adults may teach rules for cooperating and resolving conflict, the rules don't acquire peer-centered value until they are discovered, tested, or adapted in peer-centered situations. The Golden Rule is an abstract statement guiding peer-centered valuation.

THE GOLDEN RULE

"Do unto others as you would have others do unto you." With some variation in wording, this simply stated, elegant rule is honored as a moral principle in many cultures around the world. Passing it down from generation to generation gives it authority-derived value. Its moral wisdom has passed the test of time. However, its content is peer-centered.

The Golden Rule assumes a relationship of equality between people. Fairness and caring between peers is different from fairness and caring in relationships where one person is considered to be in authority over the other. Whereas we revere, obey, or show deference to authority figures, we walk side by side with persons we consider to be our equals. We show respect for an egalitarian relationship when we empathize with each other as fellow human beings, when we set limits and expectations for our relationship, and when we accommodate each other's preferences and limitations. Peer-centered valuation may be as specific as solving a classroom squabble or as extensive as finding ways to honor universal human rights.

Children and adolescents find that reaching a full understanding of the Golden Rule is an elusive pursuit. Just when they think they have figured out how the rule works, new considerations arise. What starts out as a rule governing meanness and niceness during play is later seen as a humanitarian ideal that bonds all human beings together. At each stage of development, successful egalitarian experiences with cooperation or conflict resolution are stored in the conscience as rightful ways to pursue the Golden Rule.

Parents can provide the setting for peer problem-solving and can offer suggestions. However, the actual solutions must be worked out by the children themselves in order to be considered peer-derived values. When solutions are parent-directed, they follow authority-centered values. Once in a while we hear of parents trying to run a peer-centered household, one in which all members, adults and children, are considered equals. This type of a household does not promote the development of a well-balanced conscience. Children need to develop a great deal of respect for authority before they are able to tackle moral solutions between themselves. As parents, we are our children's peers only in the most abstract sense, as when considering all human beings to have the same moral value. Parents are always responsible for order and safety.

Equality is an essential value in a democracy. We want our children to be good citizens and to incorporate the ideals of democracy into their consciences. Keeping that in mind, let us look at some defining factors relevant to citizenship as well as conscience development.

"Do unto others as you would have them do unto you." The simplicity of this rule belies the complexity of following it. In fact, the Golden Rule is better spoken of as pursued than as followed. The pursuit goes through many transformations during a person's development. Each transformation is a new realization of how to be our brother's keeper. With adult authority standing by or on call as needed, children discover the Golden Rule through balancing empathic caring with confrontation, prohibitions, and demands: "Here, let me help you [do something difficult]." "How would you like it if [something mean or unfair] happened to you? What if everybody did [something similarly mean or unfair]?" "You can't play with us unless you [conform]." Justice and peer caring develop together.

The oughtness connection of infancy lays the groundwork for discovering the moral aspects of peer relationships. Pursuit of the Golden Rule evolves from seeking goodness in mutual pleasure; it moves through various stages of understanding cooperation and conflict resolution; it culminates in an idealization of universal human rights, the practice of which is very fragmented throughout the world. Closer to home, sibling loyalty generally overrides the claim "You were always Mom's favorite" sometime before old age. The need to cooperate and resolve conflicts permeates our roles as friend, partner, coworker, and citizen. Pursuing the Golden Rule is a sometimes pleasurable, sometimes noisy and exasperating journey. Our consciences incorporate Golden Rule oughtness from these experiences and spout it back to us at crucial times.

PEERS AND PEERSMANSHIP

In the dictionary, a *peer* is first defined as an equal—a legal equal, as in "a jury of one's peers." Then the term is gradually colored with rank as secondary definitions are elaborated. A peer is a person equal to another in abilities or qualifications; a member of one of the five degrees of British nobility (duke, marquis, earl, viscount, baron); a nobleman. (These definitions come from the 1996 *Webster's Encyclopedic Unabridged Dictionary of the English Language*, p. 1063.) The narrowing in definition from peer as totally equal to peer as equal in rank is a weakness inherent in human valuing. As the pigs begin to dominate the other creatures in *Animal Farm*, George Orwell's satire about totalitarianism, they also engage in ranking practices. "All animals are equal" becomes "All animals are equal, but the pigs are more equal." Peer equality without rank erosion is an ideal that is possible to conceive but hard to practice.

THE VALUE OF PEER PRESSURE

We parents commonly use the term *peer pressure* disparagingly when we're worrying about our teenagers' vulnerability to being persuaded to participate in mischief that may lead to wrongdoing. We are proud when they resist dangerous enticements. When they fail, we want to use the power of our authority to rescue them. We easily forget that peer pressure can also be positive in its influence: "My friends got so mad at me when I [did something unfair or mean]."

If people were lumps of golden ore, we could place them on scales to determine their relative value. Equality would be a matter of weights and measures. Peer-centered morality demands that we consider all human beings to be of equal value in spite of their many differences. Our natural tendency to pick and choose what and whom we like best means that we are always "weighing" people differently. This natural tendency conflicts with our moral impulse to be fair and caring toward all. Peer pressure for fairness strengthens our moral impulse.

When people with similar characteristics, beliefs, or causes band together to form an advocacy group within our dissimilar world, their peer pressure urges the rest of us to give them and their ideas due consideration. At another time, we who have been pressured form an advocacy group centered around some other issue to apply pressure on "them." This is the equalizing value of peer pressure.

FROM SPECIAL VALUE TO EQUAL VALUE

The birth of a first child or grandchild is a special event. That child remains the ultimate in specialness, the center of our attention—until the next one appears. Then we come to our senses and remember that all children are special and that we care about each one. Parents and teachers with large broods strive to make each child feel special, and thereby equally valuable. Benevolent religious concepts affirm the inherent worth of all of God's creatures. Equality seems like a simple value—until counting wears us out.

It's hard to comprehend large numbers, whether they be stars, grains of sand, or human beings. Close your eyes and imagine a five-year-old child. Now think of two five-year-olds, now three, now four, and so on. How many does it take before the individual children become blurred into a brood, a classroom, a packed stadium, or an abstract number on a census report? In a world of six billion or more people, how many individuals can we envision as our equals? How many can we fit into our Golden Rule equation? Massive numbers cloud moral sensitivity. Fairness and caring shine best when we work together in small families, classrooms, and neighborhoods. René Dubos's maxim "Think globally, act locally" offers one response to this cloudy frustration. By treating each person we come in contact with in our personal lives as special, we contribute our small part toward respecting the specialness of all human beings. The Golden Rule is a principle that we can pursue even when we cannot fulfill our understanding of its total requirement.

When thinking about large numbers of people in practical terms, we have a natural tendency to group them into categories and classes. Our brain's ability to deal with numbers abstractly adds efficiency to our thinking. We efficiently assign stereotypical characteristics to those categories or classes. We efficiently value people en masse according to stereotypic profiles that we have learned or have constructed.

Reacting to people according to profiles can be morally dangerous. Dictators think in those terms. In contrast, day-to-day contact with real people confronts the moral limitations of profiling by pointing us to the commonality of our desires. Biographies and autobiographies can also help us understand people as individuals. Protests from the forgotten, mistreated, or wronged accentuate our understanding—unless we ignore, resist, or demean them. Working together promotes mutual interest. Commonality and mutuality provide moral logic for the Golden Rule.

EQUALITY AND EQUITY

Equality and equity are cousin concepts. *Equality* is true peersmanship; each of us has equal value. *Equity* is an effort to remove bias or favoritism from our practices when we are not equal in some characteristic, such as size, ability, or advantage. An example of equity under the law is the federal protection given to all children in the United States to receive a public education regardless of their mental or physical limitations. Formulas for achieving equity are always controversial. Some parents see placing disabled children in separate classrooms as equitable, while others see children's receiving assistance in regular classrooms as the only equitable method. At home, parents are always devising equity equations to keep the peace. Invariably, what one child calls fair, another calls favoritism.

Parents can get confused and frustrated when their attempts to be equitable are not matched by their children's efforts to be fair and caring with each other. The problem is that equity is dispensed from parent to children, while sibling caring is generated from child to child. Dispensing equity is an authority-centered value; in time, our adult children will try to be equitable with their children. In contrast, "brotherly love" is a peer-centered value. A confused mother once demanded that an older son write a letter to his younger brother, who was away at boarding school. She thought that the younger brother deserved the letter and that the older brother should want to write it. The demand was not appreciated; nor did it facilitate the brothers' concern for each other. Their relationship grew on a time line of its own, outside well-intentioned mother management.

If we save our equitizing efforts for times of real danger or harm, our children may develop equitizing formulas of their own. When these same two brothers were dis-equalized by one's having a cast on his arm, the normally more fearful but now armored brother decided to use his cast as a fist. Their father quickly intervened. But under more usual circumstances, kid-to-kid prodding, confronting, fighting, defending, proposing, and agreeing move pairs and broods toward brotherly and sisterly love year by year. And the Imp usually has something up his sleeve to level the playing field.

DIFFERENCES AND PREFERENCES

Outside the family, our young children may initially be very inclusive with other children. They eagerly make valentines for everyone in the class. They may cry when they cannot invite all of their cousins and classmates to a birthday party. Limitation introduces them to the world of human preference and choice. When they begin to prefer one child over another, they are inching toward the moral dilemma of equality versus preference.

The world of limitation motivates the study of difference, rank, and choice. It also inspires peer empathy. When we limit our child's birthday party to six guests, she must make choices. When another child, who can invite only six guests to his birthday party, excludes our child, she begins to imagine how other excluded people feel. When he is the only one in the class who is double-jointed or the only one who can't tie his shoestrings, he can imagine how it might feel to have other talents or limitations. When she is the only Asian American in the class, the only girl in a reading group, one of three students who aren't at school on particular religious holidays, or one of a handful who go to the office every noon to get a pill, she begins to know what it means to stand out or fit in. A child in these situations can be proud or ashamed, fearful or defiant: "So? You want to make something of it?" When children feel lonely, they seek out look-alikes, think-alikes, talk-alikes, and do-alikes. These peers become equals because of their similarities.

LOOK-ALIKES, THINK-ALIKES, TALK-ALIKES, AND DO-ALIKES

In Bradford Woods, Indiana, a yearly camp welcomes children who have craniofacial abnormalities. It is aptly named Camp About Face. During one early session of the camp, a nine-year-old girl was overheard telling her counselor with great excitement, "Me and Amanda [her newfound friend], we're the same age, we're in the same grade, we each have an older brother, we each like to swim, and we even have the same face problem!" Over the years that this innovative camp has been in existence, much thinking has gone into programming. No matter what activities are pursued, the main value of the camp simply seems to be the opportunity for these face-alike children and adolescents to come together summer after summer. Friendships are enduring. Two of the campers became roommates in college.

Peerage as an inclusive principle versus peerage as look-alike, think-alike, talk-alike, have-alike, or do-alike is a moral dilemma in public education. When is it morally good to group children, and if grouping is done, what is the right way to do it? What groupings will most likely promote the worthiness of each child; maximize peer empathy; promote peer-centered problem-solving and prosocial behavior; and prepare children to live in an economically complex society with democratic ideals?

GROUPING

The primary goal in grouping students in public or private schools is to place them in settings that will maximize opportunities to learn—including lessons of respect for the authority of knowledge and those who impart it. Instruction also includes the dutiful aspects of citizenship. This goal parallels development in the authority of conscience very well. When asked about rules within their conscience, children usually include ones about learning, and about respecting teachers.

A second goal in grouping students in schools is to teach them how to behave as citizens—how to strive for equality and equity in a democracy. This goal also parallels conscience development, this time related to the Golden Rule of conscience. Facilitation of this goal requires that students be placed in settings that maximize the discovery and practice of peer-centered values—fairness and caring between and among peers.

Opportunities for learning peer-centered values include situations in which students can affirm each other's basic value, empathy can be aroused, limits and expectations can be set within the group itself, issues of equality and equity can be explored, cooperative plans can be devised, and conflicts can be resolved in a systematic way. In brief, learning how to understand and practice the Golden Rule is excellent preparation for learning how to behave as a citizen in

> ### THE ADVOCATE
> Any public or private school policy in a democracy can be evaluated in terms of how it promotes conscience development and functioning. Conscience development parallels goals in teaching citizenship—its authority-centered duties and its peer-centered responsibilities. Questions to ask about individual policies, then, are these: Does it promote respect for self, authority, and others? Does it promote fairness and caring in equitable ways? Does it promote understanding and practice of the Golden Rule?

a democracy. However, like the family setting, the school setting requires that authority-centered values be accepted before peer-centered values can be explored and acted upon. Authority is always necessary to prevent harm and to assume leadership when issues are beyond the group's capacity to handle.

PEERLESS BUDDY

Individual stories bring moral issues to life. Long before special education was federally mandated, a certain neighborhood school had three classrooms of eighth-graders grouped more or less by ability. In the midst of the high-ability classroom sat Buddy. Buddy tried hard, and he often received B's for his efforts, but he definitely was not an intellectual peer in this classroom. He was tall and gangly, with large ears and an unusual face. His gait was awkward. A seventh-grade teacher affectionately pointed out Buddy's special talent for being the only student in the class who could cross his legs and keep both feet flat on the floor. His emotional responses set him apart, too: when he found something funny, he couldn't stop laughing; when he was upset, he couldn't stop crying. Many times, a classmate would put a hand on Buddy's shoulder and say, "There, there, Buddy, it's all right." Buddy's concrete style of thinking grew more obvious each year. In ninth grade, he went to the vocational high school, while everyone else in the class went to the "regular" high school. Old classmates loved to greet Buddy at football games. With great seriousness, he would admonish them to address him as "Lester" because that was his (mature) high school name.

Buddy was a moral asset to the class; he brought out other students' empathic responsiveness. One of his classmates, a neighbor, walked to school with him every day. The class as a whole was very patient. They soothed him when he was upset and were soberly patient when he couldn't stop laughing. No one objected when his assignments were modified or little was expected from him in gym class. No teacher had to tell the class how to treat Buddy, although some praised the class for its kindness. The students intuitively knew what to do. Their moral solutions were peer-derived. They valued Buddy as a peerless human being!

Differentness in tolerable amounts stimulates peer empathy, but an overload walls it off. One fall, in that same school, there was a small class of well-behaved seventh-grade students, mostly girls. There was also an "invasion" of badly behaved students, all boys. Since gang-member stereotyping had not yet been invented, these boys were not classified with that label. Perhaps "from the other side of the tracks" would have been the description at that time. An administrative brainstorm had evidently led to the grouping of compliant female students with these "bad boys." Perhaps the administrators hoped that some kind of moral-value averaging would occur.

The seating chart evenly interspersed "bad" boys with "good" girls. The girls learned a lot that fall. They learned that cigarette smoke lingers on clothing; that some students never do homework; that some bad words and doodles produce great laughter; that some jokes should be ignored; and that avoidance is a good coping skill. We don't know what the boys learned. We do know that this experiment in social engineering ended within six weeks. One day, the "bad" boys disappeared. The remaining students weren't told where the boys were sent, and they didn't ask. Their empathic responsiveness was unaroused. They simply were glad the boys were gone.

By taking into account how much differentness will stimulate moral growth and how much will traumatize it, parents and teachers can help give children a supportive setting in which to develop peer empathy. Tolerance grows in tiny steps as familiarity is balanced with exposure to differentness. Gradually, common experiences build a common ground of understanding.

NATURE'S INDIFFERENCE TO FAIRNESS

After a disastrous, disappointing event, we may hear ourselves exclaiming with moral outrage, "Life isn't fair!" At these times, we aren't complaining about a particular person who has been unfair or unkind. We aren't complaining about "man's inhumanity to man." Our outrage is focused on some act of nature that we find ourselves unprepared to control or accept.

Nature does not operate on principles of fairness. Instead, it supplies us with a variety of differences in an indifferent way. These differences may be within human nature itself or in the way our planet's bounty is distributed. Nature's indifference affects how we think about equality and equity, how we apply principles of fairness and caring to what nature has given us.

Differences and indifference in nature are relevant to parenting. We teach our children to find blessing in whatever nature gives them. Children's natural blessings include their parents. Because of nature's lack of concern about fairness, the Imp gives all children the right to complain about not getting to vote on how parents were distributed. He also gives all of us the right to read humorous moral intent into nature's workings. Some factors can be interpreted as equalizing us, some as doing the opposite.

NATURE'S EQUALIZING TRICK NO. 1: REGRESSION TO THE MEAN

One of the Imp's tricks, regression to the mean, promotes kid equality. Certain human traits—for example, height and intelligence—are distributed among individuals along what statisticians call a normal curve. That means that most people have a tendency to grow to an average height, while a few at either end of the curve are unusually tall or short. Now, the equalizing part of this tendency is a mathematical principle known as *regression to the mean*. Think of it as nature's Imp-inspired leveling principle. The leveling principle provides hope for children who are born to parents with not so much of this or that quality.

Two illustrations will demonstrate why the Imp enjoys this principle. When two very short parents have a child, it is highly likely that his height will be somewhere between the population mean (average) and his parents' heights. Such a boy will have to learn how to equalize his status with other boys without resorting to the threat "My dad can beat up your dad." Likewise, when

THE ADVOCATE
Equalizing opportunity among all children benefits the entire community, including children of privilege. If all children are protected from disease, well-fed, securely attached, and emotionally healthy and have full opportunity to learn, achieve, and morally strive, all children's lives in the community will be safer, fairer, and happier. They will all be readier to pursue the Golden Rule.

two brilliant parents have a child, her intelligence quotient is likely to be somewhere between their high scores and the mean score for the population. When this child brings home an excellent report card, the grades may reflect much more effortful study than her parents ever exerted. She may develop more capacity than her parents to empathize with students who "don't get it" or with those who live in a chronic state of test anxiety. She may live in that world herself.

Regression to the mean is a wonderful justification for public education. It keeps the proverbial American dream, progress through effort, alive! If normal distributions of talents and shortcomings did not equalize us, the world would be separated into geniuses and imbeciles, giants and midgets, as well as other alarming contrasts. We would never have the satisfaction of seeing a brilliant child rise to the top in the midst of impoverished circumstances or a state-winning basketball team emerge from a tiny town.

Picture two ninth-grade wrestlers, Kyle and Mark, on a mat in a school gym. The boys on the mat come from amazingly different backgrounds. Kyle comes from the lowest socioeconomic rung, has had many adversities in life, and is in a state school for the visually impaired. Mark comes from the highest socioeconomic rung, attends a private school, and has traveled widely. However, he and his family have also suffered from a number of problems, including trauma, chronic physical illness, and emotional disorder. There, on the mat, none of these samenesses or differences matter. There, on the mat, only wrestling ability matters. Kyle and Mark are of equal rank in this sports arena. Their school programs have cooperated to provide equal sports opportunity among boys who would otherwise compete in separate worlds.

NATURE'S EQUALIZING TRICK NO. 2: RANDOMNESS

Nature distributes harm and bounty with moral indifference. Natural disasters affect good and bad people alike. True, certain areas of our world are more vulnerable to earthquakes, droughts, floods, hurricanes, or tornadoes, but all areas have some natural force ready to wreak havoc. People who live close to the earth know about bountiful years and stingy years in crop production.

Natural disasters quicken moral awareness. They make us ask, "Why did this happen? What did we do wrong? How can we guard against further harm?" These questions, especially when accompanied by feelings of shame and guilt, may be answered with stoic resignation—this is the way life is; intensification of religious faith—God has reasons; or superstition—a hex has been placed on our family. The moral result may be callous and embittered self-centeredness, as when looters move in on chaos.

Alternatively, pondering the moral meaning of events may stimulate peer-centered valuation and action. People are known to "come together" during disasters, at least initially. At these times, commonality of experience makes concern for one's neighbors a natural response to nature's harm. However, moral energies may dissipate when problems become chronically overwhelming. Neighborly concern can also wear thin or be forgotten if we move on to greater opportunities, leaving others behind.

NATURE'S NON-EQUALIZING TRICKS: GENETIC DISORDERS AND TEMPERAMENT

Nature does not always follow rules of central tendency or randomness in the distribution of its bounty or harm. Genetically inherited diseases are distributed in more or less predictable ways. Diseases carried by single dominant or recessive genes are highly predictable. Others, carried through multiple genes interacting with environment, are much less predictable.

Maladaptive behavioral traits, such as excessive aggression, moodiness, anxiety, or the tendency to become dependent on alcohol, fall into the latter category. Negative behavioral traits can interfere with conscience functioning. For example, a highly distractible youngster may "want to be good" but is always getting into trouble because of this trait. By empathizing with the "want to be good" part of the child, adults and peers may remind themselves to be more gentle in their efforts to keep him focused.

Behavioral traits, adaptive or maladaptive, also interact with environment to give each of us a temperamental style. This style shapes how we interact with one another, what kind of a playmate, classmate, partner, or group member we are. Temperament makes us more or less inclined to treat each other kindly, harshly, patiently, abruptly, or indifferently. Temperament also colors how independently or interconnectedly, how actively or passively we pursue the Golden Rule. So does the community that tames or supports expression of our temperament. A highly structured classroom may shelter shyness and timidity, while a dangerous neighborhood may support behavior that is defensive and quick in response.

BEYOND NATURE'S HARM AND BOUNTY

Each of us may see nature as capricious, directed, kind, cruel, or indifferent. We may consider our own nature to be under the direction of an intelligence that is beyond understanding and control. We may even believe that intelligent understanding of nature is illusionary and futile. Buddhist ways of seeking Enlightenment are based on this premise. No matter how we humans approach intelligent understanding, we are inclined to come together for joint commiseration or celebration. Our peer-centered moral connection is enhanced through the commonality of human struggles.

Wherever moral truth lies, catastrophic events, everyday struggles, human maleficence, and new discoveries allowing command of nature periodically generate the need for new rules of conduct. Although authority-derived guidance brings the best of past moral truth forward, new knowledge requires moralization through egalitarian processing. Egalitarian processing means using democratic forums and legislative action to maximize benefits and eliminate harm caused by new discoveries, technologies, or procedures. In time, parents and children become peer citizens, jointly pursuing the Golden Rule in new territories.

INJECTING CARE INTO FAIRNESS

FROM TATTLING TO PEER EMPATHY

Imagine a group of kindergartners sitting around a table with a large box of crayons in the center. Brian voraciously grabs the best ones, those that haven't been whittled down to little stubs. "Brian grabbed all the good crayons!" screeches Ryan to the teacher. Tattling is front-line moral communication. Parents even recommend it when our children's only choices seem to be tattling or fighting. Depending on teacher patience, time, and the children's readiness, the teacher may expediently divide the crayons according to her formula for fairness. Or she may caringly think of a negotiation exercise that will arouse peer empathy and help the children reach their own solution. Peer empathy injects care into fairness.

Children who become too dependent on grownups for meting out fairness will have stunted Golden Rule searching skills. Learning how to become our sister's keeper while simultaneously eliciting fairness from her requires practice. Adult children in highly patriarchal or matriarchal families often come to that realization when their kingly or queenly parents pass on. Sons and daughters left with unclear authority-mandated rules for settling estates and continuing businesses may be ill-equipped to make fair and caring decisions.

SIBLING LOVE REQUIRES PRACTICE

Young children often greet a newly arrived sibling as an interesting toy, and soon after suggest that it be returned to where it came from: "Couldn't we get a puppy instead?" On the other hand, only children often long for siblings. An only child is heavy in authority-bestowed moral wisdom. Everything done right is likely to get too much praise, and everything done wrong may never be forgotten. The Imp is forced to live secretly in the only child's pocket. Without the Imp, cousins, and playmates, the only child grows up skill-deficient in mischief-colluding, setting another kid up to get in trouble, secret-keeping, and mock fighting to aggravate adults. An only child never learns what it is like to make up with a sibling just because no one else is available to play. These Impish and awkward exercises in early peer cooperation and conflict resolution require practice.

Children benefit from knowing that their peers have as much difficulty as they do in dealing with siblings. Picture a child psychiatrist with a practice in her home. One day, a very upset mother makes an emergency appointment for her fifteen-year-old son, Nick. Nick had become overly aggressive with his sister that morning while his mother was shopping. Nick sits in the chair looking sheepish and nervous. He cracks his knuckles in a syncopated rhythm while hemming and hawing about the details of the morning's frustrations. Suddenly, blood-curdling screams come from another section of the house, where the psychiatrist's two sons are resolving a difference of opinion. Nick heaves a sigh of relief, smiles broadly, and says, "Wow, that sounds like home!" He then settles his awkward, joint-cracking body deeply into the upholstered chair and has no further difficulties describing the problems he and his sister had that morning.

THE ADVOCATE

Divorced parents struggling with their own animosity must continue to inject care into fairness when making decisions about their children. Ethnic communities, wishing to preserve individual identities, must inject care into fairness for the common good. Empathy-building is a child, adult, and community pursuit.

PEER GROUP EMPATHY

A kindergarten teacher divides her class into two groups. The two groups are not pitted against each other in competitive challenges. That will come later in school. However, the groups are publicly compared in terms of their efforts at restraint and cooperation. They work for stickers and seasonal treats.

Throughout the school year, the children gradually learn that they must think and act as a group. Group empathy, or team spirit, develops. The teacher's incentives to bring about group cohesiveness facilitate growth of group pride and peer initiative. Natural child leaders emerge to persuade others to behave so that the whole group will be rewarded.

During times of crisis, individuals and groups are known to come together in heroic rescue efforts. The late college professor, storyteller, and mythologist Joseph Campbell, author of *The Power of Myth*, argued that the impulse to help a perfect stranger in need without thought for personal safety or benefit may tap feelings of union with another that were originally felt in infancy. Perhaps these deep kinship feelings underlie cooperation and courage displayed in groups. To become our brother's keeper is to generalize through group empathy. Pursuing the Golden Rule is a peer-to-peer and a group-to-group search linking caring to fairness.

DEVELOPMENTAL CONSIDERATIONS

SEARCHING FOR THE GOLDEN RULE AT THE EXTERNAL STAGE (0–6)

Golden Rule Challenges on the Playground

Imagine a fully equipped playground. A group of young children, including our own, is enjoyably exploring every inch of the play structures. We stand by, ready to assist and rescue as needed. The children who are shy may need encouragement to venture forth. Those who are bold may need admonishment to take it easy. More or less following adult-modeled rules, the children take turns, offer assistance to the younger ones, object to pushiness, and tattle on sand throwers.

When solitary exploratory needs are satisfied, spontaneous games emerge: "Let's race to _____." "Let's hide and then _____." "Let's play like _____." With no planning at all, moral issues permeate these play plots. Concerns about fairness may surge in disputes over resources, roles, methods, or duration of play. When conflict escalates to parent-arousing levels, we must then decide whether to use our authority to settle the conflict, let the children work it out on their own, or become mediators in conflict resolution. Those options are stated in the order of increasing energy requirements. The first option is the most efficient, the second is the noisiest, and the third requires the most adult creativity.

Imagine the scene suggested by this interview:

Interviewer: How did you get in trouble?

Young child: We were at Billy's. Well, that was Billy's fault, not mine. We were playing splish-splash with his water toy and he was like kicking it, flicking the thing off and blaming it on me. So I tried to dunk him.

It's a beautiful summer day by the pool. We parents are reclining in lounge chairs, soaking up sunshine while keeping one eye on our children so that they don't drown. Our child and Billy are getting noisier and noisier over that toy that we wish we had never purchased. When the fussing reaches a critical level, our lounge chair response is to noisily downgrade the importance of the toy, to minimize the children's emotional distress, and to tell them to "quit fighting" or we'll take the toy away. We lazily reason that, short of holding someone's head under water, splashing and dunking fights are basically safe. Having read the beginning of this chapter, we further justify our inactivity by claiming that the children are merely searching for the Golden Rule. These thoughts give way to rescue actions when words of danger signal our protective impulses. Billy's parents responded to that alarm.

Interviewer: Why did you dunk Billy?

Young child: Because I hate him. I wanted to kill him.

Interviewer: What did you do?

Young child: My parents took away the toy and gave us time-outs.

The Long Road to Peer Empathy

Injecting caring into fairness requires peer empathy. As the last vignette illustrates, peer empathy can take a dunk when one toy is contested by two children. In spite of fierce competition over resources and rules for playing a game, many in-play discoveries facilitate peer empathy. Four such discoveries are mutual enjoyment, turn-taking, reciprocal tolerance, and mutual misery. Each discovery is on the pathway to the Golden Rule. The following interactions show bonding between Krysta and Michelle.

Like most six-year-olds, Krysta likes to do what Krysta likes to do. Since she is also naturally social, she doesn't mind when Michelle joins in. With increasing frequency, she invites her to join in. When Michelle joins in, she usually likes the activity, too. Their enjoyment is shared. Soon Michelle gets an idea for an activity. She initiates it, inviting Krysta to join in. Krysta enjoys that activity. They learn that going back and forth this way is fun.

One day Krysta wants to do something that requires a partner. Michelle joins in, but she is in a grumpy mood. She plays in a very annoying manner. Krysta puts up with Michelle's annoying manners because she wants to keep on playing. It doesn't occur to her to ask Michelle why she is grumpy. Krysta's attitude is similar to the one in this interview:

THE ADVOCATE

Increasingly, American children are exposed to violent resolutions of peer-centered problems. Embedded in deeply hurt or disturbed relationships, violent solutions are shown daily on the evening news; in movies and video games; and, for some children, within their own families and neighborhoods. We must jointly seek Golden Rule pathways throughout the community.

Interviewer: How did you help your friend?

Child: I helped her play her new game. I play with her, even though she can be a pain.

Another day, Michelle invites Krysta over to play. Michelle insists on one particular activity. Krysta doesn't like that activity, but she participates in it anyway. She has learned that when she doesn't play what Michelle wants to play while at her house, Michelle will just keep bugging her until it's time to go home. Besides, she's found that it's sort of lonely playing alone. After a while, though, grumpiness gives way to fighting over the rules of the game. Parents overhear and threaten mutual punishment. Krysta and Michelle try to get along because neither one wants to get in trouble. Finally, they do get in trouble. Activity and enjoyment are cut off for both of them. They sit in their time-out chairs, looking at each other in mutual misery. If they express what they are feeling, they'll just be in more trouble.

In the next interview, a brother expresses his difficulties on the pathway to sibling empathy.

Interviewer: How do you and your brother get along?

Child: My brother is a blabbermouth. So I tell him to shut up.

Interviewer: How do you feel when you say that?

Child: Good! Quieter—my head doesn't start to hurt as much.

Interviewer: Are you supposed to tell him to shut up?

Child: No.

Interviewer: Is it wrong?

Child: Sometimes.

Mediating Kid Conflicts

Once we parents spring into action, we are inclined to handle kid conflicts at the behavioral level. In our best authority-centered style, we curtail negative behavior and demand positive behavior. Sometimes that's all we *can* do. At other times, we sense a moral teaching moment and bravely move into the energy-consuming task of kid mediation. Kid mediation requires that we place our empathic concern between the conflicted children. Physically placing ourselves at eye level between them helps us identify with their peer-centered point of view. Our in-between presence also establishes a zone of emotional safety. In that zone, our task is to maintain order while they share hurt feelings, differing perspectives, and frustrated efforts. We commiserate with the jointness of the failure and share hope for joint resolution.

The Mediation Steps

Having established a zone of safety, we take the first mediation step: to frame the problem as a joint one. "Are you children having trouble getting along?" The second mediation step is to help the children practice listening to each other's point of view. Listening requires being calm and attentive. If emotional expression starts skyrocketing, we may have to exercise parent authority and separate the children until those pouts, frowns, cries, stomps, or threatening postures begin to relax.

Sometimes child-generated solutions are so simple that we can hardly believe them. Mr. Anderson, a first-grade teacher, experimented with a peer-centered technique. Every time a student tattled to him about another student, he simply gave the two children permission to talk to each other. After a week of practice, he marveled at how much energy he was saving himself. He complimented the pairs whenever they moved in a problem-solving direction, even when he had no idea how they were doing it.

When children can't work out solutions by themselves, we initiate the third step. We become somewhat more active while still hoping that the children will come through with a plan of their own. Put the kids in a freeze-tag position while offering suggestions. Offer at least two reasonable compromises. Sometimes offering the same suggestion in two different ways works. Take any opportunity possible to turn conflict into a game. Winning a contest is always better than winning a fight. When everything fails, there's always the power play of an authority-mandated cease-fire. This fourth step, to be avoided whenever possible, puts all of the responsibility back in the hands of adults.

Remember to implement the same truce conditions for all fighting partici-pants. Parents are never right when they try to determine fault.

Noisy Solutions

Occasionally, children's squabbling sounds dangerous to adults, but fails to be acknowledged as such by the children. The combatants' relationship may be so sound that their everyday lives include practiced routines for wading through conflicts. The children may already have a well-rehearsed script for the plot, the lines, and the outcome. Threats and counterthreats, mock battles and peace negotiations are part of the play. Adult intervention would only louse up the plot. In these dramas, all adults need to do is unobtrusively observe how these narratives unfold.

—— **ADVICE TO PARENTS** ——————————————————————————

Nurturing the Golden Rule at the External Stage (0–6)

- **Children at play are searching for the Golden Rule.**

- **Peer empathy is a requirement for finding the Golden Rule.**

- **The pathway to peer empathy includes mutual enjoyment, turn-taking, reciprocal tolerance, and mutual misery.**

- **Intervene in child conflicts when harm is threatened.**

- **Look for moral teaching moments when kid mediation may be productive.**

- **Steps in mediation:**

    Create a zone of physical and emotional safety between the children.

    Frame the conflict as a joint problem.

    Teach each child to listen calmly to the other child's point of view.

    Offer solution choices.

- **When the moral teaching moments fail, resort to author-ity-mandated solutions.**

- **Children are noisy when they search for the Golden Rule on their own. Determine your level of tolerance.**

SEARCHING FOR THE GOLDEN RULE AT THE
BRAIN-HEART STAGE (7–11)

Friendship

Interviewer: How do you get a friend?

Child: Be nice, so people will want to be with you and be your friend.

Another child: Don't be a "show-off" because people won't like you.

New ideas about friendship change the ways in which our children pursue the Golden Rule at the Brain-Heart stage of conscience development. A friend is no longer just a generic being of nearly the same age who likes similar activities, not just someone to invite over when you're feeling bored or lonely. Between the ages of seven and eleven, a friend becomes a special someone. Friends giggle over the same silliness, go ape over the same celebrities, and find the same advertised trinkets to be absolute necessities of life. Values and emotional reactions are privately shared. Secrets are fun.

Friendship requires continuity and predictability. A friend's reactions can be more or less guessed ahead of time. A friend is dependable, calls at the promised time, and doesn't change plans just because someone else called with a better offer. A friend knows how to be a "bestest friend." In short, friendship is defined by being nice.

Being Nice

Younger children are motivated to be nice in order to share activities and stay out of trouble. At the Brain-Heart stage, being nice means identifying with and responding to the feelings and desires of a friend. Identification with a friend allows our children to wholeheartedly place the friend's interests ahead of their own — part of the time. Sharing similar values makes the search for nice things to do fairly easy. In the following interview, a mother's monetary restriction helps her daughter find a niceness that was not store-bought.

Interviewer: What's an example of being nice to a friend?

Child: Once I wanted to give [name of friend] a present. I couldn't think of what to give her 'cause my mom wouldn't let me buy anything. So, I sorta looked around. I couldn't decide 'cause I was choosin' all the little things that I didn't really want. So my conscience helped me there 'cause I picked this one little thingy that I got at McDonald's. It made me feel pretty good since I found something good to give her. I didn't play with it because it really didn't do anything.

Interviewer: What did she think of it?

Child: She was pretty surprised 'cause a lot of people don't go to McDonald's and she hadn't seen it.

Niceness reinforces friendship, and friendship reinforces niceness. Mutual niceness becomes a model for cooperation. As our children will later discover, cooperation requires niceness even when values diverge.

Rules for Niceness

A certain seven-year-old boy loved to play with his nine-year-old neighbor. The boys both had the same first name, so they were known in the neighborhood as Big Max and Little Max. Among their many shared interests was wrestling. They could wrestle for what seemed like hours at a time without injury or loss of enjoyment. What was amazing to a mother observer was how equitably they handled their differences in strength. The two boys would laugh and play-wrestle up to the point where the younger one was pinned. At a certain point of distress known to both of them, Little Max would signal Big Max with a near-cry that it was time to let go. They would then separate, only to start the play fight all over again.

On the same block, another seven-year-old boy had an entirely different kind of relationship with his eight-year-old neighbor. One would call the other to come over to play. No matter what their chosen activity, within an hour they would invariably get mad at each other and separate for the rest of the day. The following day they, too, would get together and do the same thing all over again. To the mother observer's awareness, they never had a knock-down, drag-out physical battle. But neither did they get very far into cooperation.

These two sets of boys approached the Golden Rule through different play routines that both consolidated into a common rule: Do no harm to each other. The first set's practices seemed to say, "Let's wrestle in ways we have done before because we both enjoy it and we know when to stop." The other set's practices seemed to say, "Let's do with each other what we've done before, because even though we never like it, it keeps us connected." (Sounds like a bad marriage!) The first set of boys always seemed to have fun; the second set never seemed to have fun. Within each set, however, the boys respected each other enough to do no harm.

Lopsided Niceness

Play requires both cooperation and conflict resolution. Friendship is built through cooperative adventures, but it is maintained through conflict resolution. Adventures consolidate into routines. Routines consolidate into rules. To an observer, some of the routines may look unfair: One child always has to _____, while the other child always gets to _____. However, to the participants, this lopsidedness may be quite satisfactory. Each pair defines their complementary relationship in ways that only the twosome may understand. They are engaging in peer-defined equity.

As in marriage, some role-bound activities enhance a friendship, while others make the relationship rigid and boring and bring forth accusations of unfairness. Friend-designed routines give dependability and predictability to the relationship. Other factors keep the relationship lively. Novelty—in the form of new kids on the block; adventure—in the form of new things to do; or maturity—in the form of reaching greater understanding—brings forth new rules. Each developmental loss of balance brings new challenges for cooperation and conflict resolution. The search for the Golden Rule goes on.

Losing a Nice Friend

We are a transient society. We move around, or other people move us around, frequently. Sometimes, we fail to understand how these changes affect our children. We forget that our children have put real effort into making friendships, and that change is a psychological loss for them. The following child expresses how a gain, in terms of academic opportunity, was also a loss to her, in terms of friendship.

Interviewer: What made you unhappy?

Child: I was unhappy when my friend was tested and didn't get into the EXCEL program. I wanted to be with her. I still get to be with her in Brownies.

Will the New Kids Be Nice?

Moving to a new neighborhood or school can be very stressful for the child who has just gotten a good start at understanding friendship and the rules that govern it. A move at this point in development can put the child's evolving Golden Rule understanding to an anxious test: "Will the kids in my new school be like the ones at my old school? Will they include me if I try to be nice to them? Will I know what to do to be thought of as nice? Will they have mean kids there, too? What should I wear the first day?" Although parents may think that seven-to-eleven-year-olds are pretty much the same everywhere and predict that our child will have a new friend before the weekend, if not nightfall, rapid transfer of friendship-making skills is by no means a certainty for the child going through a transition.

In the decades of the 1960s through the 1990s, many children, mostly African Americans, faced an anxiety-producing test of Golden Rule understanding when they were bused to distant schools in behalf of what was hoped would be the greater fairness of school integration. Fortunately, most of them did not have to go alone like the legendary first-grader Ruby Bridges. Friends, or at least one good friend, who ride the same bus to the same school can serve as a buffer—preserve a child's sense of connectedness—while the child addresses the task of making new friends or participating side by side with new acquaintances. Friendships grow, first out of finding similarities and developing comfortable routines, followed by discovering differences and finding comfortable routines for dealing with them. Cooperation and conflict resolution reinforce and build on each other.

Responding to Meanness

Well-nurtured children at the Brain-Heart stage feel morally obligated to respond to niceness with niceness. They also grope to understand meanness and how they should respond to it. These quandaries are at the cutting edge of their pursuit of the Golden Rule.

Interviewer: What are your best reasons for being nice to people?

Child: I'm nice to people whenever they are [nice]. Sometimes when they're mean to me. But most of the time when they're nice to me.

Seven-to-eleven-year-old youngsters usually do not run to an authority figure as their first response to meanness from another child. They may consider it useless because they have heard and memorized all the advice we have to offer. Repetition is boring, especially when the advice only works half the time anyway.

Interviewer: What do you do when [name] does things you don't like?

Child: I just ignore her when she gets on my nerves.

Interviewer: What are your best reasons for not being mean?

Another child: I shouldn't be mean to the littler kids because they don't understand.

What do we mean when we advise a child to "ignore" irritating behavior? She may think that we mean that "ignoring" will make the nuisance behavior go away. Sometimes it does, but it can take forever. Mean kids can be very persistent, and children like immediate results from their efforts. A better point to get across to children is that ignoring irksome behavior is a way of controlling personal distress. For example, if they don't let name-calling bother them, then their self-worth cannot be deflated by nasty epithets. Looking beyond nuisance behavior is hard, but not impossible.

Justifications for Being Mean

School-age children prefer niceness over meanness in themselves as well as others. Therefore, when our children consider their own meanness—or lack of niceness—they will probably feel obligated to justify those nasty feelings, thoughts, or actions. "I know it was a mean thing to do, but _____." A major justification is tit-for-tat reciprocity: one mean deed deserves another. In-kind revenge is hard to resist when we don't like the mean person in the first place or when the meanness is severe and unrelenting. Meanness among siblings may be a way of begging parents to accomplish the impossible—make life fair for everybody.

Interviewer: What are your best reasons for not hitting your sister and brothers?

Child: Because I would like to play with them.

Interviewer: What are your best reasons for hitting them?

Child: When they kick and hit me.

Interviewer: Are there good reasons to hit your sister?

Child: Sometimes, when she's bad and makes me mad.

Interviewer: Are there good reasons for leaving someone out?

Child: If you don't like them and you don't like their tastes and you don't like what they want to do.

Interviewer: Are there reasons to not make up after a fight?

Child: If they are real, real mean to you and you don't like them to begin with.

Group Meanness

Tit-for-tat meanness explodes in the story of a certain fifth-grade class on the day they had an inexperienced substitute teacher. Miss Jones was pretty and kind, and wanted to please. The class put on their worst "Sub Today!" behavior. They tested her kindness and agreeability to the limit. Sensing her vulnerability when she was unduly nice to them, they moved closer and closer to regressive chaos. Miss Jones became more and more exasperated. Finally she declared, "If I hear one more person speak out, you are all staying after school."

Julie, who happened to be very unpopular with her peers, "spoke out." With her silly, buck-toothed grin, she took the class over the edge just when they were collectively beginning to sense that they had gone far enough in tormenting Miss Jones. Everyone stayed after school. Revengeful thoughts buzzed through the room in the language of silence. As soon as the class was dismissed, all of ten minutes later, mob dynamics took over. Contagious revengefulness robbed most of these fifth-graders of their moral sensibilities.

They marched after their one-step-too-far classmate all the way to her front porch. They taunted her with ugly epithets. They even threw rocks at her porch as she ran inside. Julie's silly, buck-toothed grin was replaced by grim tears. When her distressed and angry mother came onto the porch, the crowd regained their senses and dispersed. Scared into moral sensibility by an "authority figure," the children ran home. None were late enough getting home to arouse suspicion of wrongdoing. "We had to stay after school a few minutes," they said blithely to their parents. They were too ashamed to tell the truth. The Golden Rule hid beneath the porch, while deception tap-danced above.

The next day the regular teacher was back. The children soberly went to their seats. Without introduction, the teacher read from the Bible and then gave a lecture about the respect for authority, the Golden Rule, compassion, and forgiveness. Meanness and niceness were clearly differentiated. No one complained about this breach in separation of church and state. The class was then directed to write apology letters to Julie and Miss Jones and to deliver them in person, one at a time.

Religious teachings generally support the search for the Golden Rule. Parables, folktales, family stories, and other narratives can make an important instructional impact at the Brain-Heart stage.

Interviewer: Why do you want to be nice?

Child: Probably because God wants us to be nice to other people. Jesus was always being nice. He wants us to be nice to other people, too, even our enemies. Jesus never fighted with anyone because he was a good person. He had no sins in his heart.

─── **ADVICE TO PARENTS** ───────────────

Nurturing the Search for the Golden Rule at the Brain-Heart Stage (7–11)

• **Help your child equate friendship with niceness.**

- **Realize your child's need for continuity in friendship.**

- **Teach your child how to maintain self-worth through ignoring meanness.**

- **Help your child understand justifications for her mean feelings.**

- **Help your child think very carefully about consequences if she decides to return meanness with meanness.**

- **Help your child find Golden Rule morality in literature and movies.**

- **Rescue your child when someone's meanness is overwhelming.**

SEARCHING FOR THE GOLDEN RULE AT THE PERSONIFIED STAGE (12–13)

Hanging Out

"Hanging out" largely replaces play for emerging teenagers. "Hanging out" means thinking and talking about what is "really important"—personality and presentation. Studying personality means figuring out psychological interiors—our own and each other's. Presentation involves strategizing what should be shared, with whom, and in what manner. Talking about people is easier than sharing interior selves. A proper presentation helps cover a teenager's occasional fantasy of being like no other, an alien entity walking the planet.

To avoid unwanted exposure, our emerging teenagers adhere strictly to peer standards. Clad in peer-approved, look-alike exterior camouflage, they hope that their inner selves, full of new complexities, are as private as they will them to be. Staying cool means saying very little when parents and siblings are around. Invariably, emotional coolness is periodically blown. Everything comes tumbling out.

Expressing boy-girl attraction is an exercise in coolness. Sending messages of attraction via third parties hides anxiety about self-revelation. If a reciprocal message is not returned, face-saving justifications can be made in private. If the attraction is reciprocal, more anxious moments lie ahead, more plans to process while "hanging out."

Beneath our teenagers' socially protective camouflage, their interior moral selves are being customized. Expansion in brain functioning allows their thoughts to flow from the specific to the general and back to the specific many times over. The idea of private psychological space and time is appealing to them. They conceptualize conscience as a personified moral force that keeps check on them all the time, whether external authority knows what they are up to or not. They develop a plan of personal oughtness, a protocol for the moral person they want to present to their consciences. They abstract virtues and vices. In fantasy, they project themselves in command of goodness as leader, spy, or rescuer. Fantasies of sacrifice, martyrdom, or sainthood may surge through their heads. The Imp lets them play at being the bad guy, too, as long as it remains a fantasy. In real life, the issue is how to be cool but good. Showing too much goodness can make a teenager look weird.

Interviewer: What are your best reasons for not being kind or helpful?

Emerging adolescent: A lot of times, people look at me weird because they're not used to other kids in school doing anything good. Sometimes they just glare at me.

Patience on the Bridge of Reciprocity

Patience allows an emerging teenager to explore the workings of the Golden Rule more carefully. If he is nice to his friend, he can wait longer for a hoped-for return. If the return doesn't come, he can imagine plausible justifications that will allow him to forgive his friend: "I wonder what's going on with Jason; maybe _____ is eating at him." Friendship is his motivation. Justifications preserve friendship in difficult times. Empathy for any possible distress justifies our teenager's justifications. That is, until his breaking point is reached and he shouts out, "Quit making excuses for yourself!" And maybe he walks away from the friendship. Trying to look at moral obligation from the other side of the bridge of reciprocity can be very taxing. Our emerging teenagers are learning that friendship is like that.

Interviewer: What are your best reasons for helping people?

Emerging teenager: If you want people to be happy, then you help them. They'll be happier than if they have to do it by themselves. Or if they needed some help, if something happened to them. And you'll have another friend, maybe.

Interviewer: Why do you think it's important to be a good listener?

ET: I'd want somebody to listen to me if I had a problem. So I listen to them.

Conscience as Friend

When real friendships go sour, thinking of conscience as a friend is very comforting. If our teenagers personify their consciences only in terms of restraints and demands, they are bound to have trouble with moral self-worth. A friendly conscience is empathic and forgiving as well as restraining and demanding. It lets the Imp paint a twinkle on its judging eye. Friendship with peers and conscience is a matter of reciprocal understanding. We feel best when we are in good standing with both conscience and friends. When friendship ends in a moral breach in the real world, a friendship-maintaining relationship with conscience is necessary to maintain moral self-worth. When we see a teenager in the dumps over a failed friendship, we might want to talk to her about maintaining friendship with her conscience. It may affirm self-worth when we are not there to do it.

Interviewer: What is your best reason for being nice?

Emerging teenager: I used to call my brother names, but now I don't because that's mean. I don't want to think of myself in that way [lose the friendship of my conscience].

Interviewer: What is the reaction of other people when you've done something good?

ET: Dunno. They can think what they want to. I know what I did is right.

Virtue as an Unlimited Pursuit

When we choose to arbitrarily pursue a virtue, we have no idea what the results will be. Good deeds do not guarantee return or appreciation. Our conscience may be the only empathic being on the other side of the bridge of reciprocity. Emerging teenagers are attracted to the idea of pursuing virtue for its own sake. They also have some understanding of the risks.

Interviewer: What are the things that are good about you?

Emerging teenager: I love to help other people.

Interviewer: What are the things that are good about you?

Another ET: I defend people who are made fun of. When I was in third grade, I made friends with a girl that nobody really liked. She was kind of annoying, but I made friends with her anyway. I do that a lot. She was kind of weird, and people would pick on her—picked on me too some before I changed schools.

Driven to Secrecy

Being good for the sake of being good is risky business. It can drive a person to secrecy. *The Conscience Celebration*, our companion electronically published book for emerging teenagers, is a story about someone who chooses moral secrecy. Cynthia, the agent of moral secrecy, conducts a major experiment that nearly drives her younger sister, Rachel, crazy. Cynthia starts being nice to Rachel for no reason at all—or at least, for no reason to which she will confess! Rachel is really confused because Cynthia doesn't seem to want anything in exchange; she doesn't ask to borrow anything, doesn't ask Rachel to baby-sit her pet rabbit, doesn't even ask her to keep a secret from Mom and Dad. She just starts being nice! She doesn't pick on Rachel, doesn't accuse her of anything, and even helps her unscrew the lid on a new jar of peanut butter instead of calling her a baby. This change in behavior turns their prior relationship on its ear. In fact, it disturbs the relationships within the whole family.

Cynthia's and Rachel's previous Golden Rule practice had consisted of day-after-day, night-after-night routines in which they would "do unto each other every nasty thing you can possibly think of doing, short of murder"— including always accusing the other one of starting something when Mom and Dad were around. These routines kept the girls connected and fed their sibling-designed contest to win the Favorite Daughter Award. The girls had different ways of working on their parents, and both of them were deadly clever. Cynthia had the more fiery temper, the louder voice, better argumentation skills, and redder hair. She generally won her battles with noise. Rachel was quieter but more devious. She knew just which buttons to push to get her sister to blast off—right when Mom or Dad was coming down the hall.

Cynthia's sincere experiment in niceness upset all of the family dynamics. Suddenly it became obvious to the parents that Rachel was now the instigator of all of the set-up-a-fight maneuvers, whereas Cynthia just tolerated them, kept on reading her library book, or offered to share her saltwater taffy from the state fair. Of course, Cynthia didn't say a word about her intentions. She merely started putting into practice the type of Golden Rule behavior her parents, her Girl Scout leader, and her youth minister had been preaching to her all along—with a little twist of her own design. Why had she started inflicting this advanced Golden Rule practice on her sister? Was she working on a special Girl Scout badge? Or had she simply gone weird?

The secret is that Cynthia had started thinking about "Do unto others as you would have them do unto you" in a new way. She began to think of her sister as a person, a real human being like herself—a little more immature, of course, but with feelings and all of that stuff. She began to feel guilty that she had used all of those oneupmanship skills that her advanced years (two, for the record) and superior intelligence (her own estimation) allowed her to inflict on her sister. That had been really mean! It was time that she owned up to the fact that her sister was probably going to be her sister for the rest of her life. Furthermore, Mom and Dad were probably never going to have the Favorite Daughter Award ceremony. She began to speculate on the wild idea that she and her sister were equals in the eyes of their parents, God, and the United States Constitution.

Cynthia's expanding ideas about time, space, and person allowed her to think of her sister in new ways. Instead of having now a friendship, now a non-friendship, she thought of them as having an ongoing sisterhood, one that was never going to cease, even if they wanted it to disappear. Abstracting the situation, Cynthia thought, "How should a sister, not just Rachel, but any sister, be treated?" She reasoned that what ought to be fair between her and her sister ought to be fair all the time, not just when one or the other wanted it to be that way. And if Rachel had feelings like Cynthia's—even though she showed them in goofy ways—Cynthia should honor them. "Do unto Rachel as I would have her do unto me" meant putting herself in Rachel's shoes to see how that would feel. Whew! Wearing Rachel's shoes was really a weird thought—she would need a lot of sneaker sweetener! Back to the abstract sister! Cynthia's final argument to herself was that since she was the older sister, she ought to take the lead in being nice, considerate, kind, and all that stuff.

Golden Moments

How long did Cynthia's experiment last? Well, school was about to start, and it wasn't long before she was involved in all kinds of activities with her friends, and she didn't even think about sisterhood at all. In fact, she came home from school, went right to her room where the door still said "PRI-VATE," turned on her music, talked on the phone, and did her homework until Mom called her down to set the table for dinner. Sometimes she was nice to Rachel, and sometimes she wasn't. Sometimes Rachel was nice to her, and sometimes she wasn't. Her parents never did figure out what had been going on with Cynthia at the end of the past summer. However, they did notice that she seemed to be getting along with her friends better this year, and on her first school report, her social studies teacher, who also had taught Cynthia the previous year, wrote the comment, "showing more maturity." Cynthia had experienced a Golden Moment, a flight into more developed moral thinking about the essential issues in the Golden Rule, injecting fairness with caring.

More or less, this Golden Moment had made an impact on all of her relationships, sisterhood being but one.

Golden Moment thinking can wear you out, especially when you're only twelve or thirteen. Even if teenagers had a personal moral trainer, they could run the course of expanded reciprocity for only so long. Then the Imp would just have to have some fun on the Golden Rule track. He would probably find Golden Rule situations to test parents, wanting to know if they are capable of Golden Moments.

Seven Reasons for Moral Secrecy

Why was Cynthia driven to secret sincerity during her Golden Moment? There are seven possibilities. First, she didn't want her sister to think she was weird. She knew that Rachel was committed to the view that sisters just don't act that way. Second, she knew Rachel would accuse her of deviousness, thinking that Cynthia was trying to "suck up" so that she could get something out of Rachel later. Third, Cynthia knew that Rachel would think that her niceness was only part of the competition for the Favorite Daughter Award. Fourth, Cynthia knew that if her parents knew what she was doing, they would heap praise on her and say something to Rachel like "Rachel, why can't you be more like your sister?" That would be like throwing gasoline on an already blazing fire of sibling competition, and then Rachel would really make life hard for her. Fifth, Cynthia suspected her parents would upgrade their expectations of her. Any time she slipped back into her old ways, they would say, "Why can't you be that nice all the time?" Sixth, it was only an experiment; Cynthia just wanted to try it out. Seventh, announcing a planned moral improvement would have made Cynthia doubt her own sincerity. Advance billing of her plan would only make her look like a moral braggart.

Did Cynthia really think through these seven reasons for moral secrecy? Doubtful. Was she consciously aware of making a contract between her conscience and herself? Maybe. But certainly (1) she was being reared in a value-sensitive environment—that is, her parents were trying hard to support goodness in their daughters; (2) she approached the tired-of-fighting-with-my-sister situation with a thoughtful but playful sense of experimentation; and (3) she was sincerely trying to be a better person. Secrecy makes goodness more golden:

Interviewer: Have you ever done a secret good deed?

Emerging teenager: When I give money to charity stuff, I don't tell people.

Deception in Behalf of the Golden Rule

Complete honesty is an asset in childhood. When a certain six-year-old granddaughter gets to the Personified stage of conscience functioning, she probably will no longer say to her grandmother, "Playing with you is fun, even though you are my grandmother!" or "Why do you have so many spots and wrinkles on you? Why does your stomach stick out? Are you going to have a baby?" Instead, she will begin developing Golden Rule deception: "Thank you for inviting me over, Grandma, but I've got [places to go, people to see, things to do]." She probably won't say, "Nobody hangs out with her grand-mother!" She will probably reason like this teenager:

Interviewer: What is your best reason for lying?

Emerging teenager: Sometimes you have to lie to protect the feelings of another person.

Is moral deception in behalf of the Golden Rule a good thing? That's a moral dilemma. As our teenagers enter mid-adolescence, they will have more opportunities to figure that out.

—— **ADVICE TO PARENTS** ————————————————————

Nurturing the Search for the Golden Rule at the Personified Stage (12–13)

- **Expect "hanging out" to emerge from play. Provide protective environments for "hanging out."**

- **Expect self-consciousness to emerge. Expect everyone to go silent when you enter a room where there are young teenagers.**

- **Look for thinking that involves specific-to-general (inductive) and general-to-specific (deductive) reasoning. Look for growing understanding of the attributes of virtue and vice.**

- **When given the opportunity, engage your teenager in discussions about "the person I want to be."**

- **Affirm your teenager's efforts in seeking psychological understanding of others.**

- **Use the concept of conscience in discussions, but don't get**

too nosy about your teenager's conscience. Honor moral privacy.

- **What looks like a random act of kindness in your young teenager may be part of a secret moral plan.**

- **When moral behavior improves, don't turn it into a demand. It may only be a Golden Moment.**

SEARCHING FOR THE GOLDEN RULE AT THE CONFUSED STAGE (14–15)

Parents' Peer Group Fears

Peer groups become a major influence in conscience development during mid-adolescence. There may be several peer groups who have influence on our teenagers' lives, but the one we are usually most concerned about is the one that our fifteen-year-old hangs out with on Saturday night. We often worry about moral healthiness within that group. Even when we judge its members to be basically goodness-seeking as individuals, we fear that, in the spirit of fun and adventure, group contagion may overtake our individual teenagers' moral sturdiness, leading them into high-risk activities or behavior that is clearly wrong. If the group has bold anti-authoritarian tendencies, we fear that our teenagers will turn against our values. If the group is composed of members who are totally disengaged from moral nurturance, demoralized about the future, and pursuing a course of futility, we fear contact in any form.

Group Loyalty

During mid-adolescence, peer groups become social anchors as our children move from conforming child to morally autonomous young adult. Moral issues are interwoven into all group activities. Adolescent group participation is preparatory to community participation in adulthood. Group loyalty broadens the scope of caring interwoven with fairness. Pursuing the Golden Rule is now focused on group relationships: member-to-member, member-to-group, and group-to-group.

Interviewer: What are your best reasons for making others happy?

Mid-adolescent: Usually with the group I hang around with, if one person is down, the whole group is. If one person is happy, everyone else is happy. Last year, one of my friends tried out for basketball. Everyone else but her made it. No one wanted to be like "Yeah, I made it." They didn't want to make her feel sad. She was sad and no one wanted to say anything about it. So no one even talked.

Multiple Groups Define the Teenage Community

Teenagers readily identify social groups within their school community. Categories repeatedly described are the academically oriented types, ranging from "preppies" to "nerds"; the physically oriented "jocks"; and the politically oriented "popular" people. Non-achievement-oriented groups may be identified as "druggies" or "losers." One social group within the school may appear to "have

> ### THE ADVOCATE
> The healthiness of parental peer group fear rests in the motivation it gives us to support not just our teenagers, but teenage culture as a whole. Since we obviously cannot dam up the adolescent passage in the stream of life, it behooves all adults to provide creative opportunities for teen group thriving, learning, and virtuous striving. Every time we take on the roles of chaperon, coach, youth-group sponsor, or school-board activist, we are living up to that goal.

it all." This privileged group may be a composite of high achievers in academics and sports, winners of honors and awards, and holders of student political office. They are the ones who will be nominated as "most likely to succeed" in the senior yearbook. When this group or a member of it strays from the social norm, the gossip includes the question "How could it happen?"

Near the other end of the spectrum of social labeling, another teen group is characterized by school absenteeism, poor academic performance, nonparticipation in school organizations, gravitation to out-of-school friends, thrill-seeking activities, use of illegal substances, and even juvenile court appearances for status offenses. Although this group may live on the fringes of moral and academic expectation, it is not antisocial. There is no criminal orientation. Concern for others is merely overly focused on the group itself and its "now" orientation. Academically, it is known for its underachievers. Plans for the future are foggy or undefined. When a member of this group goes morally astray, gossip includes the question "What else could you expect?" However, at the twenty-five-year class reunion, one or more individuals in this group will surprise everyone with some kind of unique and successful achievement. Gossipers marvel.

What is similar about the groups at both ends of the socially labeled spectrum is their intense intragroup loyalty. "Do unto others as you would have a member of the group do unto you" and "Do for the group what you would like the group to do for you" mean a strong commitment to fairness and caring within the teen group. Loyalty to outsiders may be dormant or weakly expressed. Attitudes toward other groups may range from healthy competition to condescension and contempt. Family loyalty may go dormant. Going to a family reunion may be as boring an activity as parents could possibly impose.

Teen groups collectively shape the identity of the teenage community. Each group deserves as much moral support as adults can give them. In time, loyalty learned in the teen group will expand to neighborliness, political party affiliation, work-group allegiance, willingness to fight for one's country, international cooperation, environmentalism, or other loyalties yet to be defined. President Kennedy's often-quoted "Ask not what your country can do for you, but what you can do for your country" arouses the kind of emotionally charged loyalty that is first engendered in adolescent groups.

Anna, a fifteen-year-old high school sophomore, came home from school one day infused with school spirit. No pep rally had taken place. It had just been a regular school day with a substitute teacher in social studies. The sub, however, happened to be the dean of girls. She had an inspirational presentation that she saved for those last-minute need-somebody-quick substituting occasions. She rallied the students to think about the meaning of their school community. What were its flaws and strengths? How could they improve it?

Later that year, the high school was targeted for possible closing by the school board. Inspired students immediately volunteered to be part of the protest group at the school board meeting. They marched into the meeting with banners and school colors flowing. Their elected leader spoke passionately for the continuation of their school. Although their cause was lost, the students, solidified in their loyalty, had an important experience in democratic process.

Maintaining Well-Being within the Group

High school groups may be tightly knit known-each-other-from-kindergarten units or come-together-from-many-places groups bonded by common interests or aspirations. Loyalty seals an unwritten covenant of cooperation within a well-functioning group. Fairness and caring, formerly focused on two-person sibling or peer relationships, now includes concern for the whole group. Maintaining a sense of well-being within the group is a top priority: "Everyone was in a good mood today!" Unwritten rules evolve that maintain the solidarity of the group—rules for leadership, decision making, turf defense, or pairings within the group. For example, a member may be chastised or even excluded for being too dominant, stealing another member's boyfriend or girlfriend, or letting out a group secret.

Confidentiality is an important aspect of loyalty. Teenagers naturally want to know about and solve each other's problems. That's one of the reasons for all those phone calls. Decisions are being made regarding when to get into or stay out of other people's private affairs; what to do with rumor and gossip; when to disclose concerns to adults and when to keep those concerns group secrets.

Interviewer: What are your best reasons to mind your own business?

Mid-adolescent: I have a tendency to get into people's business without them asking me to. Like if something is going on with them and, this is an example, if two of my friends are into something, I get into it. Even adults—I like to know what it is. I have to know everything.

Loyal friends want to protect each other, even when that protection involves the possibility of personal harm.

Interviewer: What are your best reasons for fighting?

Mid-adolescent: You should fight to protect someone. Like you should at least try and help if nobody ain't there.

Pitfalls of Peer Group Secrecy

Teenage secrecy justifies parent concern. Our sense of caring, protectiveness, and wisdom mandates that we balance respect for privacy with vigilant alertness. While fostering peer-centered responsibility, we want to be informed and ready to intervene when our teenagers are in dangerous situations. We must be alert to unsupervised social gatherings; curfew violations; sexual activity, pregnancy, and abortion; gun ownership or accessibility, cigarette, alcohol, and drug use; irresponsible driving; vandalism and nuisance behavior; classroom cheating; value-deficient entertainment; and more. As a support to our teenagers' social network, we parents must have our own network of concerned adults within the community.

Loyalty Conflicts

Loyalty is a moral asset. It can also be part of a moral dilemma. Our teenagers' loyalty to friend, group, or adolescent community can place them in desperate moral straits when that friend, group, or community is doing something wrong. When there's potential for harm to any human being, it is no time for confidential intragroup loyalty. Human loyalty is the greater good. When peer loyalty is overdone, we hear too late that a teen committed suicide when her boyfriend dropped her; that we harbored someone else's teenager in our house overnight when he should have been home working out a conflict with his family; or that an abortion or drug overdose occurred. These tragedies open our teenagers' hearts to the fact that there are times when we all belong to the same human community. Pursuit of the Golden Rule is not age- or group-specific.

Peer-centered discussions of moral issues benefit from adult leadership. However, outside of emergencies, parents are usually not ranked in first place to lead them. Establishing independence from parents, even when parent guidance is valued, is a strong motivator for aloofness in mid-adolescence. That raises the village concept of raising a child (or teenager) to a new level of importance. School teachers, counselors, coaches, youth workers, ministers, godparents, or mental health workers all make excellent facilitators of such discussions. In fact, they may be idealized as "really cool" people. Little do our teenagers know that their parents may also be "cool people," but only to some other group of teenagers.

Group discussions about peer-centered values may emerge casually, around a campfire, after practice, or in lieu of "the topic" in the classroom. Allowing teenagers to lead a teacher beyond the confines of an assignment is a "cool" way of generating value-centered discussions. "We got Mr. _____ off the topic today. We had this really neat discussion about _____. Now those papers aren't due until Monday." More formal discussions about peer-centered values may be deliberately programmed into the school curriculum, integrated into problem-centered group therapy, or included in adolescent programming in youth-oriented organizations.

Is This the Right Group for Me?

Sometimes a teenager's moral assessment leads to the feeling that he is in the wrong group. If he chooses to leave a peer group, he may find a healthier one to join. If he has had a bad peer experience at one school, he may transfer schools, resolute in knowing what kind of friends he will make this time. Or he may be more satisfied to stand outside of any social group. If he stands resolutely alone with his values, he may be morally sturdier than he was before he felt a part of the group. In fact, this stance may mark the transition to the Integrating stage of conscience development.

Some teenagers never have the experience of being part of a social group. Yet their conscience development may proceed on schedule. They mentally separate from parent-pleasing conformity, formulate a sideline view of teenage culture, and go on to become mature moral decision-makers. Another type of sideline teenager is just plain lonely. These teenagers need others to reach out to them. They need to be the focus of a group that is looking for good things to do.

Looking for Good Things to Do

Morally healthy teens want to be well thought of by peer groups, by parents, by the teen community, and by the larger community: "People think teenagers are all [bad characteristics]; they never notice when we do [virtuous things]." Mid-adolescents have a readiness to idealize virtuous possibilities—goodness that will impact the future of the larger community they are entering: "If we all help a little, the world will become _____." Individual altruism inspires the group. Group moral enthusiasm can contagiously inspire individual members. In this enthusiastic mode, the Golden Rule expands to "Do unto others as you would like them to do in the future." This means giving more than you expect to get back—no immediate return or no return at all. Reciprocity tips to the side of generosity in the two following examples.

Interviewer: How do you help with your stepsister?

Mid-adolescent: I try to be nice to her. She doesn't get told right from wrong a lot since we've been growin' up 'cause she's my stepsister. So she's been passed around to all these different people. I have to be in the mood to get along with her. It's like effort. It's like a bridge and here's me and here's her. She won't come meet me halfway. I have to go over there. I should be glad I can make the effort to get along with her, but it bugs me, sometimes.

Interviewer: What are your best reasons for helping others?

Another MA: My mom has a friend, and they don't have much money at all. They can barely buy bread. Her daughter wanted to play softball, but they didn't have enough money to let her play. So I gave her the money and bought her a mitt to play.

Interviewer: How did you feel?

MA: It kind of made me feel good that I did something like that for somebody.

Adults do well when we provide opportunities for altruism for teenage groups. It is important that we acknowledge acts of kindness and generosity every time we see them. We also should affirm our teenagers when we see them assuming the role of mediator or counselor—as long as the responsibility isn't too much. How do we know when it is? When the junior counselor is in more distress than the conflicted parties. The following teenager is functioning somewhere between counselor and ally.

Interviewer: What are your best reasons for being fair?

Mid-adolescent: If two of your best friends are fighting, you don't want to pick sides. You want to listen to both sides of the story first and see if you can work it out between them—before you choose sides. If I don't care about the person, then I won't listen to their side of the story.

───── **ADVICE TO PARENTS** ─────────────────────────

Nurturing the Golden Rule at the Confused Stage (14–15)

• **Expect the growth of peer loyalty and confidentiality.**

• **Expect peer-group labeling and judging.**

• **Be alert to over-involvement in peer problems.**

• **Strike a balance between nosiness and aloofness from your teenager's peer activities.**

• **Be alert to potential harm. Intervene.**

• **Be loyal to the whole teen community by getting involved in teen groups.**

• **Provide opportunities for altruistic behavior in teen groups.**

───

SEARCHING FOR THE GOLDEN RULE AT THE INTEGRATING STAGE (16–17+)

Emancipation from Group Dependency

Two important changes in conscience functioning begin to appear sometime after our teenagers' sixteenth birthdays. First, they demonstrate a more definitive moral self within their group. Their dress-code camouflage may even relax. Second, they show psychological movement away from the group. Group emancipation will soon be necessary for them to move on in life.

A specific moral dilemma may bring these changes into evidence. We may overhear our teenager saying to her friends, "Take me or leave me, this is what I believe." A stronger moral identity within the group and outside of the group affects her pursuit of the Golden Rule. She begins to see the "other" in more universal terms. "Do unto others . . ." means honoring universal human rights separate from gender, class, ethnicity, religion, intelligence, popularity, talent, or attractiveness. The very characteristics by which she formerly grouped her peers may now be negated in defining the moral "other."

Interviewer: What are your best reasons for not fighting?

Older adolescent: Everybody is created equal. There is no right for anybody to beat on anybody else.

Non-violence is a commitment to an ideal, and therefore may be impossible to achieve. Living with ideals in a not-so-ideal world is always a struggle.
There may always be situations in which self-defense or loyalty is a chosen
justification for fighting. We keep an ideal in mind through personalizing universal recipients. Seeing one as representative of all, again, fits René Dubos's
mandate, "Think globally, act locally."

Courage to Be Fair and Caring

Moral courage is required to confront an immoral action practiced by self,
friend, or group. We described how courage emerges as a "relaxed but morally
alert state" in Chapter 3. Now we discuss another aspect of its development.

At the Confused stage, our teenagers were hesitant to take a moral stand
that would upset friend or group. When pushed beyond their moral limits, they
were more likely to seek new friends than to stand alone on an issue. Since
courage develops in steps, this was developmentally appropriate.

At the Integrating stage of conscience development, our adolescents show
more resilience in the face of group sneers or mockery. Once they break
through the courage barrier with one moral decision, they are likely to do it
again. Moral courage may become habitual: "Here is where I must draw the
line." Drawing the moral line will gain them more respect from some peers,
while others continue to sneer. The following older teenager reflects on her
less courageous years:

Interviewer: Why should you avoid peer pressure?

Older adolescent: I think back to when I was in middle school. I hung
around with this friend a lot who always liked to tease people. She was
really rude to them. She would do cruel things. A lot of times I would
go along with it, even though the whole time I was thinking I shouldn't
be doing this. Sometimes I'd even chip in and tease a little bit. I felt
really bad during that, and I felt bad afterwards. I didn't really act like
myself. Some of my friends would go along with it and think it was
funny, and other ones would feel really bad for the ones that were being
teased. Other ones that weren't really involved, they would probably
think bad of me.

A few individuals move through adolescence and into adulthood without
strong moral challenge. They may be, by nature, cautious, compliant, and
value-oriented. They may be comfortable standing outside the social main-

stream in mid-adolescence. They may be fortunate in having a few select friends with similar personalities and values. Peer pressure may be foreign to them. How do they learn to be morally courageous? Perhaps through vicarious learning or study of hypothetical moral dilemmas. Such experiences ready us for challenge. Challenge will certainly come when they become parents.

When Universal Care Defines Fairness

Our teenagers' ability to envision universal human rights strengthens moral courage. However, no individual's courage has yet changed the world. Understanding the odds may intensify a teenager's admiration of people whose courage has had major impact. She may become an impassioned admirer of Mahatma Gandhi, Martin Luther King, or Bishop Tutu. He may strongly identify with masses of people who have suffered at the hands of others— victims of the Holocaust, slavery, child labor, famine, hostage-taking, war, and the like. Religious worship may include adoration of saints and prophets. Moral imagination, fed by idealism, may prepare our teenagers for a courageous act later in development.

"Do unto others as every human being ought to be treated." Note that the doer and recipient are identical in this restatement of the Golden Rule. There is no "be nice to those who are nice to me"; no "return meanness with meanness"; no ignoring; no setting an example so others will learn; no allowances made for in-group loyalty or group-to-group alliances. When the Golden Rule is interpreted as the obligation to pursue (or demand) universal rights, unconditionally, for all of us, care overrides fairness.

In predicting his own demise, Martin Luther King undoubtedly grasped the dangers of unlimited moral commitment. His pacifism meant taking a stand for the equal and non-violent treatment of all human beings, regardless of danger to his own life or the lives of his followers. By letting go of self-defense and loyalty-to-group justifications, he moved his Golden Rule beyond reciprocal considerations, which placed him in great danger. If he had pursued universal human justice to ensure honor in heaven, his Golden Rule would still have retained reciprocal features. By pursuing universal human justice as an end in itself, he placed living the Golden Rule above the consequences to any particular person, including himself.

Do sixteen- and seventeen-year-olds have the capacity to understand unconditional giving or unconditional resistance? Well, listen to the words of this seventeen-year-old:

Interviewer: What are your best reasons for not hurting people?

Older adolescent: Because if you hurt one person, you hurt more than one.

Like if I was, for instance, to hurt you, well, then your friends would know how I am and they wouldn't want to be my friend. And then if I ran into your brother, he wouldn't want to be my friend because of what I did. So, it's like a train that has a cart added on each side. You hurt everybody.

This boy does hang onto reciprocity in terms of desiring friendship in return for not hurting. However, he universalizes the consequences of hurting to include everybody. What is particularly interesting about this boy is that he grew up without family support. He was abused in childhood and legally removed from his home. He had spent most of his seventeen years in residential placements or psychiatric hospitals. His IQ test scores were repeatedly around 80. Of most interest is how he struggled with his ideals. When he went home for a visit with his foster parents, he invariably "messed up." An aggressive response over some issue would prompt them to return him to the hospital early. Whatever justifications he had for striking out at his foster siblings or parent ultimately failed him. He would sink into grief because he could not live up to what he believed in—a world in which people did not hurt each other.

The Interconnectedness of Humankind

In the last example, the boy used the image of a train "with carts added on each side" to represent the interconnectedness of humankind. In the following example, an adolescent girl combines her own experiences with cheating with the effects of a friend's cheating, and then focuses, in turn, on how the entire class was affected. The competition with her cheating friend inspired her to think of the fairness issue in terms of the whole class. With just one more mental association, she might have expanded her ideas to include students everywhere.

Interviewer: What are your best reasons for not cheating?

Older adolescent: The reason I don't think I'd do it again is because one time, my friend—she cheated on a real big history test in a class where we have the hardest teacher in the school. And she got an "A" on it and I got a "C" on it, and I studied the night before so hard. I was so mad. And she just sat over by this girl that's like really, really smart. And she just cheated off of her. I wanted to tell on her so bad 'cause when we got our report card, she got a better grade than I did. She did that on two tests. When you're studying, that's just not right. So that kind of taught me a lesson how I felt when she did that—like the rest of the class [was wronged]. So, I mean I've never done it on a big test. If I cheated on a big test now, I'd go tell the teacher. A year ago I wouldn't have.

SUMMARY

Living with others as siblings, classmates, or neighbors gradually leads our children to pursue the Golden Rule. "Doing unto others as you would have them do unto us" becomes a challenge to balance caring and fairness in egalitarian relationships. As children figure out ways of cooperating and resolving conflicts at different stages of development, their concept of responsibility between self and other grows in complexity. Along the way it takes into account samenesses, differences, limitations, preferences, and equity. Incorporating the Golden Rule into conscience keeps all of us searching for ways to be fair and caring in uncharted moral waters.

At the External stage, parents demand and show pleasure in small episodes of Golden Rule behavior in sibling and playmate interactions. We commend sharing and generosity. We allow noisy peer negotiations up to the point of harm, frustration, or our own intolerance. We mediate conflicts by showing egalitarian, empathic concern; facilitating moral listening and negotiating; or offering a menu of moral suggestions. When all else fails, we resort to authority-mandated fairness.

At the Brain-Heart stage, our seven-to-eleven-year-old children become more independent in pursuit of the Golden Rule. Having a friend requires niceness. Dealing with meanness is a challenge. Sometimes a child justifies responding to meanness with niceness if the other child is younger and lacking in understanding. Ignoring meanness, as recommended by adults, doesn't always work. Responding to meanness with meanness may teach a lesson about why not to be mean. Some days meanness grows from mischief, especially when an authority figure isn't keeping order. Contagious meanness in a group can lead to real harm.

Expanding concepts about time and space affect Golden Rule thinking at the Personified stage. Emerging adolescents are more patient when niceness isn't immediately reciprocated. They can speculate on acceptable excuses and forgivability. Conscience is now conceptualized as an interiorized friend. This calls for an interiorized Golden Rule: Be the kind of person your conscience would want to think of kindly. In the exterior world, self-consciousness is a moral concern. Other people may think that pursuing goodness in public is weird. Moral secrecy may be the solution.

At the Confused stage, our fourteen-to-fifteen-year-olds are mainly concerned about caring and fairness within groups. Loyalty becomes an important moral issue. Do unto others in the group as you would have others in the group do for you. Do for the group what you would like the group to do for you. Consciousness of group similarities and differences leads, eventually, to respect for group diversity. Prosocial activities are chosen to enhance the moral reputation of the group. These activities may be seen as an investment in the future of the community.

At the Integrating stage of conscience development, our sixteen-to-seventeen-year-olds begin to comprehend universal human rights. The "others" in "do unto others . . . " means absolutely everybody—all of humanity. It takes courage to take a moral stance in behalf of all people. It may involve peer criticism. However, like a chain reaction, one person's actions eventually affect all others. Including everybody leads to the concept of unconditional caring. Universal caring becomes the definition of fairness, even if it is only a hope or a dream. Unconditional caring may mean personal sacrifice. Conceiving an ideal Golden Rule and living by it are two different things. People are fallible and courage is limited.

THE STORY SO FAR

Our definition of conscience now includes a basic sense of human connectedness; moral-emotional responsiveness; respect for authority and authority-derived moral wisdom; and a Golden Rule for understanding fairness and caring among equals. In the next chapter, we will add self-derived values and will power.

Developing Moral Willpower

6

In this chapter, we explore the developing relationship between self and conscience. We examine how children develop self-worth; how self-worth becomes an obligation of conscience; and how children develop moral willpower. *Moral willpower* is using personal choice to follow, not follow, or temper the guidance of conscience. The effect of willpower on conscience development has been interwoven into discussions in previous chapters. Now we bring willpower into full focus.

Children value living from the very beginning. Survival instincts give infants a kick-start in expressing their needs and asserting their wills. Life appears to value life, even at pre-conscious levels. Conscious discovery of self-worth comes through being loved and cared for as well as through discovering the pleasure of being in the world. Our parenting efforts to induce compliance and pleasing are always balanced by our children's efforts to be themselves and to discover the world on their own terms.

Very young children explore, learn, enjoy, and create with vigor. When frustrated, they fuss, fume, fight, and flee with vigor. Gradually, we parents learn how to comfort or curtail their fussing, fuming, fighting, and fleeing. Gradually, our children accept help with their exploring, examining, enjoying, and creating. With further help, they develop skills, mastery, and self-control. These abilities add power to their sense of self-worth and willpower.

Children grow up to have their own ideas about how the world ought to be and how they ought to live in it. As their moral vision broadens and sharpens, they actively choose which behaviors they will restrain, whom they will please, what virtues they will pursue, and how they will measure moral satisfaction. Gradually, they assume responsibility for being persons of conscience. As persons of conscience, they decide when they want to accept life as it is and when they want to work at change.

Now let's go through the relationship between self and conscience, self-worth and willpower, in more detail.

AUTONOMY AND WILL

WILLFUL ACTIONS: ME DO

When a child is born, we are captivated by the miracle of this new life. We affirm the worth of this precious human being by bestowing a carefully selected name, a gender role, and other messages of specialness generously intermixed with hopes and dreams for the future. We also come to appreciate our child's own statement of worth as she begins to assert preferences and demonstrate willfulness. Disappointed or pleased, accepting or amazed, or experiencing some combination of these feelings, we come to appreciate that, to a greater or lesser extent, this child is as this child wills to be.

Contrasting photo images of child-as-angel and child-as-Imp express our parental ambivalence about autonomy and will. All dressed up, sitting still and looking perfect, is the child-as-angel picture we mail to grandparents. However, a video of our child in action, getting into things, demanding this and refusing that, manipulating us alternately with temper and with cuteness, portrays with greater accuracy our child-as-Imp. In a particular family scrapbook, two-year-old Will is pictured innocently looking at the camera while plunging a finger into his sister's birthday cake. Imp and young child have a strong bond.

"Me do" is an early expression of willpower. Transforming "me do" into "me do what me ought to do" moralizes willpower. Children's initial compliance with adult authority depends mostly on the parents' will. Committed compliance with parent values comes with our children's exercise of moral choice. Inspiring child will to move in a moral direction is an art in parenting. More anxious children respond best to gentleness in parent demands and reprimands. Bolder children respond best to our appreciation of their spontaneous efforts to please. Gradually, our children internalize parent values, process them with their own values on their own time schedules, and then willfully choose what courses they will follow, situation by situation.

Ms. Bolton, a skilled preschool teacher, always acknowledged the autonomy of her four-year-old students. "You be the boss" was her frequent statement when urging compliance with her sit-in-the-circle-and-be-quiet routines. She affirmed each child as boss of his own body parts. The children usually responded to her gentle requests that they sit still, keep their hands to themselves, close their mouths, and open their ears. Once in a while, sternness was required. Rarely, physical holding had to be done. Each child's effort at restraint was praised. When they were all quiet and attentive, Ms. Bolton's committed compliance came into play. She demanded of herself that each story and activity be an absolutely captivating performance.

SELF-CONSCIOUSNESS: I SEE ME

The establishment of self-concept (knowing who I am) precedes the development of self-consciousness (knowing or wondering whether I am doing right or wrong). Imitating an Impish but harmless procedure of psychologists who have studied self-concept, place a dab of rouge on a toddler's cheek, then ask him to look in a mirror. If he tries to remove the rouge from the mirror's surface, self-concept may not yet be developed—the blemish belongs to the mirror. If he tries, instead, to remove the ruddy spot from his own cheek, seemingly ashamed of the blemish, self-concept is present. Adding a bit of self-evaluation to self-concept results in ready-to-be-moralized self-consciousness.

POWER PRONOUNS: I AND ME; ME AND YOU

Personal moral narratives involve the "I" and the "me." "I" evaluates "me." Our very young, "me do" children are not capable of self-evaluation. They know they are good only because we tell them so. In time, they understand that "I" do things, while things happen to "me." Later, we challenge them with "Why did you let that happen to you?" or "Why did you do that to me?" Still later, they will ask such questions of themselves. We want each of our children to have a courageous moral "I." We want them to make sound moral choices.

In adulthood, exercising moral choice involves using our observing, critiquing self to evaluate our self-in-action. Conscience is an observing and critiquing moral monitor. Its demands and prohibitions make for lively internal debates and choices. We may consider it friend or enemy, helper or nuisance. Or we may feel it needs an overhaul.

NEGATION: I WILL NOT; YOU WILL NOT

Negation may be our children's first volitional act. Deliberately spitting out mashed carrots is an act of will. A toddler late to acquire speech uttered his first word when he was nearly two. It was a clear and firm "NO!" Why mess with preliminaries when you can go straight to what is important, expressing your own will? The same child responded to a neighbor boy's presence in his backyard by standing behind the screen door of the porch, repeating loudly, "Tyler, you can't come in." Tyler didn't want to come in. He wanted to play in the sandbox: "Michael, you can't come out." Two negating minds asserted their respective wills. Side-by-side guarding of their respective territories was their chosen form of cooperation.

Negation is an act of preference long before it becomes a moral refusal. Likewise, want-to-do and will-do precede ought-to-do. Once moral learning brings oughtness into place, dedication to rules can be quite literal and forceful. A six-year-old first-grader, Amanda, having just been exposed to the "Just say NO" component of a drug education program, remonstrated vigorously when her mother ordered a margarita at Chi Chi's. "Just say NO, Mommy, just say NO!" Amanda had willfully chosen to join the "Just say NO" campaign.

CONTROL: GRASPING AND DISPOSING

Imagine being the parent in this scene. Dad has just placed his adorable older infant, Jamie, in the high chair. Dad places toys on the tray to amuse Jamie while he warms his son's food. Jamie repeatedly holds onto the toys, smiles gleefully, and lets them drop to the floor. He looks at Dad with wide open eyes, anticipating that Dad will pick up the toys. Dad does. If he doesn't, Jamie cries and pounds on the tray. The routine is repeated until Dad feels like he needs a back support. Jamie has Dad, his toys, and gravity under his control.

Dad becomes annoyed with this game, believing that control is in the wrong hands. Parents should be in charge of lessons about gravity. He doesn't think it's right for Jamie to manipulate him. He knows it's too early in development to pound home a rule about not throwing. He could ignore Jamie's behavior and disengage from the game. But he doesn't really want to do that —not because he can't tolerate hearing Jamie cry and pound while Dad extinguishes this unwanted behavior, but because he wants to stay engaged in interaction with his son. After all, every minute counts in a parent-infant lifetime.

Manufacturers of infant toys know this dilemma well. So we buy their toys with suction cups on them. We hope that strike-down-and-watch-it-bounce-back will produce as much pleasure as throw-it-down-and-watch-Dad-bounce-it-back. We feel very clever to be able to remove ourselves from the control game while still giving our children something to control. There's a catch, though: Kiddie crackers and cookies don't come with suction cups. We'll have to protest over that kind of throwing. Perhaps we'll ignore cookie throwing and refuse to replace them: "All gone!" Surely we'll do something to reverse the direction of control. Germs are handy. They give us a child-protective duty to assert firmness and take control. That will prepare us for being on the controlling end of other games soon to emerge, like write-on-the-walls, lost-my-shoes, and let's-run-into-the-street.

To control something—a ball, a paintbrush, a sailboat—is a powerful pleasure. To control something in someone else's hands—toys being picked up by a child, shoes being tied by a parent, anniversaries being remembered by a spouse, or a special concern being remembered by an elected official—can be an even more powerful pleasure. A person in control invites respect from others.

Words of control, power assertion, and efficacy permeate our moral language. We *hold* tenaciously to our beliefs, *rise* bravely to the occasion, *stand up* for our rights, go on the *march,* or *strike back* at the enemy. When our energies are spent or we develop different purposes, we *let go.* It all begins with childhood stubbornness. Therefore, when on a selective basis we honor our very young children's "NOs" and throw-aways, we may be nurturing their future moral willpower.

SELF-DOUBT AND SHAME

Self-consciousness brings forth doubt, self-doubt, and shame. Will, our boy captured on camera with his finger deep in his sister's birthday cake, will soon move from a position of innocent pleasure to questioning the goodness or rightfulness of his actions. He will soon become aware that other people are judging his actions. Self-doubt will arise. If his moral antennae pick up a judgment of wrongness, shame will be aroused. The scrapbook picture recorded him in position one, innocence. Positions two and three, self-doubt and shame, are not Kodak moments. Self-doubt and shame do not like to meet the camera's eye. As an adult, he will enjoy thinking of himself in position one and laugh at the picture.

The clash of innocent and Impish autonomy with shame and doubt forms a developmental crisis that was first described by the child psychoanalyst Erik Erikson. His clinical studies led him to postulate a series of normal developmental crises in which an individual is confronted with opposing forces requiring resolution. Each resolution leads to more psychological maturity. He identified the crisis of *autonomy versus shame and doubt* as emerging during the second and third years of life. Here we highlight the moral aspects of Erikson's scheme of psychological maturation.

During the developmental crisis of autonomy versus doubt and shame, our children's self-awareness, me-looking-at-me-doing-something-fun, changes from playful autonomy to doubt, self-doubt, and shame. Doubt induces intellectual curiosity: "Can I make this [toy, person, etc.] do what I want done?" Self-doubt introduces the moral dimension: "Should I be doing this?" Self-consciousness opens the issue to the observing world's judgment. "What do others think of me when I do this?" A harmful activity accentuates self-doubt and shame: "Vases break! I was told not to touch it." Sensitivity to others' behavior may do it: "No one else has her finger in the cake." Sheer wonder may do it: "Why is everyone looking at me? Is there something wrong with what I'm doing? Am I bad?"

Doubt and self-doubt herald intellectual and moral curiosity: "What happens when I mix this substance with that substance? Is it good or bad to do so? Why?" In particularly bold children, investigation may be the prominent learning mode. Telling them not do something only feeds their curiosity. For shyer children, anticipating approval or disapproval may guide their investigations. Both modes of investigation are important. Intellectual discovery invariably leads to moral questions. Remember the atom bomb!

CRITICAL MOMENTS IN NURTURING MORAL WILLPOWER

Episodes of self-doubt and shame are critical moments for moral learning. Our children's typical response to self-doubt is to socially reference their parents. They peer at us inquisitively, as if to ask, "Have I done something wrong? Tell me what to do." When a harmful consequence has occurred—a burned hand, a broken collarbone—soothing our children is our best response. The incident is self-teaching. An "I told you not to" statement is unnecessary. Gentleness and empathy with the pain lets our children know that we are sorry when they have to learn "the hard way." Shaming a shame-filled child only leads to emotional disaster. When shame spills over into feelings of anger and retaliation, moral progress goes into reverse. Being humiliated prompts deceptive justifications, and may feed an antisocial will.

Pretend that the flash of the camera awakened Will's moral curiosity. "Why is someone taking a picture of me doing this?" thinks Will. "Why are my sister's guests all snickering?" If his action is met with an approving response, let's say chuckling forgiveness, embarrassment will be his primary emotion. However, if Will receives messages with overtones of annoyance, disgust, disappointment, or frank disapproval, shame will mount.

Shame is an emotion of acute sensitivity. If his parents vigorously disapprove of fingers in birthday cakes, especially someone else's, self-conscious Will may run for cover, leaving a trail of frosting behind him. Or if distressed to the point of feeling retaliatory, he may mess up the whole cake. Either way, he will probably be a more restrained child at the next birthday party. Something inside him is beginning to morally assess cake-investigating behavior. Self-doubt and shame are beginning to trigger his moral willpower.

Although we hate to see any child uncomfortable, we parents may feel relief at the appearance of self-doubt, shame, and social referencing—looking to us for instruction. Monitoring a free-spirited toddler's every move is taxing.

Inducing compliance from the little Imp wears us out. We welcome our children's self-doubt—that is, unless it's overdone and turns into obsessive worry. We welcome shame—unless it turns into mortification. The parenting challenge is how to gently mold our children's self-doubt and shame toward the pursuit of goodness.

SHAME AND SHAMING

Shame is like salt; there can be too much or too little. When a child has a shame overload, parents must respect the resulting pain. One Fourth of July, six-year-old Tyrone participated in a club swim meet. His goggles came off during his one and only event. He finished last. He pleaded with his parents not to tell their adult friends at the party they were going to after the meet. The parents laughed in surprise at this concern. To Tyrone, their laughter was humiliating. His feelings were very, very hurt. Apologies and soothing were in order. His parents soberly soothed him until he was out of the room. Then they burst into laughter again.

Sometimes children benefit from shame induction. A classroom volunteer was reading to some kindergarten children. He noticed that they were paying a lot of attention to each other, but not to the story. They giggled, talked, and acted silly to the point that the volunteer felt he had lost control of the group. His wonderment turned to frustration and then to disgust. He threw the book down and said he was getting their teacher. When the teacher arrived, the story came out. A boy sitting next to the reader was pretending to be very interested in the story while making bunny ears over the volunteer's head. Impish autonomy was in need of moralization.

The teacher rose to the occasion with a magnificent show of moral outrage. Among other strong statements, she told the children that she was ashamed of their behavior and directed them to sit at the library tables with heads down. A few of them cautiously peered up from the head-down position to check expressions on the adults' faces. They were probably worried that notes would go home to their parents. Adults held their faces in stone-like poses of disgust. At the next reading session, the children were very, very good. They restrained the Imp's influence magnificently.

The power of shaming depends on the strength of attachment between the shamer and the shamed. Miss Douglas, an art teacher, was a legendary woman of will in the high school where she taught. She had snowy white hair and a penchant for wearing flaming red dresses, and she took patriotic pride in demanding that all of her students learn the second verse of the "Star-Spangled Banner." She commanded her class with long speeches containing before-the-fact praise. She was of the persuasion that predicting behavior would make it occur. She stated that *all* of her students *always* became so absorbed in their work that she could leave the room at any time and they would go right on working. Principals, superintendents, and dignitaries from far places had been impressed!

One day, after all of her students had mastered the second verse of the "Star-Spangled Banner" and were allowed to resume their art projects, Miss Douglas left the room. Upon her return, she caught one ninth-grade girl talking to her easelmate. "Ellie, I am so ashamed of you for marring the reputation of this class." As Miss Douglas glared and made more shame-inducing statements, her target failed to become humiliated. In fact, it was all the girl could do to keep a straight face. She wanted to burst out laughing because, since her name wasn't Ellie, she couldn't possibly deserve all of this shaming. She controlled her laughter muscles enough to get through the lecture. She did become more careful about talking when Miss Douglas was out of the classroom. However, she didn't feel ashamed, and her restraint was not a moral conviction. Years later, she wondered if people with multiple personalities felt like this when the wrong "personality" in them was being addressed.

Mild shaming incidents often induce amusement in bystanders. A grandparent watching a stone-faced parent shame a big-eyed child over a relatively minor misdeed is an example. The grandparent feels an internal tension because she identifies with both sides in this moral teaching session. She identifies simultaneously with the parent's desire to raise a good child and the child's desire to maintain allegiance with the Imp. The grandparent would like to put her fingers in the cake right along with the child. In contrast, severe shaming situations induce severe discomfort in bystanders. Watching a stressed-out parent unmercifully shame a child in public is unbearable.

VALUING THE SELF

Our infants come wired to value their own survival. Watch a baby aggressively mouth a nipple as if competing for a world championship. It is we parents, however, who affirm our children's goodness. Children first value themselves because we value them. By the time their autonomy meets self-doubt and shame, we need to step up the pace of our affirmations. We do so with words, emotions, and deeds.

Self-worth is an unstable belief. If it were a sturdier belief, "self-" words wouldn't be so frequent in our language. We speak of needing more self-confidence, self-control, or self-esteem. We want a better self-image. We read self-improvement books. When self-valuing goes sour, we speak of self-effacement, self-degradation, or self-destruction.

SELF-INTEREST

Self-interest is a nasty term. We sometimes accuse our older children or teenagers of being interested only in themselves. We suspect grown-ups' altruism when it receives glitzy recognition. Yet focus on the self is necessary to build and maintain energy, especially moral energy. We are certainly not much good for others when our energy is depleted. Energy depletion make us just want to let the world go by. Remaining de-energized for prolonged periods of time invites cynicism, callousness, and moral apathy.

Envision a moral value triangle in which obligations to authority, self, and others exist in dynamic tension. We build energy for moral investment in others when we attend to our own

THE ADVOCATE

Excessive shaming produces anger and defiance in children rather than the moral conviction to be good. Excessive shaming is a form of emotional abuse. But shaming the shamer only make matters worse. People who report to or work in Child Protective Services meet this challenge to restraint everyday. Abusing parents are excessive shamers. Temporarily removing a child from a shaming situation while simultaneously directing parents toward therapeutic resources is the ideal goal. Such parents need to be soothed and taught to adopt parenting methods that involve milder doses of shame. They need to learn tolerance and forgiveness. They need to discover self-tolerance and self-forgiveness.

nurturance, health, learning, and creativity. We nurture moral energy in our children when we allow them time for self-soothing, rest, and free play.

SPONTANEOUS MORAL ENGAGEMENT

With energy restored, we become more aware of our surroundings, including wrongdoing and neediness in others: "What can I do to help?" Energy renewal moves us toward spontaneous moral engagement. Young children always have energy for moral engagement. A two-year-old reaches out to comfort another crying child, plays the clown to make a depressed parent laugh, becomes disturbed over something that is broken. When young children become frustrated, they look to their parents for help. They lean on our supply of energy and beg for our moral engagement.

CLASHES OF WILL

Willpower requires energy. A young child's will is playful, innocent, investigative, and engaging. A parent's will is naturally protective, watchful, committed, instructive, and admonishing. On highly charged days, a parent's electrified will may become overprotective, excessively emotional, overly goal-determined, harshly instructive, demoralizing, or abruptly forceful. In response, a child's humiliated will may then become sour, entrenched, irritable, or destructive. In adolescence, it may become *dangerously* destructive.

We do not want life with our children to be a clash of wills. We want to share a common goodwill. Parent-child goodwill involves a gradual transfer of responsibility from parent to child. How gradual a transfer is the tricky part.

TEMPTATION AND FREE WILL

Temptation and free will are universally pitted against each other in moral narratives. Recall the Old Testament Garden of Eden story. Imagine Adam and Eve as innocent children, God as parent, and the snake as tempter. Playful, innocent Adam and Eve lost their innocence when they investigated the fruit of the Tree of Knowledge of Good and Evil.

Doubt, self-doubt, and shame transformed them into intellectually curious, morality-seeking beings. God, sustaining a protective, instructive, but confrontational style in the story, cast them out of the Garden before they could get into any more trouble. He set their limits! "No trespassing" signs were posted. If they had been allowed to stay, they might have stolen the secret of everlasting life from the Tree of Life. That would have empowered them beyond their ability to handle it.

After being booted out of the Garden, Adam and Eve and all of their descendants would forever long for a paradise of absolute goodness. Getaway vacation advertisements would tempt them forever. They had to learn how to deal with curiosity and temptation on a moral journey of their own. They continued to have the freedom to "just say no" or "just say yes" as their growing wisdom directed them.

As mythical descendants of Adam and Eve, parents have a lot of free will in child-rearing. Some of us respond to this challenge by being very willful parents. Some of us are very permissive parents. Overly willful parents operate from a power base of self-righteousness. They act as though they have already tasted the Tree of Knowledge. Excessively weak parents operate from a dream state of innocence and playfulness. They act as if they were still living in the Garden. Here we will deliberately over-dramatize these two extremes to show that in the extreme, neither position works out very well.

PARENTS EMBLAZONED WITH CERTAINTY AND POWER

Very willful parents try to protect their youngsters from learning from the Tree of Knowledge of Good and Evil on their own. Their parenting messages are fiercely protective and dictatorial. They know in no uncertain terms what is good for their children. When crossed by repeated child willfulness, particularly during adolescence, they will cast their children out the door — as soon as the law allows. "When you're out of this house, you can do anything you want. As long as you are under my roof, you will do as I say." These parents scream, shame, forbid, and punish. They bind, hand and foot, their children's desires to make their own moral choices.

PARENTS ENCHANTED WITH FREEDOM AND INNOCENCE

In contrast, extremely permissive parents are enchanted by their children's innocence, free spirits, and investigative natures. They dance with the Imp. They relish the notion that doubt leads to discovery and inventiveness, but they find the idea of their children experiencing self-doubt and shame abhorrent. They are love-and-peace parents. They affirm their children, as well as any other child found under their roof, incessantly. Their love knows no boundaries. Their children know no limits.

Love- and peace-enchanted parents may become morally outraged over the fact that the Garden of Eden is being destroyed by pollution, herbicides, and mismanagement of soil, water, and wildlife. Beyond Garden issues, however, they want their children to be absolutely free of encumbering, civilizing practices. They minimize the importance of household routines, incessant lessons, status-seeking peer groups, competition, and team spirit. They do admire virtuous striving and spontaneous goodness. They know no prejudice, but occasionally despair over people who don't agree with them. Commitment to peace hides overt anger in hostile dreams, where they unconsciously throw hard-to-love people out of the Garden again and again. Peace-and-love parents have problems integrating good and evil. Their children have trouble figuring out the moral distinction between feeling good and being good. As teenagers, they get lost in relativism. When they reach adulthood, they often go looking for revealed truth. Religious fundamentalists wait eagerly to hand them this truth.

DOWN-THE-MIDDLE PARENTS

Most of us parents chart an uneven course between these two extreme positions. We strive to balance our will with our children's will. We want to influence their will in ways that build respect for both of our generations as well as our mutual heritage from the past. We respect our children's curiosity and doubt as we variously safeguard their explorations with enclosures, fire extinguishers, helmets, or knee pads. We value their pleas for freedom, but we keep linking freedom to responsibility. We consider self-doubt and shame to be moralizing opportunities to gently teach them our views about good and bad, right and wrong. We set limits, establish consequences, and passionately speak our minds when we are upset. We are pleased when we see our children develop anticipatory anxiety over wrongdoing. We want them to feel bad when they have done something wrong, but we want that feeling to emanate from their own hearts, not ours. We expect reparation. We are willing to forgive. We want them to learn from experience. We want them to take pleasure in an ever-developing moral wisdom. We want them to use their willpower for moral restraint and action.

Down-the-middle parents strive to balance their child-rearing practices in ways that give equal weight to respecting authority, peers, and self. Each family develops its own ways of establishing order and hierarchy, teaching skills, developing routines of fairness and caring, encouraging spontaneous goodness and virtue, prioritizing responsibilities, groping with moral complexity, and fostering individual decision-making. No parents have ever found the perfect formula for teaching children how to honor their parents, their siblings, and themselves simultaneously without experiencing tension and making mistakes. Whatever course we parents take, we expect our adult children, when their autonomy has fully matured, to alter or improve upon the course we have laid out for them. The Imp notes that our assessment of our children's maturity always lags a little behind their own assessment.

We will now look at how children and adolescents describe autonomy, will, self-doubt, shame, self-evaluation, and moral responsibility in their own words.

DEVELOPMENTAL CONSIDERATIONS

DEVELOPING MORAL WILLPOWER AT THE EXTERNAL STAGE (0–6 YEARS)

Life Valuing Life

Looking at a struggling plant in the garden, we say with anthropomorphic license, "You are really trying hard to live!" A child's scabby knee shows us nature's healing work in progress. After nursing a pet through a final illness, we note that he "put up a good fight." Anxiously watching a relative with lung problems come off of a respirator in a hospital intensive care unit, we marvel at her struggle to breathe on her own. Each of these examples illustrates nature's commitment to survival. We could call it natural willpower.

Interviewer: What are your best reasons for taking care of animals?

Young child: So they can live.

Affirmed Goodness

Our very young children come to know their goodness through parent affirmations. They also begin to judge themselves in comparison to others who are also recipients of parent affirmation. Listen to these siblings' comparative analyses:

Interviewer: What are all the good things about you?

Young child: I'm better than [brother]. He's bad and I'm good.

Interviewer: Were you born good or bad?

Another YC: I was born good because my mom had two boys and she wanted a girl and she finally had one.

Interviewer: Were you born good or bad?

Another YC: Both good and bad. When [younger brother] was in my mom's stomach, he wasn't good because we were climbing on him and he was kicking on us. I didn't think it felt good on my mom because it was like boom, boom, boom. My mom was pregnant so we climbed on [younger brother]. He didn't like that.

Interviewer: Do you think you kicked on your mom when you were in your mom's stomach?

YC: Yeah, like boom, boom, boom.

Me Valuing Life: Having Fun and Being Safe

When clinicians interview a child who is reluctant to be interviewed, the safest question to ask is, "What do you do for fun?" Moody children may look away in irritation because they aren't having any fun. Anxious children may give shyly expressed, hope-you-approve answers. Stubborn children may stick to their answer of "Nothin'." Children with conduct disorders may provocatively tell about one of their risk-taking deeds. Universally, children indicate that having fun is their childhood right. We believe that this is their way of saying that they value their own lives.

Interviewer: What are your best reasons for having fun?

Child: Having fun is—just being a kid. It's what you're supposed to do.

Morality and fun become integrated in play. Give a three-year-old some toy people and ask him to make up something about children being good or bad. Ask him to show grownups being good or bad. If he's in the mood, he will readily perform. If he feels that we are interfering with play-in-progress or getting too close to his self-consciousness button, he will refuse. Later, he may do it out of his own free will. Play helps our children consolidate values from parent-directed routines. They take command of those values as they play out different consequences. They exercise moral willpower in their play. Facilitating play is a conscience-nurturing activity. Parents who see themselves portrayed in play may choose to modify their parenting style.

An emotionally safe environment is necessary for play to be free, creative, self-revealing, and self-instructive. Unsafe conditions, particularly those involving maltreatment or chronic hardship, result in play that is survivalistic, defensive, and stifled. Having fun and being afraid are diametrically opposed. Games of fear and terror come out of drastically unsafe conditions. Games of fairness and caring come out of environments permeated with adult protection and emotional support.

We create an emotionally safe environment for our children by enforcing rules of safety, protecting them from violent television programs, monitoring sibling fights, resolving most spousal conflict out of earshot and view of the children, and commending them when they transform their own emotional unrest and aggressive actions into even-tempered words or play. After a traumatic experience, we comfort them and listen attentively when they choose to tell and retell the scary events. Our sustaining and comforting presence helps them build defenses that distance them from trauma, affirm their basic goodness, assure their current safety, and help them think brightly about the future.

Mirror, Mirror, on the Wall

Self-evaluation precedes the development of moral willpower. External stage children evaluate themselves in terms of their ability to get attention and approval. Physical attributes and size capture their interest.

Interviewer: What are all the good things about you?

Young child: I'm the tallest and the toughest one here.

Interviewer: Tell me all of the good [bad] things about you.

Another YC: I don't like the color of my hair. I wish my teeth were straight.

Although these criteria appear to be outside the realm of morality, they are building blocks of self-worth. A special challenge exists for children whose bodies are different from others in cosmetic or functional ways. They may need added doses of basic affirmation from their parents to buoy up their reasons to self-affirm. The way we express that affirmation is very important. It should be genuine, natural, and free of negative feelings about having a physically or functionally imperfect child. Our children's self-worth will not thrive if they sense that we are pitying them. Neither will it thrive if they see us become ashamed, demeaning, or nasty toward people who ask curious questions.

Facing facts imbues self-worth with courage. David Roche, a San Francisco therapeutic storyteller—who happens to have a large vascular malformation covering one side of his face—was invited to talk with a group of children and adolescents with cranio-facial abnormalities at Camp About Face. Gathered in a shelter by the lake, he prompted these campers to ask in unison, "What happened to your face?" Then he told them—matter-of-factly. He showed them how to face that question. Then he told other parts of his life story, emphasizing "moments of grace." He defined a moment of grace as a time when a seemingly impossible-to-open door of opportunity does open. An example was his first mutually desired boy-girl kiss. If he had been self-pitying, self-effacing, ashamed, and afraid, he might have fled from this op-

---

THE ADVOCATE

All children deserve a safe environment in which to play. Protecting our precious children from those children who are growing up defensively and defiantly in environments unsafe for play only delays our children's eventual encounters with them and their dire circumstances. What harms one child's life harms all children. Our parenting responsibilities extend to the community. We exercise community responsibility when we work to keep guns and drugs away from all children; when we teach or coach; when we remove lead from soil and houses; when we say, "That's enough television for today"; when we search for alternatives to child labor around the world; when we support UNICEF or the Children's Defense Fund; when we—you fill in the blanks; you know the needs of your community. If we exercise moral willpower by making the world a safer playground, our children may take up the responsibility for the next generation.

portunity, thinking, "I'm too ugly." Instead, he seized the opportunity. He had been schooled in self-worth and readiness to ally with others who were smart enough to value him.

Willing Restraint

Children are spontaneous and energetic. We teach our children how and when to restrain these characteristics in behalf of moral concern for others. There are times to ask, "What happened to your face?" and times not to ask. A child once told her grandparent at the family dinner table, "We were trying and trying to find someone to come over for dinner. We couldn't find anyone, so we called you." Innocence is invariably honest.

Some restraint is a natural part of survival:

Interviewer: Why don't you hit your sister back?

Young child: If she does hit me, I don't hit her back 'cause she'll probably beat me up or something.

Restraint in behalf of survival is vital to life valuing life. Other restraining efforts are directed toward living up to a standard of goodness.

Interviewer: How do you keep yourself good?

Young child: I walk around in the store and keep my mouth shut.

Interviewer: Any other way?

YC: I keep my hands in my pockets.

Restraint often defines "being good" at the External stage. Just as our very young children seem to say "no" many more times than "yes" or "yes, please," they consciously put effort into a morality of restraint sooner than a morality of virtue. Virtuous behavior does occur at young ages. However, these niceties are more likely to be spontaneous rather than the result of ongoing effort.

The Imp thrives on sibling rivalry. However, when Impish foolishness gets out of hand, it also must be restrained.

Interviewer: Tell me all of the good [bad] things about you.

Young child: Sometimes I think that I wanna—um—call my friends and invite 'em over for a bad party. We'll call my sister "stupid."

Interviewer: Do you do it?

YC: No, not really.

Interviewer: Why not?

YC: Mom wouldn't think it was nice.

Interviewer: Any other reason?

YC: I guess it wouldn't be nice.

Memories of Mom's opinions guide this child's moral choice. Mom's rule, "Be nice," is very close to becoming a self-chosen moral rule.

Rewarding Restraint

The more curious, spontaneous, or downright impulsive our youngsters are, the more effort they have to put into restraint. Walking around in a store while not touching anything probably doesn't make our children think about what good museum patrons they will be someday. Sometimes they need immediate rewards for their effort.

A nagging question that children invariably and repeatedly ask on a long car trip is "Are we there yet?" Some parents brace themselves for this nagging question by bringing along a carload of entertainment. Others nag back. Clinicians particularly enjoy working with parents who agree to co-design behavioral strategies. One such set of parents contracted with their hyperactive twelve-year-old son, Ben, for incremental amounts of spending money for each hour that he did not pester them with the how-much-longer question during a twenty-plus-hour drive from Michigan to Florida.

The incentive challenged and satisfied Ben. The parents also found it to be much more satisfying than playing the cow-counting game or constantly reprimanding him. Emotional harmony between Ben and his parents was maintained throughout the trip. Attachment was also facilitated because the parents had to listen for possible slip-ups and Ben had to pay attention to whether they would count any near slip-ups. The Imp got Ben to vocalize, "Are we there yet?" with his mouth closed. Family goodwill turned this trickery into a fun-filled game.

Bribery or Behavioral Management?

Some parents call a reward-based contract with a child good management. Others call it bribery. Parents who see these contracts as good behavioral management usually say so in neutral tones. Their faces do not reflect strong emotions when describing their experiences, except for a smile of satisfaction when they report that a procedure worked well. They affirm that the negotiation was a win/win contract, with all parties getting something desired in a fair and equitable manner. Parent will and child will work together.

In contrast, parents who feel that behavioral contracts with children, whether involving money, possessions, or privileges, are somehow wrong may call them bribes, saying the word in disapproving tones. This perception of wrongness is related to a faulty sense of parent power. These parents say that children have a *duty* to respond to parental commands. If a child spontaneously chooses to be obedient for no better reason than being in a good mood that day, his parents get really demanding. They reason that if he can choose to be good once, he can do it all the time! If he didn't rock his chair back and forth at the table even once while Grandma was visiting, he can do it at every meal. They shouldn't have to bribe him into being good!

Parents who are sadistically power-hungry think of a behavioral contract as an offer a child can't refuse. Taking pride in their cleverness, they gleefully propose a "deal" to the child. That is, indeed, a bribe!

Alternatively, parents who despondently interpret child disobedience as a loss of parent power approach behavioral contracting as personal defeat. In tones of despair, they pronounce that exchanging goods for good behavior is absolutely wrong. However, since "nothing else has worked," they grudgingly give into that psychologist's silly ideas.

These disgruntled responses imply that children's moral willpower can be built only through submission to parent willpower. But fearful submission is not moral willpower. Self-chosen restraint is. Encouraging our children to assume authority over their goodness is more productive than keeping authority all to ourselves. When our children show spontaneous goodness, we should express appreciation. When they can't hold it together, we should be patient and forgiving until the right behavioral contract comes to mind.

A behavioral contract can be differentiated from a bribe in the following ways:

(1)   An effective contract with a child makes an offer that is in no way coercive. It preserves freedom of choice. It is not an offer the child "can't refuse."

(2)   The targeted behavior is one that both the child and the parents more or less agree should be changed.

(3)   The incentive is meaningful to the child at the child's developmental level. It is not so small that the child will feel demeaned nor so large that the child will feel undeserving. The incentive is not ridiculously excessive. Neither is it an embellishment of a basic right, for example, food, clothing, shelter, companionship, or age-appropriate freedoms.

In the example above, Ben approached the contract as a game. He and his parents had fun anticipating whether he and his hyperactive impulsiveness could handle the challenge. The ability to control his mouth was within his developmental reach. If his parents had suggested the same contract when he was seven years old, his attentional and impulsive difficulties would have defeated him—with or without Ritalin. The money he earned for self-control was an "extra." He would have had a fun time in Florida without it.

In contrast, a bribe is coercive and demeaning. The contract is lopsided. Parents are much more invested in the behavioral change than the child is. If the child complies, the parents' sense of power is rewarded, while the child feels ashamed, demeaned, or angry. The parent may rub salt into the wound by saying, "See, I told you that you could do it; you just weren't trying." The child may then cry out ragefully, "I was too trying!" or sink into stubborn silence. Or she may be gutsy enough to say under her breath, "I wouldn't do that if you gave me a million dollars!" While this struggle is going on, the Imp is sitting on the child's side of the power teeter-totter with weights on his ankles.

How do behavioral contracts or other procedures nurture conscience development? Does paying a child to keep his mouth shut facilitate the development of moral willpower? A "yes" answer, which ours is within the context of the above example, requires some explanation. If a child with a flapping tongue gets the hang of verbal restraint, it empowers him later—when he has more understanding—to refrain from saying things that hurt other people's feelings; bothering others while they are concentrating; blurting out secrets; tattling; or cursing and talking back to parents, teachers, coaches, referees, or other people in authority. With verbal restraint under control, the child will, in time, have more energy to express himself with words that are kind, humorous, helpful, instructive, or wise. The community will appreciate his training in articulated diplomacy if he chooses to exercise his First Amendment rights in public. The ultimate payoff for the parent is pride in a grownup child.

—— **ADVICE TO PARENTS** ————————————

Nurturing Moral Willpower at the External Stage (0–6)

- **Affirm your child's basic goodness.**

- **Create a safe environment for play. Encourage play. Take note of the moral themes incorporated into play. Enter into play with your child. Don't try to control the play; follow your child's lead.**

- **Use rewards to teach your child restraint. Choose restrain-**

ing tasks that your child is ready to master. Cheer success; in time, your child will find the cheering more rewarding than the trinket.

• **Model restraint.**

DEVELOPING MORAL WILLPOWER AT THE BRAIN-HEART STAGE (7–11)

Excesses in Restraint

Restraint centers our children's attention on the "do nots" in their lives. If moral willpower involved only restraint, our children might grow up to look like those see-no-evil, hear-no-evil, speak-no-evil monkey carvings. The Imp wouldn't enjoy himself at all. Comedians wouldn't have any fun-to-remember childhood antics as material for their routines. In order to keep comedy from dying out altogether, the Imp would have to work overtime enticing children to draw artful masterpieces on walls, walk along dangerous ledges, and fill the ears of grownups with embarrassing truth. If he couldn't make those temptations work once in a while, he would feel he wasn't earning his board and keep. He would have lost his moral purpose in life: balancing mischief and goodness in behalf of fun.

Skill Mastery: Doing It and Doing It Well

Mastery captures the interest of seven-to-eleven-year-old children: How many things can I learn to do, and how well can I do them? Can I learn to read well enough to retell the story? kick a ball well enough to be on the team? act well enough to be in the play? do my chores well enough to get my allowance?

Interviewer: What are all the good things about you?

Older child: I clean my room and make my bed.

Another OC: I'm good at reading, art, and sports; I'm not good at math, and I don't always do as I am told.

Another OC: I play piano well. I do my homework as soon as I get home.

Effort and Sufficiency

Mastery is linked to competition in our culture—competition with others and competition with self. Seeing what others can do sharpens our children's self-evaluations. Basic goodness isn't enough. They want to be good at _____ or better than _____. They ask themselves if they have tried hard enough.

When they are stressed, they complain that too much is expected of them. They come to know when they have tried hard enough through feeling fatigue, getting to a certain page in the text, or winning the award. In the midst of pressure from grownups and competition with peers, they carve out personal standards for effort and sufficiency. We must place our demands somewhere between their willingness and what we believe to be good for them. Some days, they just need to have fun.

Truth, Rules, and Boundaries

Games combine fun with opportunities to practice skills. Success may or may not involve winning. If winning is involved, the winner may be a single person, the team, or everybody who tries. Board games moralize the play life of seven-to-eleven-year-old children through procedures for handling lying, cheating, and stealing. Values for truth, rules, and boundaries undergird these procedures. Our children cannot lie without learning something about truth. They cannot cheat without learning something about rules. They cannot steal without learning something about boundaries. Moral standards for effort and sufficiency grow to include these values. Truth, rules, and boundaries give moral meaning to the maxim "It doesn't matter if you win or lose; it's how you play the game."

Don't Get Bored with Board Games

Board games are a favorite activity of children at the Brain-Heart stage of conscience development. Many of us parents cringe a little when we see a child approaching us with a Monopoly game. All of a sudden, we have sixty million reasons why "we'd just love to play, but _____." Perhaps we can revitalize the game-playing energy we had in our youth by thinking about games as a way to underscore the values of truth, rules, and boundaries. The game of Monopoly adds a built-in moral dilemma. Although the stated objective of the game values fairly pursued greed, the objective of most adult players is to end the game. Other than arbitrarily calling time, the most expedient method is to encourage spendthrift habits in all players. Thus the moral dilemma for adults.

Breaking Rules

School-age children define conscience growth as accumulating a bank of rules:

Interviewer: Does your conscience grow as you do?

Older child: [As you grow] your conscience gets smarter. You can think of rights and wrongs faster. You know more do's and don'ts because you've lived longer and you have more experience.

Rule-breaking upsets us parents. We are inclined to push harder for compliance. Sometimes we can approach the problem from another angle by discussing decision-making with our children. We'll explain with this example:

Interviewer: What are your best reasons for not obeying your parents?

Jason: Mostly I do what my parents ask—so they'll do things for me. But if they ask something that's really unreasonable, like not to go someplace that will cause no harm—like the park—I might go and just not tell them about it.

Jason bypassed the truth and boundary features of his parents' rule to make his own rule: "Go where you want to go, as long as you believe no harm will come from it." What should Jason's parents do when, let's say, Jason's little brother tells on him? Should they emphasize their authoritarian duty to make rules for him and his duty to follow them? Should they punish him? Or should they talk to Jason about the moral aspects of his willpower? how he makes decisions? what risks he takes when he acts on his own? what benefits come from independent choice? what values lie within his rules?

We don't have a "right" answer. The solution is tied to Jason's maturity, his overall respect for his parents, the dangerousness of the park, the maturity of his companions, and his style of learning. We do know that the more Jason feels free to participate in the discussion, the more he will learn about morality. Any time we engage our children in identifying and weighing the values inherent in their decision-making, we are supporting their moral willpower. They may even choose punishment as part of their solution.

When our children get the hang of moral choosing, perhaps they'll have the willpower of this youngster:

Interviewer: What are your reasons for not cussing?

Older child: You can be really cool and not cuss. Some of my friends cuss and they're really not that cool. Most of my friends don't cuss. It's just something I choose not to do.

ADVICE TO PARENTS ────────────────────────

Nurturing Moral Willpower at the Brain-Heart Stage (7–11)

- **Support skill development of all kinds.**
- **Help your child find balance between effort and sufficiency.**

- **Explore the values of truth, rule-following, and boundaries.**

- **Don't get bored with board games. There are moral lessons in playing them.**

- **Help your child construct his own rules.**

DEVELOPING MORAL WILLPOWER AT THE PERSONIFIED STAGE (12–13)

Private Self and Public Self: Another Moral Connection

Emerging adolescence is an exciting time. True, it was fun being a kid, but transforming into an adult-in-the-making is downright exhilarating. What is morally intriguing at this age is discovering the coexistence of a private life and public life. There is the self that a teenager knows himself to be—monitored carefully by his conscience—and the self that he presents to others—monitored carefully by parents, teachers, and friends. Living up to internal standards and maintaining a good reputation become dual motivators for assuming moral responsibility.

Interviewer: Why is it important to feel good about yourself?

Emerging teenager: If you don't feel good about yourself, you're not going to do it [follow an expectation]. If you say, "I can do this," then you're gonna do it.

Interviewer: Why should you hang out with the good crowd?

Another ET: You should hang out with the good crowd so you have a good reputation. If you hang out with the type of people that do drugs and stuff, they're gonna think you do it, even if you don't, because you hang around with those people.

It might seem that the watchful eye of an internal conscience combined with the desire to maintain a good reputation in the community would lead to moral perfection. Alas, perfection is never reached, because conscience, parents, friends, teachers, coaches, community, and individual all have slightly different expectations. Furthermore, all standard-bearers are fallible. Conflicted expectations bring our young adolescent to view moral living as a matter of virtuous striving.

Virtuous Striving

Emerging adolescents define rules of conscience as try-to-be-this (nice, generous, kind) and try-not-to-be-that (mean, selfish, rude). In earlier years, their rules were more absolute always-do-this and don't-ever-do-that statements. They are beginning to understand virtue and vice, moral striving and imperfectibility. A virtue is a category of goodness toward which we strive. Although younger children define and perform virtuous acts, they don't appreciate the elusiveness of virtue—how pursuing it can be likened to chasing a mirage on the highway. A vice is a category of badness that we work to eliminate or restrain. Younger children also know about vice. They don't know that avoidance involves a lifetime of effort.

Interviewer: What is good or bad about you?

Emerging teenager: I try to be fair and have good citizenship in sports.

Is There Virtue in Making a Bed?

Parents can squelch virtuous striving by getting over-determined about compliance. Among families who come into therapy, bed-making—or some other task involving cleanliness, orderliness, and timeliness—is a repeated source of family conflict. Bed-making can be a powerful symbol of many interrelated and conflicting values in a family. As teenagers' self-determination increases, conflicting values are accentuated. If bed-making is not an issue of contention in your family, substitute one that is in the following discussion.

What does bed-making symbolize? There are distinct generational differences. To parents, bed-making may represent normal compliance, respect for authority, respect for property, self-respect, orderliness, cleanliness, aesthetic appreciation, or . . . something too trivial to fret about. We may feel that beds made, grass mowed, or dishes washed are tension-reducing signs that our household is functioning smoothly. Everyone is doing his share to organize the chaos. Unmade beds may symbolize procrastination, laziness, slothfulness, or disrespect.

In contrast, the teenager may see bed-making as representative of little-kid obedience, a waste of time and effort, a meaningless task. A few teenagers will make their beds out of an inherent enjoyment of tidiness (the Imp rations these types one to a family). An unmade bed may represent autonomy, relaxation, freedom, and choice. Combined with other family issues causing emotional discomfort, an unmade bed may be one marker of defiance, insubordination, or downright insurrection. Or it may represent something too trivial to bother with.

Even when bed-making has been a long-established household routine-become-rule, an emerging teenager will probably rethink its meaning. At the

External stage, our children make their beds to please us and avoid negative consequences. Positive reinforcement makes it an accepted ritual. When consistently reinforced from an early age, bed-making and other chores are performed at the Brain-Heart stage as implicitly internalized rules. Periodic monitoring and reinforcement maintain the procedures. Our children can be challenged to improve quality and speed for minimum rewards, especially in competition with a sibling.

Duty, Virtue, and Autonomy

Beginning with the Personified stage of conscience development, bed-making is likely to be examined in terms of duty, virtue, and autonomy. When bed-making is an issue, a teenager asks herself, "Why am I letting my parents make me do this? What sense is there in doing something that is just going to be undone at the end of the day?" Thoughtful, caring, fair-minded parents then ask themselves, "Why am I making bed-making into an issue? What is important about this ritual?" In therapy sessions, moral motivation and will-power become the under-the-bed topics. Resolution then becomes a matter of a negotiated choice that brings duty, virtue, and autonomy into new balance. Contrasting points of view are described below.

MOTIVATORS FOR TEENAGE BED-MAKING

Duty

Dutiful compliance with non-essential tasks is an uncommon value in American culture for adults or children. Outside of camp or military school, emerging teenagers are not likely to think of duty as a good enough reason to make the bed. Therefore, if a teenager isn't being sent away to military school, other motivators will have to be sought.

Generosity and Other Virtues

Once virtue is worked into the discussion, oughtness is released from duty-bound meaning. It moves from the do-or-get-[punished, shamed, restricted] position to the want-to-because-I-am-a-[helpful, kind, generous]-person position. Virtue comes into focus. Bed-making can be conceptualized in this scenario as a favor or a gift. Now, favors and gifts usually don't come every day. They would lose their beyond-expectation generous meaning if they were habitual. Bed-making as gift-giving requires joyful initiative. Furthermore, favors and gifts are usually not extended to angry, demanding people, especially when they are parents. Therefore, if the favor or gift-giving rationale is pursued, parents need to learn to be smilingly grateful for what we receive, while removing it from the class of expected behavior.

Teenage-Initiated Contracts

Another bed-making motivator in adolescence stems from our teenagers' sense of initiative. They begin to offer us contracts. Earlier in childhood, we were usually the designers of such contracts. Now our teenagers begin to approach us with propositions like "If you'll drive me to [here and there], let me do [this and that], let [so and so] spend the night, I'll make my bed, your bed, my brother's bed, and [whatever else might be a convincing kindness]." Usually these offers can be shaped toward healthy win-win solutions—that is, unless we refuse to work with our teenagers' contracting initiatives and whine, "You only offer help when you want something!"

We may think that a bed-making contract is all about bed-making. Our teenagers may think that it's all about bed-making. It's time for a paradigm shift. As parents we need to start taking pride not in a bed well made, but in our teenagers' initiative and negotiation skills. When parents and adolescents each use willpower to the benefit of themselves and others, everyone is assuming moral responsibility. And the bed may get made, too!

MOTIVATORS FOR TEENAGE NON-BED-MAKING

Filing Disorder

Has your teenager been screened for filing disorder? Those afflicted with this age-confined disorder can remember where anything important is filed only when it is hidden under piles of stuff on the bedroom floor. They develop strange blind spots for objects in full view. If they are forced to neatly put things away, they can't find those items again. If we make the kindly intended mistake of putting things away for them, they will accuse us of losing, misplacing, or taking their things every time they can't find them.

The unique memory capacities associated with filing disorder appear to deteriorate with age. Only a few cases have been reported beyond the age of thirty. In addition to having filing disorder, our teenagers may claim that an unmade bed added to piles of stuff on the floor of the room is a statement of unique personality. Clutter helps them define themselves! What is confusing to adults is that, just as with their clothing, music, demeanor, and hair, this definition looks like a cloned copy of their friends' clutter. The only known treatment for this disorder is a closed bedroom door. With time, our teenagers will get lost in their own chaos and become annoyed with their own smells. Their unusual thinking will disappear through natural decay. They will emerge to see the light of day. Many parents have retreated into this distant, patient, but hopeful resolution.

Possessiveness and Property Rights

"It's my room! It's my bed; I'll make it when I'm ready!" These statements imply that the speaker or shouter is feeling not only willful, but possessive as well. Things must be very important to these teenagers. We could get into a debate with them over legal ownership, stewardship, loans, rental space, or gifts. We could show them the deed to our house. We could charge them rent in the form of bartered services—like bed-making.

Rather than engage in a battle over property rights, let's pretend that our teenagers do own their rooms. The right to own property is a principle of democracy. Pride in ownership generally means more attention given to upkeep. Acting like they own property in adolescence may be good training not only for future real ownership, but for development of how-to skills useful in working on community projects such as Habitat for Humanity. Perhaps we should encourage these highly possessive adolescents to develop whatever design-and-construct skills appeal to them—painting, building, refinishing, quilt-making, sewing, and so on—to create signature rooms of their own. Perhaps bed-making rules should get lost in pursuit of an artistic personal statement. A bedspread of the teen's own design may just have to be spread out neatly to get proper recognition.

What balance between duty, virtue, and willpower have you achieved in your family? Working out the balance is all part of nurturing moral responsibility.

Dialogues between Self and Conscience

Moral responsibility emerges from dialogues between self and conscience. When moral questions arise, we knock on conscience's door. We ponder why we did or didn't follow a certain course of action in the past. We brood over what we should do now. These dialogues accumulate in memory, especially those that arrive at workable solutions.

Our twelve-to-thirteen-year-olds are just beginning to engage in this internal process. From time to time, in little bits and pieces, they begin to interpret themselves to themselves. They evaluate personal characteristics and beliefs. They examine how they present themselves to others. Their consciences serve as moral consultant-in-residence. The following two teenagers answer the interviewer's direct questions with indirect, hypothetical speculations. They avoid self-disclosure, yet reveal personal beliefs about responsibility derived from contrasting their own life experiences with others'.

Interviewer: Were you born good or bad?

Emerging teenager: I think that everyone is probably born good, but it is how they were brought up that makes them turn bad. If their parents abuse 'em and always yell at 'em and keep gettin' mad at 'em. And they [parents] were influenced by working at a dirty place or sold guns. . . .

Another ET: If you played with a friend a lot that was mean, then you would grow up being scared.

Conscience as Motivator of Self

Our young adolescents envision conscience as an internal voice prompting self-improvement through the pursuit of virtue and the avoidance of vice.

Interviewer: What changes would you like to make in yourself?

Emerging teenager: Sometimes I'm grumpy and not nice. I don't like myself when I'm that way.

Another ET: I don't like it when I want to just be mean to other people. Like I wonder what I could do to them because they did "that" to me, and do it back. I hope, as I get more mature, I'll outgrow that.

Another ET: To be calmer—to not get mad at my brothers and sisters. To not hit 'em or turn my sister upside down and hold her by the ankles.

Self-initiated reforms of this kind require quiet time and space for introspection, reflection, and resolution—self-evaluation, choice, and action. For young American teenagers living in a spacious home, this may mean long hours in the privacy of their own bedrooms—bed made or unmade. On the other hand, self-evaluation may require no more than a private space within the mind, where introspection is enhanced through conversations with make-believe others, God, or conscience. With no more need to play out dialogues and action sequences with toys for props, introspection can even occur on a crowded school bus.

Interviewer: Are there changes going on in your conscience now?

Emerging teenager: When I was little, I would just get mad at my mom when I was in trouble. Now I get mad at myself.

Another ET: You learn from your past mistakes.

Interviewer: What changes need to be made?

ET: If you accidentally step on someone's glasses and they get mad at you so much and start yelling at you, you don't really want to say "sorry" because, well, you should be sorry, but they should be sorry, too, for yelling at me.

Moral reflection is not always difficult or painful in early adolescence. The following youngster tells us how simply insight can emerge:

Interviewer: What did you like about the interview?

Emerging teenager: I liked [the interview] because I've never gotten the opportunity to answer those kinds of questions, and now that I know what I am, I can maybe start not fighting with my brother and start obeying my conscience.

—— **ADVICE TO PARENTS** ————————————————

Nurturing Moral Willpower at the Personified Stage (12–13)

- **Affirm your teenager's awareness of a private and public self.**

- **Admire your teenager's ability to abstract moral meaning from experience and memory.**

- **Affirm virtuous striving.**

- **Study family rules in terms of duty, virtue, and autonomy.**

- **Be open to negotiating teenage-initiated contracts.**

- **Make your own bed and lie in it. Find satisfaction in your own virtuous striving.**

DEVELOPING MORAL WILLPOWER AT THE CONFUSED STAGE (14–15)

Belonging and Valuing the Self

As teenagers move into mid-adolescence, they continue to experience life as an exciting adventure, particularly if they are solidly embedded in a social network focused on academic and extracurricular success. In contrast, mid-adolescence can be a period of excruciating pain and disappointment for those who feel outside the peer network. Popularity may not be their demand, but a sense of belonging is. When our teenagers feel lonely, we naturally try to console them. Sometimes, we tell them that friends are not important. They do not believe us. No matter how much we affirm them, they remain dissatisfied. Valuing themselves means having friends. Self-evaluation means meeting the expectations of those friends.

Our mid-adolescents make self-judgments and feel judged in ways that they will trivialize later in development. Heather, an eighth-grade girl plagued by psoriasis, entertained suicidal ideas when she felt like an outsider in her class. She struggled with belonging all the way through high school and into her freshman year in college. She read and applied every popular psychology book she could find. Finally she said to herself, "Why am I trying so hard? Why is this belonging stuff so important?" When she let go of that striving, she became more comfortable with herself, relaxed with other people, and concentrated more on her pre-law curriculum. In that step, she affirmed the moral value of her individuality.

Adolescents must affirm the moral value of their being. Parent affirmation is vital as an engendering influence, but self-valuing is beyond our doing. Valuing the self is a steppingstone to assuming moral responsibility. Moral responsibility involves vigilant monitoring of personal behavior. It means following rules of conscience. It means figuring out when rules of conscience are deficient, flawed, or absent. Mid-adolescence is a time when our teenagers discover that they must work with the conscience rather than simply obey it. They must work with elders rather than simply obey or defy them. They are about to discover that they must assert themselves with friends when they experience value clashes with them. The volitional aspects of moral responsibility begin to sink in during mid-adolescence.

Coming of Age

Whether our teenagers are observers or participants, their moral identities are strongly influenced by how they and their peer community interact with historically important events occurring during the decade of their emerging adulthood. To some degree, moral identity is decade-specific. Recall the decade between your fifteenth and twenty-fifth birthdays. How were your values influenced by new inventions; social practices and political issues; national or international conflicts, exploitations, or cooperative efforts; or planetary concerns? Many of us recall our decade-specific response to these events with nostalgia, pride, and the urge to advise: "Back in [the '40s, '60s, '80s], we _____. We weren't afraid to _____. What you young people need to know is

_____." In contrast, a few people respond with regret, despair, or outrage. Both viewpoints influence the transmission of values.

Watching our teenagers decide what, where, and with whom to be on a Saturday night hardly resounds with anything so profound as the moral impact of social change. In between Saturday night choices and larger social concerns stand the enticements of the popular culture. Vendors of the popular culture depend on adolescent desires, and vice versa. Together, they encode values through fashion, language, products, entertainment, and sports. The central value is youth itself. Youth-oriented messages highlight popularity, fast-paced sensation-seeking, immediate gratification, pseudo-maturity, and freedom.

> **THE ADVOCATE**
> Most adolescents use their peer group as a social buffer while psychologically emancipating from parent dependency and moving toward individual responsibility. However, we also honor those teenagers who accomplish the same goal by traveling a more solitary path. Both paths lead to assumption of moral responsibility.

Adolescents tap into parent elder wisdom rather infrequently during the time that they are intently focused on developing individual and peer identity. They may totally tune out the fact that their families continue to be a value resource center. Nonetheless, the way we live our lives continues to be a background reminder of values they may choose to adopt—now or later. Furthermore, through carefully worded commentary on popular culture, we may continue to influence their ideas about moral restraint, learning, virtuous striving, egalitarian issues, or individual responsibility. Some evenings, we might even get into an interesting dialogue.

Freedom

Teenagers love the imagery of freedom—going where you want to go, doing what you want to do, being responsible to yourself alone. Stacy, a fifteen-year-old who usually conformed to family rules, decided one Sunday night that she would go out on her bicycle after dark without her parents' permission. She reported later how exhilarated and free she felt riding in the neighborhood at night. Alarmed and confused, her parents called her boyfriend's house, only to find that he was home with his family. Calls to a couple of girlfriends produced no information. They decided to adopt a "wait and see" stance. After enjoying her ride, Stacy went to a youth minister's house, where she learned to play euchre. She came home a couple of hours later. Upset but relieved, her parents pretended to be asleep when she arrived home. The next day the youth minister called Stacy's mother to reassure her that "she had nothing to worry about."

Instead of imposing a punishment, the mother decided to let Stacy's conscience do the work. It was hard for her father to keep a sour look off of his face when he left for work the next morning. No comments were exchanged between parents and daughter. Later that day, Stacy's mother drove her to her orthodontist's appointment. Music on the radio covered the silence between them. On the way home, Stacy broke the silence with "Mom, you want me to sign up for chemistry next semester, right?" We can surmise that a struggle between compliance and independence was going on in her mind. Stacy appeared to be seeking a way to assure herself that mother-daughter attachment was intact. The mother said, "Yes, I think that would be great. It's good preparation for college." The Imp in the mother grinned. Stacy never did a night ride again, but she had to do that one. Months later, she commented, "I just wanted to see if I could do it."

Risk-Taking and Risk-Management

Stacy and her parents each took a risk. Stacy risked the dangers of the night. Her parents risked the possible consequences of not tracking her down. Stacy's risk-taking was associated with feelings of freedom, excitement, and challenge. Her parents' risk-taking was associated with feelings of anger, fear, and betrayal. Each side managed their feelings with equanimity. Fortunately, no harm came to Stacy. During the risk-taking episode, the space between Stacy and her parents stretched to a state of tension. By the next afternoon, it contracted to a more relaxed state of closeness. Stacy felt a little more autonomous. She demonstrated responsibility on her sojourn. Not the kind her parents wanted, but enough to show that she was thinking about her own safety. Risk-taking is hard on teenagers and hard on parents. Harm and trouble live in the expanded space of freedom. Risk-taking in teenagers calls forth parent risk-management. Managing risk is risky.

Teenage risk-taking decisions involve smoking, alcohol, drugs, body art, sex, theft, all forms of locomotion, work beyond approved hours, weapon possession, Internet liaisons, skipping school, running away, and some activities we have forgotten to list. Each activity offers its own kind of exhilaration. Sensation-producing activities may fit a fantasized picture of being grownup, taking control, or challenging fate. If our teenagers are not self-valuing and morally alert, they may get hurt. Parents hope that sensation-seeking activities will be of the tasting rather than the indulging kind. Vicarious participation may satisfy teenagers' curiosity while better judgment says, "No, not for me!" Occasionally, our teenagers may find themselves trapped in activities with the wrong people at the wrong time in the wrong place. Alternatively, they may be the ringleaders in such activities. An overnight stay in a juvenile lockup may be part of the lesson.

Interviewer: How do you decide what is the right thing to do?

Mid-adolescent: Your conscience is mostly right about what you shouldn't do, so you should follow your conscience. If it's something that you have to do and it tells you not to, but you have to do it, something personal, you have to do it.

Interviewer: What choices are hard for you?

MA: If something feels good and it's bad, then you want to do it just because it feels good.

Another MA: I haven't had sex yet. That's a big teenage discussion issue.

Interviewer: What decisions are hard for you?

MA: A friend gets you to do something that will get you in trouble; while you're doing it, you realize you don't even want to do it.

When choosing risk-management techniques, parents are always at risk for doing too much or too little. Our risk-management decisions include too many warnings versus not enough warnings; too much snooping versus being oblivious to behavior right under our noses; confronting boldly versus confronting meekly; intervening too soon versus not intervening soon enough; expressing too much emotion versus not expressing enough; punishing versus letting an experience be self-teaching.

Interviewer: What did you learn from that [experience]?

Mid-adolescent: . . . that I'm not going to do anything against my will.

Another MA: [When] they're, like, tempting me to take that, I'm not going to, because if I touch that, I'm in trouble.

Moral Inspiration: Idols and Ideals

When our teenagers were children, they may have played at being great people doing great deeds. By mid-adolescence, that play transforms into daydreams with heroic content. Heroism and idealism shape the characters of the protagonists. Action sequences are full of virtuous deeds. Evil people are

THE ADVOCATE

Since mid-adolescence is a time to look beyond parents for heroism, we parents can focus our attention on sources of moral inspiration in the community. If we are on the school or church board, we can assess whether curricular materials are morally inspiring; whether opportunities for moral discussion and debate are adequate; whether opportunities for group problem-solving, cooperation, and altruistic action are available; whether the teachers, coaches, and youth leaders involved with our teenagers speak in morally inspiring ways; whether movies with morally inspiring content are sufficiently promoted.

brought to justice; the rights of the disenfranchised are defended; diseases are cured; the enslaved are freed; love and peace are made secure. Morally inspired daydreams influence later moral aspirations.

In between hero-worshiping daydreams, our teenagers may sporadically devalue us, telling us that we just don't know anything. We may have moments of feeling hurt—even paranoid. The hurt really digs in if our teenagers create idols out of other adults who we know are just as human as we are: friends' parents, favorite teachers, coaches, camp counselors, or pastors. We remember when we used to be the hero. The hurt, which we know to be a parenting developmental necessity, subsides when we join our teenagers in admiring virtue-pursuing historical figures. We also admire Mother Teresa, Mahatma Gandhi, Martin Luther King, Nelson Mandela, or the Dalai Lama. We are less laudatory than our teenagers about certain celebrities.

Whereas our younger adolescents were more likely to define virtue within person-to-person interactions, our mid-adolescents begin to think in terms of groups of people: classes, races, or ethnicities. While being in the right group may dominate their social lives, exposure to out-groups or left-out individuals may capture their hearts. Being left out themselves may deepen their humanitarian perspective. While media advertising directs them to the right brand of athletic shoes, media news exposes them to pain and suffering. An assigned report on a courageous individual, let's say Ryan White or Anne Frank, may stimulate their sense of the heroic. They may aspire to superhuman goals as they formulate the hero within.

Interviewer: What is good about you?

Mid-adolescent: I strive for honesty; I try to apply the Golden Rule.

Another MA: I try to be a good Christian.

Mid-adolescents demonstrate moral responsibility and willpower in two main ways: by resisting temptation and formulating individual opinion.

Interviewer: What did you learn this summer?

Mid-adolescent: This guy I'm seeing, he wanted to have sex. I said "no," so that was good. I didn't do anything against my will. I don't share a lot of things with my friends anymore . . . 'cause I'm not gonna sin. I don't want to get attached. I'm going to grow and [go to college]. I've hardly seen any of my friends this summer. It's weird.

Interviewer: What are your best reasons for not minding your elders?

MA: If I feel they are wrong, and I know I feel secure enough that I can know they are wrong — and I can back it up and make them see — then that's a pretty good reason for not minding your elders.

The first example makes us proud. The second example can make us proud or worry us. That worry expresses our ambivalence about our teenagers' finding their own moral pathways. Our parents had the same worry.

—— **ADVICE TO PARENTS** ————————————————

Nurturing Moral Willpower at the Confused Stage (14–15)

- **Appreciate your mid-adolescent's intense desire to belong in his peer community.**

- **Accept peer belonging as a steppingstone to psychological emancipation from parent dependency.**

- **Be aware of adolescent risk-taking temptations.**

- **Become a risk manager. Intervene vigorously in times of danger.**

- **Admire your teenager's moral inspirations and aspirations.**

- **Become a promoter of moral inspiration and aspiration in the community.**

- **Affirm your teenager's moral decision-making process more than the decisions themselves.**

DEVELOPING MORAL WILLPOWER AT THE
INTEGRATING STAGE (16–17+)

Coming out of the Confusion

Sometime during their late adolescence, as early as age sixteen or as late as whenever adolescence ends (some say thirty), we notice distinct changes in our teenagers. These changes make us smile. From time to time, they seem more young adult than teenager. Their requests are more reasonable. They are less dependent on peer opinion and demand. They tackle goals with more confidence and dedication. They are even more tolerant and forgiving with us parents. We begin to feel at ease imagining an empty nest. When these feelings emerge in us, our teenagers are comfortably assuming moral responsibility.

Psychological Emancipation from Peer Dependency

Emancipating from parents is a dominant psychological task in early and mid-adolescence. Identifying with a peer group prevents our teenagers from feeling lonely and despairing about growing up. At the same time, the peer community, with its close ties to the popular culture, opens our teenagers' eyes to a variety of contrasting values. In later adolescence, our teenagers begin the emancipation process again, this time shaping a moral identity separate from peers. They and their consciences work as a team, defining what is really important to them.

Interviewer: What changes are going on in your conscience now?

Older adolescent: I used to run around with a crowd that wasn't very positive. There are friends I hang out with now. They do some odd things, too, and I don't even hang out with them much anymore. I just go to school with them. They drink (and I do, too) but they drink every weekend. I don't want to get in that mode before I go to college.

Taking Pleasure in Responsibility

The Integrating stage of conscience development is characterized by moral composure. Taking responsibility is pleasurable. When taking on a job that needs to be done, our older adolescents worry less about whether or not others are doing their share. A get-the-task-done attitude really improves relationships at home. Getting a chore done is more important than deciding who ought to have done it. Getting it done can even be more rewarding than receiving credit for doing it. Responsibility is self-rewarding.

Interviewer: What are your best reasons for caring about others?

Older adolescent: Caring, not only are you giving something for somebody else, you're giving something back to yourself for doing it.

Interviewer: Have you ever done a good deed and no one knew about it?

OA: Today I stayed after my radio class to do some work that somebody neglected. The rest of the people may not find out about it, but I got the work done. And I don't have to worry about it.

Finding Balance in Moral Judgment

Mature brain functions are required to achieve balance in moral judgment. A balanced moral view is one that can see good within bad and bad within good. It requires that we hold different perspectives in our working memory at one time. Balanced moral judgments protect us from the extremes of idealization or devaluation. Balanced moral judgments allow us to evaluate ourselves without falling apart. As the following adolescent implies, good incentives can grow out of bad influences.

Interviewer: Were you born good or bad?

Older adolescent: I don't believe people are born good or bad. It depends on what happens to them in their lives and whether they decide to do good things or bad things. It just depends on what influence— like if they have an incentive to do something good or do something bad.

Conceptual integration of good and evil enables our young adults-in-the-making to be morally even-keeled in judging themselves and others. It empowers them to modulate emotions more successfully; to abandon primitive justifications, particularly blame and spitefulness; and to tolerate imperfection in others. We benefit from our older adolescents' balanced evalutions of our years of conscience-nurturing efforts. Balanced moral understanding opens the door to forgiveness. Our teenagers can forgive us and themselves. Moral-emotional quietude allows our adolescents to ponder mysteries without getting distressed. They can use adversity, deprivation, and challenge creatively in the exercise of moral responsibility.

Tolerance and Human Fallibility

Forgiveness and tolerance of self and others are mutually reinforcing. Tolerance allows us to appreciate human differences while seeing common value in all human beings. It allows us to laugh at human fallibility. That brings us face to face with the Imp. We can tolerate poking fun at each other if we incorporate the Imp into our moral life. We can accommodate to acts of fate more gracefully with the Imp at our side. We can find humor in our own plight.

Gerald was a middle-aged man dying of cancer. Day after day he sat in his recliner chair with a child's sand pail at his side where he kept his bottles of pills. His view of the world was confined to the scenery outside his living-room window, the television set, and his wife scurrying back and forth performing caring activities. One day, Gerald said to Martha with complete seriousness:

Gerald: Martha, do you know if they have any face masks at Murphy's?

Martha: Well, they might have some left over from Halloween.

Gerald: If they do, I want you to buy three of them and start wearing them. I'm so sick of the same person walking back and forth in front of me all day long.

Ongoing Moral Alertness

Our best humorists are morally alert people. A morally alert person who can find humor in the human condition is a treasure. During late adolescence, our teenagers become aware of the benefits of constant moral alertness.

Interviewer: What changes are going on in your conscience now?

Older adolescent: It just seems like it [conscience] is there more now that I'm older.

Moral alertness is not a fear-based cautiousness that automatically says "NO" to any temptation. It does not automatically rule against anything or anyone that is new or different. Moral alertness is a value-sensitive, study-the-situation consciousness that helps us guard against bias, prejudice, and any other form of judging a book by its cover. It encourages us to pay close attention to detail, to get all the facts, to digest them carefully, to look at the situation from as many perspectives as we can imagine, to speculate about underlying meaning, and, finally, to make a moral judgment and commitment to action.

Interviewer: Why is it important not to make quick judgments?

Older adolescent: I try to get to know somebody before I make a decision on whether they're good or bad or evil or whatever.

Another OA: If they would get to know me better, they might change their minds about me.

Another OA: We never know the whole story.

Anticipating the Future

Older adolescents ready to leave the nest are especially alert to moral challenges they may face in new terrain. In time, those challenges will either strengthen existing conscience functioning or motivate further reorganization and reintegration. Right now, these adolescents are focused on applying the best moral judgment they have acquired.

Interviewer: Does your conscience change as you grow older?

Older adolescent: Your conscience doesn't really change. Situations do. You have to deal with them.

Interviewer: Are there changes going on in your conscience now?

Another OA: I don't think your conscience changes. I think your environment changes. People change. From high school to college, I'm sure is going to be a big change. You'll do different things. All along your conscience is going to stay the same. You still have to deal with doing things wrong and that feeling.

Our final quotations are from adolescents we confidently endorse as being ready to leave the nest.

Interviewer: What changes are going on in your conscience?

Older adolescent: Eating green vegetables makes sense now.

Interviewer: How does your conscience help you?

Another OA: Humor, humility, tolerance, and compassion are necessary for survival in an imperfect world.

─── **ADVICE TO PARENTS** ───────────────

Nurturing Moral Willpower at the Integrating Stage (16–17+)

- **Affirm psychological emancipation from peer dependency.**

- **Affirm satisfaction in individual responsibility.**

- **Affirm judgment that incorporates the complexities of good and evil.**

- **Affirm tolerance and forgiveness.**

- **Affirm humor about human condition.**

- **Affirm moral alertness.**

- **Prepare for an empty nest. Find new moral commitments.**

SUMMARY

Their assumption of moral responsibility is our ultimate goal in nurturing our children's consciences. The transformation of youthful willfulness into moral willpower begins with our children's valuing their own existence. Having fun is their most natural way of expressing pleasure in being and pleasure in being loved. Self-consciousness, spurred by awareness of how others react to them and their behavior, sets in motion thoughts and feelings of doubt, self-doubt, and shame. Self-worth is maintained through choosing what they feel they ought to do. For External stage children, restraint is the most frequent choice. By the Brain-Heart stage, our children's developing neurological abilities motivate them to master a variety of skills. Motivation for success also comes from their ability to compare themselves to others. They must exert willpower to balance effort with sufficiency. In all skill areas, doing the right thing involves moral decisions regarding truth, rules, and interpersonal boundaries.

Emerging teenagers at the Personified stage define moral responsibility as the pursuit of virtue and the avoidance of vice. Pursuing virtue is a matter of striving; perfection is impossible. Exerting moral willpower involves reasonable negotiations with authority—real authority and the authority of conscience.

At the Confused stage, our teenagers return to the issue of valuing themselves, this time without the support of parent affirmation. Psychological emancipation from parents is eased, temporarily, by leaning on a close group of friends. Our teenagers' peer groups influence their moral identities as they influence the peer groups. In combination with the popular culture and historically important events, a generational identity comes into being. Heroism and idealism solidify values. Moral willpower means supporting generational values.

Emancipation is a repeating theme at the Integrating stage, as our older adolescents release themselves from dependency on peer groups. Individual moral responsibility requires tolerance and forgiveness to live with fallibility in self and others. A sense of humor supports tolerance and forgiveness. Practice in individual moral decision-making builds confidence and courage. An ongoing moral alertness emerges.

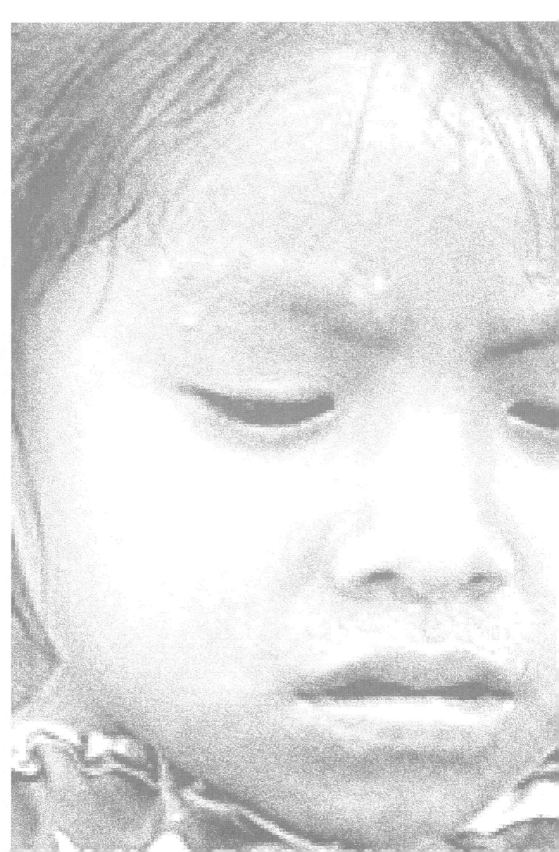

Developing the Meaning of Conscience

7

So far in this book, we have written about conscience as though it were pieces of a puzzle, threads of a tapestry, or building blocks of a structure. Conscience is really a whole, dynamic entity within the mind. It is a mental concept that ties the threads of moral being together. It functions as the heart of personality. It motivates oughtness. For most of us, oughtness is the pursuit of goodness. For a few of us, oughtness is the pursuit of badness. In all of us, conscience holds up our definition of goodness and badness to us. It asks us to be accountable. We can be pleased with conscience or feel burdened by it. We can use it, ignore it, argue with it, adjust it, or reshape it. It is there, and we live in a dynamic relationship with it.

BIOLOGICAL BUILDING BLOCKS OF MORAL MEANING

Why is it there and how did it get there? At the biological level, we observe life perpetuating life. We infer that life values life. Beyond that inference, we find no inherent moral meaning in biology, and certainly no consciousness of purpose. Nonetheless, each of the biological building blocks of human survival—attachment, caretaking, emotion, thought, memory, value, language, action, and defense—influences how we construct moral meaning. These building blocks program us to function with continuity, rhythm, structure, and alertness. Meaning grows from these functions. Moral meaning captures what we believe to be the most important aspects of life. Conscience holds that meaning in place.

DYNAMIC MORAL MEANING

Meaning is never a permanent structure. The meanings of words in a dictionary gradually change with usage over time. Conscience, our personal storehouse of moral meaning, is written and rewritten at different stages of our development. It consolidates historical lessons with fresh experience, discoveries, and experiments. We personalize its meaning through intuitive, scientific, spiritual, and practical insights. Conscience is our link between the way things are and the way we believe they ought to be.

We create moral meaning by distinguishing good from bad, right from wrong—in our relationships with each other and in relationship to ourselves. Even though certain moral truths are deduced time and time again in personal and cultural history, we sense that, just like scientific truth, moral truth is just beyond, or maybe far beyond, our reach. Some of us find that idea to be a source of motivation, others of despair. Most of us find moral contentment in making small contributions to the triumph of goodness over badness or helping rightness to win out over wrongness.

INTERLOCKING PIECES OF MORAL MEANING

As in a puzzle, each piece of conscience interlocks with the next piece. We cannot create moral meaning in our lives without emotional connection to each other. Emotions require regulation for the sake of harmony. Emotional harmony is achieved through rule-keeping within our relationships. Rules are value-laden. Basic values affirm respect for authority, self, and peers as well as the environment that supports us. Upholding values requires willpower. We must choose when to restrain and when to act. These interlocking pieces of moral meaning fit together into a dynamic, psychological form—conscience.

STAGES OF CONSCIENCE

Conscience holds moral meaning in place at any one time in our lives. Conscience grows wiser with development. Changes are subtle from one day to the next. However, specific developmental shifts can be easily identified in childhood and adolescence. In this book we identify five shifts in the understanding of conscience before children graduate from high school. Adult stages are yet to be defined. Potential for development is present throughout the life span.

When we consult our conscience, it helps us review current experience for moral action. It holds in sharp focus relevant memories of crucial moralizing experiences—times when the voice of oughtness sounded loudly and clearly.

It helps us the best it can at its particular stage in its development—which, of course, happens to be where we are in development, also. That means it takes us no further than we are able to comprehend. Children wish parents would automatically find that stopping point when they are lecturing them.

NURTURING CONSCIENCE DEVELOPMENT

Parents do not nurture children's development in pieces. We do not separate our investment in their physical, cognitive, emotional, and social development into units of time like classes in a school day. We remain completely invested in their whole beings all the time. Neither do we nurture our children's consciences in pieces. We do not concentrate one day on firming up our moral connection, a second day on evoking moral-emotional responsiveness, a third day on defining values, and a fourth day on strengthening moral willpower. We are totally invested in their pursuit of goodness all the time. We nurture that pursuit through our children's ups and downs, quiet periods and challenging periods, successes and failures.

Let's picture ourselves, like the parents of Dan in the first chapter, watching one of our children walking in procession at his or her high school graduation. As we review the stages of conscience development, we will also review the many ways in which we nurtured its formation. The methods will be familiar. They all have been described in the last six chapters. As the review proceeds, let's highlight nurturing efforts that supported our children's evolving pursuit of goodness. Let's cheer when our actions went right to the developmental target like arrows to a bull's-eye. Let's pat ourselves on the back, not for having been perfect parents, but for having pursued our goal in good conscience—to support a healthy sense of oughtness in our children. The pat on the back will encourage us to pursue further goodness.

DEVELOPMENTAL CONSIDERATIONS

THE DYNAMIC MEANING OF CONSCIENCE AT THE EXTERNAL STAGE (0–6)

Ask a kindergartner if he knows what a conscience is. Most likely, he will draw a blank. Ask him if there is something inside him that knows about good and bad, right and wrong. Maybe yes, but probably no. Ask him how a boy or girl his age knows when he is doing something good or bad, right or wrong. He will tell you short, personal stories, each of which has a moral. The stories will alternately sequence events leading to trouble and events leading to approval.

Ask him how he knows about good and bad, right and wrong. He will give his parents the credit. Our young child believes in moral heritage.

Ask this same kindergartner to draw a picture of good and bad, right and wrong. He will most likely want two sheets of paper. Or he will clearly divide one sheet into two parts. One drawing will show a boy or girl doing something wrong. He will also draw or explain that the child in the drawing is getting reprimanded or punished for the wrongdoing. A second picture will show the child doing something good or right. The child will be smiling. Any adults in the picture will be smiling, too.

Nurturance during the External Stage

By the time our children were kindergartners, they described a definite moral connection to their parents. From the day we laid eyes on them, we nurtured that connection with protective physical and emotional care. We extended that care in high-quality, high-quantity amounts. We mirrored their emotions, empathizing with each one. We had moments when we shared emotion. We took delight in their joyful feelings and soothed their negative ones. We affirmed their basic goodness.

We first defined morality to our children by rescuing them from danger. "Don't touch" and "don't go there" were our first commands. We didn't blame them for negative results from their curious explorations; we just curtailed them. Teaching them about restraint was our goal. Our children had a different goal: to explore, learn, and create. When we said, "no," they stormily showed us the qualities of potential genius, doubt, and willpower. They introduced us to their friend the Imp. They taught themselves a few things about "don't touch" and "don't go there." Gradually, our goals met in reality and reason. We came to agree that fire can harm.

Self-consciousness and self-doubt emerged to support moral growth. Those feelings prompted our children to question their own behavior. They generated the idea that they might, indeed, be doing something bad or wrong. Sad, mad, and fearful feelings began to interlock with actions that others labeled as bad or wrong. We helped them work through those feelings by showing them how broken things could be fixed and bad feelings could be soothed away. Their moral-emotional responsiveness began to function.

Slowly, we worked demands and prohibitions into everyday family routines. In this way, we introduced our children to continuity, rhythm, structure, and reasons to be alert. Through these functions they gathered a rudimentary meaning of how life ought to be lived. We underscored the value of our authority over these matters.

We provided time for our children to play with agemates. We relaxed during the times when they found mutual enjoyment. We praised them for sharing and taking turns. When they were naughty, we disciplined them fairly. We helped them negotiate ways to cooperate and settle disputes. We used our authority when they couldn't figure it out by themselves.

Smile with contentment the next time you see a child, spontaneously or on request, drawing a picture of himself being praised or reprimanded for doing something, alternatively, good or bad, right or wrong. He is developing a conscience. Pat yourself on the back if you were involved in nurturing it along.

THE DYNAMIC MEANING OF CONSCIENCE AT THE BRAIN-HEART STAGE (7–11)

Ask a seven-to-eleven-year-old child to define the word *conscience*. Sometime during that developmental interval, she will affirm that she understands the term. "I've heard of it . . . I think it means _____." The younger she is, the more difficulty she will have defining it. To help her explain what she knows, ask her if there is something inside her that knows about good and bad, right and wrong. She will readily say, "Yes." She will say that she has rules for right and wrong stored in her mind, brain, heart, or some other internal location. Although she will still attribute the source of moral knowledge to her parents and other authority figures, possibly including religious ones, she will now claim ownership of rules of conscience. These rules tell her what she should do in order to be a good person and to do the right thing.

Ask this same child to further explain her conscience by drawing a picture of it. Her drawing may be a brain, another body part, or a geometric design. It will be an organized form with a clear interior and exterior. Rules of conscience will be on the inside. They may be represented symbolically or written out in literal form. "Always do _____; never do _____."

Nurturance during the Brain-Heart Stage

Parents can take a lot of credit for their children's rules of conscience. We did not inscribe the rules in their brains like rules posted above a classroom chalkboard or commandments learned in Sunday School. Their rules of conscience were concretized from our day-to-day living routines. These routines gave their lives continuity, rhythm, and structure. They discovered which prohibitions and demands required maximum attention based on how we reinforced them: the more affirming our attitude, the more they wanted to please us. Our attitudes shaped their attitudes about rules of conscience. Our attitudes determined whether rules of conscience functioned as out-in-front guides for oughtness or drag-behind ought-to-have-dones.

Our children mastered a myriad of skills during the Brain-Heart stage. They also learned about the morality of mastery—how to manage time and effort in behalf of quality production and performance. We helped them discover a comfortable rhythm for effort and sufficiency, how hard to work and when to relax. We curtailed them from excesses. We protected them from adults who wanted to drive them too hard.

We appreciated our children's sense of moral anticipation, those times when they looked ahead far enough to avoid trouble. We took silent pride when a drop in mood accompanied wrongdoing. We expected them to feel bad after wrongdoing, but we wanted those feelings to be prompted more by their developing consciences than by us. We knew a moral-mood connection would serve them well in the future. It would motivate them to repair wrongdoing and prevent its reoccurrence.

After wrongdoing, we helped our children examine options for making things right. Sometimes we required reparations of them. Sometimes we required them to say, "When this [moral situation] comes up again, I will _____." When the wrongdoing brought disharmony to our parent-child relationship, we worked to restore good feelings after the reparation process. We laughed and joked as we forgave them. We told them about our moral failings when we were their age.

We honored our children's need for continuity in their friendships. We admired their efforts to be nice. We underscored the values of truth-telling, rule-following, and boundary-keeping in games as well as in real life. We commiserated with them when they felt left out or treated meanly. We helped them maintain respect for their moral self-worth when ignoring meanness in others. We introduced them to positive interpretations of the Golden Rule, examples of times when it might be better to return meanness with kindness. We honored their need to learn on their own, to make their own decisions, and to deal with natural consequences.

Smile with contentment the next time you encounter a child trying to live a rule-bound life. Her conscience is growing. Pat yourself on the back if you were involved in the day-to-day moral routines from which these rules emerge.

THE DYNAMIC MEANING OF CONSCIENCE AT THE PERSONIFIED STAGE (12–13)

Ask a young teenager to describe his conscience. Very likely, he will describe it in anthropomorphic terms: "My conscience is like [a voice, eyes, a someone] inside me that [tells me what I ought to do, lets me know when I've done something wrong]." Our emerging teenager knows that he is speaking metaphorically. Conceptualizing conscience as a person means that his moral connection with others has taken on internal form. The presence of a moral voice within himself means that all of his thoughts, feelings, and actions are now known to his conscience—if not to real people in the real world. The moral voice within him asks for compliance, pleasing, and self-judgment.

Our young teenager's moral-emotional responsiveness is intensified in response to his personified conscience. Rules of conscience nag or whisper to him like words coming from a real authority. He may hear the opposite words, too. He conceptualizes temptation as a real force. Fortunately, he is not as literal as he was at the Brain-Heart stage. He understands that perfect rule-following is impossible. Being well-intended or striving to do the right thing counts as moral behavior. Rules of conscience, therefore, tend to be restated as virtues. Failure is more forgivable when wrongdoing was not intended. Nonetheless, moral failings still require make-up work. Reparation and healing are now undertaken to restore internal as well as external harmony.

The ways in which pieces of conscience come together in the emerging teenager's mind are now so complex that he finds it hard to describe all of them. He may give various emphases to internal representations of the moral connection, regulation of moral emotions, the values and virtues he finds most important, or his struggles with moral willpower. He may reflect on contrasting moral forces within himself by saying that he tries to follow his good conscience rather than his bad one.

Ask a young teenager to draw a picture of his conscience. If he draws a brain, he will compartmentalize a specific section to represent his conscience. If he draws a person, moral symbols will be worked into the characterization. The conscience figure may look stern or benevolent. It may be gigantic or small. Religious imagery may be included. Horns and halos emphasize the internal struggle between good and bad, right and wrong. No matter how culturally universal the symbols, something very personal about his conceptualization will be expressed in the drawing.

Nurturance during the Personified Stage

Our emerging teenagers' internalized consciences did not turn out to be duplications of the ones we would have custom-designed for them. Their consciences became developing contracts between themselves and their own interpretations of moralizing experiences. Nonetheless, we contributed greatly to that contract. When they became teenagers, we modified our family routines to balance demands for compliance with opportunities for virtuous expression or times to exercise purely autonomous choice. We negotiated with them when they proposed behavioral contracts of their own design. We provided opportunities for them to make moral commitments outside the family.

We understood the importance of the private emotion of guilt in conscience development. We respected their closed bedroom door. We gave our young teenagers time to privately process their moral well-being while we kept our nose to the ground for signs of distress or trouble. We did not hesitate to confront them when we smelled trouble. We enjoyed those times when they spontaneously talked to us about their feelings about good and bad, right and wrong. We walked through the steps of reparation and healing with them. We smiled when they became exuberant over reinstatement of a clean conscience and worked to heal wounded relationships.

We enjoyed our young teenagers' increasing grasp of intentionality. Understanding intentionality made them more tolerant with themselves. It also made them more tolerant with us. They could acknowledge that we had their best interests in mind, even when we imposed rules that they didn't like. When we felt that their internalized consciences were working efficiently, we allowed them more freedom in the community. Their eagerness to trust themselves with responsibility was always slightly ahead of ours. They had great faith in their good intentions. We required hard evidence of moral maturity, too.

We anticipated that our teenagers would come to value the peer group above all else as they progressed into mid-adolescence. We provided protected places for them and their friends to "hang out." We knew they would become increasingly self-conscious in our presence when their friends were around. We remained distant but available. When given the opportunity, we helped them process psychological and moral evaluations of the peer community. We engaged them in conversations about "the person I want to be." In so doing we also had in mind, but did not necessarily state, "the person I want to have as a friend." We did not overload our conversation with moral terms. We walked gingerly between our young teenagers' private selves and their public selves. We knew we would be doing that for some years.

Smile with contentment the next time you encounter a young teenager seeking to be virtuous but autonomous. His conscience is growing. Pat yourself on the back for all the times you contributed to the voice of conscience in young teenagers.

THE DYNAMIC MEANING OF CONSCIENCE AT THE CONFUSED STAGE (14–15)

Ask a mid-adolescent to describe her conscience. Her definition will be similar to the one she espoused earlier in adolescence—an internal voice of moral authority. However, she will speak with less certainty about the authority of that voice. Her tone will suggest hesitation, unrest, or confusion. Peer-centered values, well-fed by the popular culture, capture her moral interest. She has a lot to sort out. When facing a moral decision involving conflicting values or loyalties, she is likely to experience great distress. Distress, in tolerable amounts, prompts moral development. Her conscience is growing.

While still more or less respecting us as her parents and respecting our contributions to her conscience, she is nonetheless on a quest for *real* authority. In that quest, she looks to adults outside her home, to the popular culture, and to her peers. She idolizes and idealizes some persons and their values, while dismissing others. Education, religious and secular, introduces her to historical, fictional, and current charismatic leaders. Her specific peer community itself becomes a source of moral authority. Certain peers will strike her as totally "cool." Popular culture, also educational, keeps her in tune with advertising- and media-guided opinions regarding the values of various celebrities and acquisitions. The value of material acquisition is inescapable in the popular culture.

Ask this same mid-adolescent to make a drawing of her conscience. Symbols denoting questioning, confusion, conflict, or tension will most likely be present. Moral-emotional disharmony will be depicted in creative ways. Specific emotions and moods may be color-coded. Anxiety may be expressed through scribbles and mark-overs. Opposing moral commands may be written out.

Nurturance during the Confused Stage

The natural desire to psychologically separate from parents had a great impact on our teenagers' conscience development during mid-adolescence. Recalling trials and tribulations from our own adolescent emancipation helped us deal wisely with this desire for separation. As we watched our teenagers join their friends in taking on the garb and language of pseudo-individuality, we winked at the Imp over the distance between them and true individuality. With our teenagers immersed in peer think-alike, feel-alike, talk-alike, and do-alike pursuits, we changed our parenting focus from supporting conscience development in our individual teenagers to that of the peer community. We worked in that community to provide teens with a network of safety as well as opportunities for pursuing goodness, especially altruistic goodness. We worked inconspicuously but remained alert to opportunities to join a moral dialogue. We remained especially alert to occasional situations that mandated moral confrontation and limit setting.

We affirmed our mid-adolescents' search for *real* authority. We pondered over the idols and ideals that appealed to them, especially those from the popular culture. Occasionally we suggested candidates of our own: "Have you ever read about _____?" We let our opinions as parents be known to the proper authorities regarding educational curricula. We affirmed teachers, religious leaders, coaches, and youth workers who became idols to our teenagers, while privately making sure that they were, indeed, adults of good conscience. We became "admired authorities" to teenagers outside our home.

We anticipated that our teenagers would experience loyalty conflicts over values. We knew that their moral-emotional equilibrium would sometimes be highly disturbed. They might express righteous indignation over issues of entitlement: "There's no reason I shouldn't be allowed to _____." We were patient as we listened to overly bold, critical, and emotionally fiery statements interspersed with sullen silence. Our attentiveness let them know that we valued their opinions-in-the-making, even when they had trouble expressing those opinions coherently. We urged them to be calm during disagreements. We emphasized that moral-emotional equanimity in the face of conflict is part of becoming an adult. We admired their efforts to be a friend's best friend, to be their brother's or sister's keeper. We honored confidentiality. However, we set limits when emotional involvement went beyond their capacity to handle it. We led or pushed the teenager in distress toward appropriate help.

We knew that our teenagers would be pulled into risk-taking behaviors as an expression of freedom. We remembered our own attraction to speed, danger, and fun at that age. We remembered our feelings of invulnerability. We helped our teenagers balance freedom with responsibility, judging their success one situation at a time. We avoided giving blanket freedom. We became risk-managers. We always remained their parents, not their friends. We cheered, sometimes privately, sometimes openly, when they made moral decisions independent from the peer group.

Smile with contentment the next time you encounter a mid-adolescent seeking the voice of *real* moral authority. Commiserate with the distress of her search and commend her efforts at resolving loyalty and value conflicts. Her conscience is growing. Give yourself a pat on the back for every time you patiently pursued a moral dialogue with adolescents like her.

THE DYNAMIC MEANING OF CONSCIENCE AT THE INTEGRATING STAGE (16–17+)

Ask an older adolescent to describe his conscience. There will be more calm in his voice than during mid-adolescence. He will pensively say that although his conscience is his source of moral knowledge, responsibility rests with him as to how to use it. Leading a moral life is no longer a simple matter of compliance with stored rules. Neither does the moral voice within always give adequate guidance. Idols and ideals may seem remotely connected to here-and-now decisions. Each moral situation requires careful consideration. Ambiguity and dilemmas are often present. There may be good within bad and bad within good. Methods for pursuing goodness may come into question. Philosophical questions regarding means-ends justifications (phrased in his own terminology) may enter his mind. When to act may become just as important as how to act.

Our older adolescent is going through a second step in psychological emancipation. Having achieved some psychological separation from parents, he is now separating from peer dependency. Group identity is still important; friends are still important; but even more important is his individual moral identity. An intimate relationship may rise in importance, only to fade into a more insistent pursuit of self-definition. The future, with all of its possibilities and uncertainties, is frequently on his mind.

Ask this same older adolescent to draw a picture of his conscience. Markers of confusion and uncertainty will be gone. He will carefully choose moral symbols that express his individual point of view. Interconnectedness, courage, or dependence on a higher power may be symbolized. Integration of good and bad will be a dominant theme. Goodness outweighing badness will be represented or described in some way. Individual choice and responsibility will be highlighted. Words need to accompany the drawing to interpret individualistic artistic choices.

Nurturance during the Integrating Stage

We greatly enjoyed seeing our teenagers emerge from the Confused conscience stage. Our relationship became more relaxed as our older adolescents demonstrated increasing amounts of sensibility and responsibility. Communication was more open. We laughed more. Sometimes their opinions sounded like our own, but we never mentioned it. Instead, we winked at the Imp. We found our older adolescents able to process dilemmas and wrongdoing with less emotional distress. Occasionally we saw them face a problem with real moral courage. We commended them.

We were proud when we saw our older adolescents assuming responsibilities of leadership with younger children, and sometimes with peers. We enjoyed seeing them more focused and goal-oriented, more cognizant of the future. We felt more appreciated as parents. Little expressions of gratitude brought tears to our eyes.

In tune with our adolescents' concerns about the future, we anticipated that new moral challenges would arise for them. We knew that even with their growing sense of psychological independence, the current structure of family, friends, high school, and community still supported their moral functioning. Soon that structure would fade into memory. As they went off to college or to other independent pursuits, we knew that new temptations and challenges would arise. They would join new peer groups. Contrasting or competing values would need to be processed.

In the meantime, we affirmed values that were already in place for them, including patience, tolerance, and forgiveness. We would continue to talk and listen, listen and talk. When they began to see their world from the perspective of societal needs and failings, we would empathize with their frustration over the gap between idealism and reality. We would be in for further chiding ourselves. We would empathize with their desire to make a difference in the world. We would side with optimism over pessimism. We would affirm realistic ways of pursuing ideals, one decision at a time. We would sometimes think of ourselves as fellow adventurers in the land of good and evil. With parenting responsibilities eased but never complete, we would take on new commitments and responsibilities.

Smile with contentment the next time you encounter an older adolescent behaving in a morally independent and responsible way. Pat yourself on the back for all the times you nurtured that sense of responsibility in him.

CONCEPTUAL LIMITATIONS AND MORAL RIDDLES

In this book we have painted an optimistic picture of individual conscience development. We have defined conscience as a mental structure that progressively incorporates, constructs, and guides moral wisdom and practice. Following the tenets of cognitive science, we believe that its formation is dependent on an interlocking, spiraling connection between nature and nurture. The conscience development we have described is optimal but not spectacular. It is what can be expected to develop smoothly when a child's natural abilities are adequate and nurture is constant in its moral attentiveness, care, and teaching.

Descriptions throughout the book emerged from the voices of real children and adolescents. They provided us with spontaneous stories about the nature of oughtness; the naturalness of their desire to pursue goodness; the ways empathic human attachments shape the pursuit; the ways emotions fluctuate in the regulation of moral harmony; the ways moral rules emerge from value-defining learning experiences; and the ways moral responsibility becomes a necessary expression of oughtness. In their own Impish ways, they also told us that mischief can be fun; that people are fallible; and that patience, humility, tolerance, and forgiveness are a natural part of conscience development. They inspired our creation of the Imp as moral humorist.

We are pleased but not totally satisfied with our work. Moral riddles remain. We will outline a few.

CAN GOODNESS BE KNOWN WITHOUT BADNESS?

Can our child learn to pursue goodness without getting in trouble or seeing others get in trouble? Is the bad kid on the block a moral standard bearer? What if the bad kid is our child?

IS HUMAN SUFFERING NECESSARY FOR APPRECIATION OF GOODNESS?

We know that nature distributes its bounty randomly, unfairly, or stingily. We find some protection and control over the cruelty of nature through manipulating genetic codes or enhancing the predictive powers of the weather forecasters. Sometimes we hear parents of a physically or mentally disabled child describe their child as a blessing. This is the child who taught them how to appreciate life, to know courage, or to find joy in small increments of progress. Can we value our lives without adversity?

IS CULTURAL DIVERSITY REALLY AN OLYMPIC COMPETITION IN THE PURSUIT OF GOODNESS?

Kinship loyalties grow into cultural loyalties that compete with other cultures in the pursuit of goodness. Goodness is defined through family life, religion, education, commerce, and government. While all cultures have certain things in common in defining goodness—for example, honoring the Golden Rule—each culture develops its own style of pursuit. Does this seeming competition increase or decrease goodness in the world? Is it better to teach our children loyalty to our own ways or to open their eyes to tolerance and acceptance of others' ways? Does the latter option strengthen or weaken their moral identity?

IS A CHAIN OF MORAL CONNECTEDNESS AROUND THE WORLD A REALISTIC EXPECTATION?

We have described how the security-empathy-oughtness bond, formed in infancy, expands to include feelings of moral obligation toward other authority figures and peers in our child's life. A triangle of respect for self, authority, and peers emerges as a dynamic moral value complex. Individual moral actions are emotionally motivated one choice at a time. Although we can fathom and advocate policies honoring universal human rights, do we really have the moral energy to form a chain of moral connectedness around the world? What are the limits of human caring? What do we teach our child about those limits?

IS IT POSSIBLE TO ACHIEVE MORAL-EMOTIONAL EQUILIBRIUM AROUND THE WORLD?

In times of patriotic passion, we hear orators speak of the conscience of a nation. From time to time, we see the formation of moral coalitions. To some degree, they are always suspected of merely being ways to support selfish interests. On the other hand, an occasional person carries a banner so clearly evil that it distinctly defines the pursuit of goodness for the rest of us. Will moral passions ever rise and fall in unison to maintain world harmony? How do we feel about moral passion when our children go off to fight for a cause much larger than themselves?

IS THERE A BETTER WAY TO CONCEPTUALIZE GOODNESS?

Is the moral value complex balancing respect for self, authority, and peers—including the environment that supports it—an adequate conceptualization of goodness? Is the pursuit of goodness always a matter of balance, choice, or approximation? Is there a goodness that is not moral? Is there a better way to conceptualize and pursue goodness? When we teach our children to pursue goodness, it is important that we know what we mean by *goodness*.

IS IT POSSIBLE TO MAKE A MORAL DIFFERENCE IN THE WORLD?

We honor leaders with moral courage for having made a difference in the world. They strongly influence our definition of goodness. They inspire us to bring about change. We make improvements. In the meantime, in other places in the world or in other time segments of history, including the present, the pursuit of goodness decays. Can we promise our children that they will have a better world if they participate in improving it?

We parents do not need to solve these moral riddles to nurture conscience development in our children. We teach our children to pursue goodness, first according to our definition, and then later in ways that follow their own discoveries. If we do our job well, our children may want to join us in solving these riddles. That's a parent's moral hope, right?

Suggested Reading

Bowlby, J. (1988). *A Secure Base.* New York: Basic Books, Inc.

Brazelton, T. Berry, and Cramer, B. G. (1990). *The Earliest Relationship: Parents, Infants, and the Drama of Early Attachment.* New York: Addison-Wesley.

Campbell, J. (1988). *The Power of Myth.* New York: Doubleday.

Coles, R. (1986). *The Moral Life of Children.* Boston: Houghton Mifflin.

Coles, R. (1993). *The Call of Service.* New York: Houghton Mifflin.

Coles, R. (1997). *The Moral Intelligence of Children.* New York: Random House.

Damon, W. (1988). *The Moral Child: Nurturing Children's Natural Moral Growth.* New York: Free Press.

Darwin, C. (1872). *The Expressions of the Emotions in Man and Animals.* Reprint. New York: St. Martin's Press, 1979.

Dunn, J. (1988). *The Beginnings of Social Understanding.* Cambridge, Mass.: Harvard University Press.

Eisenberg, N., ed. (1982). *The Development of Prosocial Behavior.* New York: Academic Press.

Ekman, P., and Friesen, W. (1975). *Unmasking the Face.* Englewood Cliffs, N.J.: Prentice Hall.

Erikson, E. (1963). *Childhood and Society.* New York: W. W. Norton.

Galvin, M., and Stilwell, B. (1998). *The Conscience Celebration.*
http://www.IUPUI.EDU\~PSYCH

Gardner, H. (1980). *Artful Scribbles.* New York: Basic Books.

Gilligan, C. (1982). *In a Different Voice.* Cambridge, Mass.: Harvard University Press.

Izard, C. E. (1991). *The Psychology of Emotions.* New York: Plenum Press.

Kagan, J., and Lamb, S., eds. (1987). *The Emergence of Morality in Young Children.* Chicago: University of Chicago Press.

Kidder, R. M. (1995). *How Good People Make Tough Choices.* New York: William Morrow.

Kohlberg, L. (1981). *The Philosophy of Moral Development.* New York: Harper and Row.

Kushner, Harold S. *How Good Do We Have to Be.* Boston: Little, Brown.

Lickona, T. (1983). *Raising Good Children.* New York: Bantam Books.

Piaget, J. (1932/1965). *The Moral Judgment of the Child.* New York: Free Press.

Selman, R. (1980). *The Growth of Interpersonal Understanding.* New York: Academic Press.

Thomas, A., and Chess, S. (1977). *Temperament and Development.* New York: Brunner/Mazel.

Index

DR. STILWELL is a retired, voluntary faculty member of the Department of Psychiatry at Indiana University School of Medicine. During her career she has been involved in medical school teaching programs; the private practice of child and adolescent psychiatry; consultation with various agencies, including the Indiana Blind School, the Indiana School for the Deaf, and the Indiana Girls School. She has been a member of the editorial board of the *Journal of Child and Adolescent Psychiatry* and director of an inpatient unit for middle-school-aged children. Together with the co-authors of this book, she has written numerous articles, published in professional journals, about conscience development in normal and disturbed youngsters.

DR. GALVIN is currently voluntary faculty at Indiana University and involves himself in child adolescent psychiatry teaching and conscience-centered professional-ethics courses for faculty, students, and residents. He continues research in the effects of maltreatment on conscience formation and functioning and writes children's books, including the companion book, *The Conscience Celebration.*

DR. KOPTA is Chairman and Professor, Department of Psychology, at the University of Evansville as well as a clinical psychologist in private practice. He received his doctorate from Northwestern University in 1983. He is a leading expert in the area of psychotherapy research, with over 60 publications, chapters in books, videos, and scholarly paper coverage on network television as well as in *USA Today, U.S. News & World Report, Vogue, Glamour, Self,* and *Der Speigel,* the European news magazine. *Encyclopaedia Britannica* noted that Dr. Kopta's research papers delineating how much psychotherapy is needed to successfully treat the variety of diagnoses and symptoms have become two of the most cited scholarly works in psychotherapy research.